FIGHTING THE RUSSIANS

FIGHTING THE RUSSIANS

French Soldiers' Letters
1799–1815

BERNARD WILKIN & RENÉ WILKIN

Pen & Sword
MILITARY
AN IMPRINT OF PEN & SWORD BOOKS LTD.
YORKSHIRE – PHILADELPHIA

First published in Great Britain in 2024 by
Pen & Sword Military
An imprint of
Pen & Sword Books Ltd
Yorkshire - Philadelphia

ISBN 978 1 39905 962 6

A CIP catalogue record for this book is available from the British Library.

Typeset in INDIA by IMPEC eSolutions
Printed and bound in the UK by CPI Group (UK) Ltd, Croydon, CRO 4YY

Pen & Sword Books Limited incorporates the imprints of Archaeology, Atlas, Aviation, Battleground, Digital, Discovery, Family History, Fiction, History, Local, Local History, Maritime, Military, Military Classics, Politics, Select, Transport, True Crime, After the Battle, Air World, Claymore Press, Frontline Publishing, Leo Cooper, Remember When, Seaforth Publishing, The Praetorian Press, Wharncliffe Books, Wharncliffe Local History, Wharncliffe Transport, Wharncliffe True Crime and White Owl.

For a complete list of Pen & Sword titles please contact:

PEN & SWORD BOOKS LIMITED
George House, Units 12 & 13, Beevor Street,
Off Pontefract Road, Barnsley, S71 1HN, UK
E-mail: enquiries@pen-and-sword.co.uk
Website: www.pen-and-sword.co.uk

or

PEN AND SWORD BOOKS
1950 Lawrence Rd, Havertown, PA 19083, USA
E-mail: uspen-and-sword@casematepublishers.com
Website: www.penandswordbooks.com

FSC
www.fsc.org
MIX
Paper | Supporting responsible forestry
FSC® C013604

Contents

Acknowledgements

The authors would like to thank all who have helped to produce this book. We are particularly grateful to the employees of the State Archives of Belgium, especially Sébastien Dubois and Michel Trigalet, and let us not forget the readers of our previous books and those who have shared their enthusiasm for the period with us. As always, we need to express our gratitude to Heather Williams from Pen & Sword, without whom this project would not exist.

As usual, the support of our family proved essential to overcome the many frustrations associated with writing a book. We cannot thank enough Stéphanie Podgorski, who has endured many holidays in places where nothing has happened for over two hundred years. We are also extremely grateful to Phileas Wilkin, who still makes his father and his grandfather proud.

Introduction

At the time of completing this book, Ukraine and Russia have been involved in a lethal conflict in Eastern Europe for over two years. The involved parties have shown a desire to use historical events to validate their current actions or to caution foreign powers. As an instance, in February 2023 President Putin and his associates, while addressing President Macron,[1] referenced the French soldiers' fate retreating from Moscow during the 1812 campaign. There is no denying that the Patriotic War of 1812, known as such in Russia, has had a lasting impact on collective memory, particularly in Eastern Europe. The campaign has been distorted by both Czarist and Soviet propaganda, and presented as a people's war and a symbolic precursor to the fight against Germany in the Second World War, known in Russia as the 'Great Patriotic War'. However, the conflict between France and Russia, spanning from the French Revolution to the downfall of the Corsican emperor, was significantly more intricate than the stereotypes perpetuated by two centuries of state messaging. Given the growing number of inquiries our societies are making about Russia, it seemed fitting to delve into this tumultuous past through a new publication, particularly as there is an unexpected void in the literature. Much has been written about the campaign of 1812, but far less about previous campaigns. While writing this monograph, various points came up. The question of how the French perceived the Russian military, and how this perception subsequently evolved, was deemed important. Additionally, it was necessary to clarify the notions of hatred and contempt between the opposing sides.

The sentence '*C'est la bérézina*' is still commonly used in the French language to describe a disastrous situation. However, few native speakers are aware that the term has historical roots and reflects a violent past shared between France and Russia. During the Revolutionary War, France had been engaged in battle with a number of European countries for several years when Russia joined the Second Coalition on 29 November 1798. After being defeated in Switzerland and Holland, the Czar quickly withdrew from the conflict. In April 1805 Russia joined the Third Coalition, but suffered a humiliating defeat at the battle of Austerlitz on 2 December 1805. The Fourth Coalition in 1806–1807 resulted in the bloody but inconclusive battle of Eylau and the Russian defeat at Friedland. Following the treaty of Tilsit, Russia formed an alliance

1. *Indian Express*, 21 February 2023.

with France and engaged in minor skirmishes against Austria during the Fifth Coalition war. After the catastrophic invasion of Russia in 1812, a coalition of several countries emerged victorious over Napoleon in 1814. During the War of the Seventh Coalition, in which the French emperor suffered a decisive defeat at Waterloo, Czar Alexander I dispatched a substantial army towards the Rhine, although it arrived too late to engage the enemy.

As in *Fighting for Napoleon* and *Fighting the British*, this book draws upon a wealth of primary sources penned either during or shortly after the Napoleonic Wars. All material was originally written in French and translated into English by the authors. We endeavoured to remain as close to the original texts as possible, having carefully chosen and analysed hundreds of personal diaries and letters to include. Official after-action reports and proclamations, which were sometimes more detailed than any form of correspondence, are also included in the primary sources. These sources are unequally qualitative and possess specific issues, which require comprehension. The letters were authored over extended periods, primarily by young and uneducated men. Less than 38 per cent of these individuals could read or write, with illiterate soldiers often relying on their educated comrades to communicate with their families. Low-ranking soldiers wrote letters to keep in touch with their relatives, as well as for practical reasons. French soldiers often portrayed their situation as worse than it was to elicit sympathy and almost systematically requested money from their parents. These reports were often kept by educated men, primarily young officers, who comprehended the historical significance of their observations. Personal journals often suffer from self-absorption and overstatement, but are also replete with details and devoid of post-war alterations. Official after-action reports are equally fascinating and informative but require a certain level of critical scrutiny. Surviving officers from a lost battle were often eager to attribute the defeat to their deceased colleagues. Reports served as their only opportunity to vindicate their own actions and, sometimes, to salvage their military careers. Proclamations posed a challenge as their primary purpose was propaganda, targeting both civilians and soldiers. This book aims to document a prolonged and arduous time in history. Consequently, there are unavoidable absences in the archives, especially for the initial operations, fought by a handful of men, and for the 1812 campaign during which the majority of letters were intercepted by the Russians. In rare instances, the only recourse for us was to employ memoirs and souvenirs written after the conflict to make up for the scarcity of surviving records. The memoirs in this book were mostly written shortly after the collapse of the French empire. By contrast with the previous two volumes, we have also included Napoleon's letters. The importance of comprehending his psychological processes during decisive campaigns, such as the one in 1812, was particularly notable.

This book is divided into seven chapters. Chapter 1 explores early operations, including the obscure Swiss campaign of 1799–1800 and the botched Anglo-Russian invasion of Holland in August 1799. Moving forward, Chapter 2 focuses on the war of the Third Coalition, demonstrating the French soldier's overwhelming superiority over the Russian during the operations, which was confirmed at Ulm and Austerlitz. In the following chapter, 3, we investigate the war of the Fourth Coalition. Our contention is that the French demonstrated their superiority on the battlefield once again, although the Russians proved a formidable opponent, particularly in the contested battle of Eylau. Chapters 4–6 are exclusively dedicated to the study of the invasion of Russia, an event of significant historical importance that warrants in-depth analysis. Chapter 4, in particular, examines the early phase of the campaign. Using letters and diaries, this study provides evidence that the French army embarked upon the invasion of Russia with unabated confidence, despite having just escaped Spanish territory. Chapter 5 details the chronicles of the battle of Borodino and the great fire in Moscow. Napoleon's hasty advance towards the city, without due consideration of the possibility of a retreat, revealed his overconfidence in compelling the Russian emperor to submit. Consequently, these missteps set the scene for the catastrophic events that were to follow. Chapter 6 examines the apocalyptic retreat and the significant number of casualties suffered by the French army. The Russians, who were greatly aided by the cold weather, dealt a severe blow to the French forces. The loss of numerous valuable officers had a debilitating effect on the Grande Armée. The final chapter, 7, is dedicated to the 1813–1814 campaign, in which one of the bloodiest battles took place at Leipzig, and the occupation of Paris.

Bernard Wilkin & René Wilkin
February 2024

Chapter 1

Wars of the French Revolution

The Swiss campaign

Before the eighteenth century, there was limited knowledge of Russia amongst the French. Peter the Great's involvement in European politics acted as a catalyst, leading the western powers to become interested. The French encountered Russian troops for the first time during the Seven Years War (1756–1763). However, despite these miscellaneous interactions, the sprawling empire remained shrouded in mystery for several years. Its sheer size, climatic conditions, inadequate roads and numerous language dialects rendered any exploration of Russia an arduous task. Only a few books described this distant land. During Napoleon's reign the French used a translated version of a work by British geographer John Pinkerton, in which he claimed: 'The Russian empire may be the most extensive ever to exist, with a length of approximately 9200 English miles and a width of 2400. Nevertheless, the eastern regions feature vast deserts and a sparse population.'[2] Estimating the population of Russia at the start of the nineteenth century is challenging. William Tooke, a British resident of Russia for several years, approximated the population at that time to be 36 million. However, modern researchers base their estimates on other sources. Catherine the Great's final census in 1794–1796 mentioned 18,707,000 men, while the count in 1815 had increased to 21,943,000, including 3,947,000 non-Russians predominantly in the Baltic and Polish regions.

Pinkerton had a dim view of the country's government: 'The government of Russia appears to have always been despotic, there being no legislative power distinct from that of the sovereign … This vast empire is divided into about 40 governments or vice-royalties, of which 34 may be assigned to the European part. The whole frame of the government may be pronounced to be military; and nobility itself is only virtually estimated by rank in the army.'[3] During the latter half of the eighteenth century Catherine the Great, who ascended to power by overthrowing her husband, pursued a policy of rapid

2. John Pinkerton, *Modern Geography, a Description of the Empires, Kingdoms, States, and Colonies; with the Oceans, Seas, and Isles; in All Parts of the World*, vol. 1, p. 299.
3. Pinkerton, op. cit., p. 305.

expansion. Focused on governing her extensive empire, she refrained from joining the European powers' declaration of war against France following the execution of King Louis XVI. Catherine passed away on 17 November 1796, and her son Paul I succeeded her as Czar.

The new leader pursued a foreign policy different from that of his mother. Opposed to the French Revolution, in 1798 he formed the Second Coalition with the United Kingdom, Austria, the Ottoman empire and the Kingdom of Naples. Some 50,000 Russian soldiers, commanded by Alexander Suvorov, were dispatched to fight against the French in the United Provinces, Italy and Switzerland. This was the first time that the French army had faced Russian troops. Paul I's troops initially targeted the Cisalpine Republic, which was established by the French in 1797 as a sister entity to the French Republic.

The Russian-Austrian army in Italy defeated the French at Cassano d'Adda[4] on 27 April 1799 and entered Milan two days later. Several French soldiers encountered the Russian enemy during and after the battle. One example is Alexandre Boutroue, who was assigned to cross the Orba river with his infantry regiment but became engaged in a violent clash with Russian horsemen. In a letter Boutroue detailed the events:

> A river was being inspected, but the appearance of the enemy cavalry had begun to create disorder in the troop and the approach of night increased it still further. Many men had already perished, victims of their haste; a large number, frightened by the cries of those who were drowning, had fled up the river to avoid a death which they considered certain. Berger set off in pursuit, outpacing them and stopping them; reminding them of their courage, he asked only for order and tranquillity in order to preserve their lives and their honour. He succeeded in bringing them back, arranging them in battle; in their turn they imposed themselves on the enemy and effectively supported the arrangements made by the battalion commander for the crossing of the river. By his firmness, his prudence and above all the confidence he was able to inspire in his comrades, Sergeant-Major Berger played a large part in the results of this day, when the battalion was able to escape from an enemy that was far superior in numbers and that was manoeuvring to envelop it, while General Victor believed it was infallibly lost. This honourable action earned him the rank of second lieutenant.[5]

Suvorov's troops captured Turin on 26 May 1799 and reinstated King Charles-Emmanuel IV to the Piedmontese throne, the French having compelled him

4. Near Milan.
5. Alexandre d'Hauterive, *Lettres d'un chef de brigade 1793–1805*, Paris, 1891, p. 121.

to abdicate in December 1798. The young Etienne Béniton[6], a French soldier taken prisoner in Switzerland by the Russians, noted in his memoirs:

> By the new road we had taken, we crossed the Russian camp. It was the first time we had seen these new enemies of France. They were strange men, singularly dressed. The infantry was composed of small, robust men. Their clothes were of a dark green cloth; the clothes came down to the ankle; their headgear was a sort of pointed shako which was not less than eighteen inches high, so that these men, seen from the front, at a certain distance, appeared to have their faces in the place of their stomachs. Their rifles seemed enormous; their bayonets were not less than two feet long. This paraphernalia gave them a heavy appearance and a sombre ensemble. There were few horsemen.[7]

Republican General Becker recounted his initial engagement with the soldiers of the Czar during the battle of Cassano to his family:

> Going down the Adda, Adjutant General Becker managed to repel several Russian parties; but Suvorov having forced a passage at Trezzo, separated the Becker brigade from the bulk of the Serrurier division. Although General Grenier had come to the aid of this brigade, which was making the greatest efforts to stop the enemy, the Russians had already gained a great deal of ground, when the general-in-chief sent fresh troops to Adjutant Commandant Becker, with orders to seize with the bayonet a village where the left of the French army was to be supported. This village was taken, although defended by more than three times the attacking forces, and 400 Hungarian grenadiers were taken; but when one wanted to break through, one found oneself in the presence of a considerable mass of enemy infantry, supported by a large artillery unit firing at the French columns. Adjutant Becker, knowing the importance of the position he had taken, defended it with the most courageous obstinacy; but his left being soon overrun, and his right being discovered by the retreat of Grenier's division, his brigade was compromised, and he then ordered the retreat, which was carried out in the best possible order. He had already had two horses killed under him, when a Biscayan went through his stomach. A faithful servant remained with him under the rain of cannonballs and grapeshot,

6. Étienne Béniton (1799–1858) joined the army in 1793. He reached the rank of captain and was awarded the Legion of Honour. He retired in 1814.

7. Etienne Béniton, also known as commandant Gervais, *A la conquête de l'Europe, souvenirs d'un soldat de la Révolution et de l'Empire*, Paris, 1939.

> and continued to lavish his care. The Austrian general Zopf arrived, who had the wounded man relieved and bandaged and gave orders to transport him to the headquarters in Milan, with the recommendation that he be protected against the Russians, who at that time hardly took any prisoners. While the Austrian soldiers were taking the unfortunate officer away, Suvorov arrived with his staff. Seeing that it was a French general, he stopped the stretcher, placed it on a barrel and said: 'You are mortally wounded, General, you have murdered your king, destroyed religion, overthrown the monarchy, commend your soul to God; let him be taken away and cared for.' The wounded general was fully conscious while Suvorov addressed this singular apostrophe to him, which he has never forgotten, and said to himself: I have done none of this.[8]

By mid-May 1799 the early successes of the Austro-Russian forces resulted in low morale among the French soldiers. The Austrians took advantage of the opportunity and launched an attack on Zurich in June. Between 4 and 7 June 1799 Archduke Charles and General Friedrich Freiherr von Hotze led their troops and attacked the soldiers of André Masséna, resulting in the French general being forced to retreat from the city. Pierre-Charles Duthilt, a corporal who was part of the 14th demi-brigade, witnessed the catastrophic event:

> On 3 June (15 Prairial) the enemy, having collected all his forces, crossed the Glatt and attacked us vigorously; we were, after resisting for long, forced to withdraw into the intrenched lines which covered Zurich. We lost many men in this fight, notably Captains Detamacker and Jacob Bouillet, Sub-Lieutenant Stohlcars, a very distinguished young man, and a large number of non-commissioned officers and chasseurs; the particular and average loss of each of our companies amounted to eight to nine men.[9]

However, the allied forces did not pursue the Republican army. Several days later the French and Russians crossed paths at the battle of Trebbia in northern Italy. Duthilt, who was absent but had learned from French propaganda newspapers that his side had emerged victorious, stressed the significance of such a victory, even if so-called, for the morale of those engaged in the fight in Switzerland:

> On 1 July (13 messidor) one announced the first victory gained in Italy on the Russians by generals Macdonald and Moreau; it was qualified

8. Félix-Victor Martha-Beker, *Le général Beker, comte de Mons*, Paris, 1876, pp. 18–19.
9. Camille Lévi, *Mémoires du capitaine Duthilt*, Paris, 1909, p. 86.

> of the name of moral victory, because it was more important for the opinion than for the fact; one had fought the Russian army of firm foot and for the first time one had resisted it effectively. The most frightening reputation had preceded this army which came from the depths of the Ukraine and which was said to be formidable. Our discouraged soldiers yielded the ground to them without almost disputing it; such was the unfortunate effect which had resulted from the little confidence inspired by the old general Scherer, who had succeeded in the command of the army of Italy to general Bonaparte, under whom the army had always marched from victory to victory; this army had then lost all its energy, through the imperiousness of its general; and in the circumstance in which we found ourselves, we believed in the resurrection of its strength by the efforts which it had just made.[10]

The battle of Trebbia proved to be a conclusive triumph for the Austro-Russian forces. Despite losing 5,500 men, the allies succeeded in inflicting 16,500 casualties on the French, causing them to withdraw. Moreover, the French suffered another setback at the battle of Novi on 15 August 1799. As a result, Macdonald was compelled to retreat, relinquishing any ability to pose a threat to northern Italy.

Back in Switzerland, after the initial Austro-Russian successes, General Korsakov,[11] one of Suvorov's subordinates, faced a French offensive on both banks of the Limmat river and in the city of Zürich. Between June and September 1799 General Masséna had managed to regroup and reorganise. The *Journal de Toulouse* newspaper of 11 October 1799 (19 *vendémiaire* year 8) published three letters concerning the second battle of Zurich:

> 1° General Masséna, by telegraphic bulletin: 'the enemy made a surprising resistance. It was cut in pieces. One can put the number of its dead at 6000; the ground was all covered with them. Among the prisoners, whose number is not yet known, there are 2000 wounded. General Hotze was killed; we buried him yesterday with military honours. Three Russian generals were taken. Masséna.
>
> 2° General Chabran, in Basle, on the 7th Vendémiaire: 'The two Russian and Austrian armies are completely destroyed. The Russians crossed the Thur. One is with the continuation of the debris of the

10. Lévi, op. cit., p. 86.
11. Alexander Korsakov (1753–1840) was disgraced after the campaign in Switzerland. He became nonetheless a cavalry general in 1801 and served as Governor-General of Lithuania from 1806 to 1809 and 1812 to 1830.

Austrian corps and Bavarians, who were already joined to them with the number of 8000 baggage, effects of corps camp, six flags, more than 100 pieces of artillery, are in our possession; the loss of the two enemy armies, both in killed and wounded and prisoners, [is] of more than 10,000 men. The Russians, those barbarians of the North, are no longer in Helvetia.

3° Extract of a letter of an officer of the army of Helvetia:Zurich, 7 Vendémiaire. I announce to you, citizen representative, the capture of Zurich. You could not imagine of the rout of the enemies. Luggage, gold, money, generals' car, all was the prey of our soldiers; four generals killed (among which General Hotze), one made prisoner, 15,000 men killed or taken, including 13,000 Russians; such is the result of our attack. The enemies were so frightened that they only stopped at Constance, where we made a reconnaissance. It is surprising that those people who have very little cash in their country, had so much wealth in the army. The poor devils took great pains in bringing us the most beautiful furs from 800 leagues away. Thanks to their kindness, I am very warmly dressed for the winter: to see most of us in our fox and bear skins, one would think we were inhabitants of Kamchatka. The Russians know no manoeuvres; they are rather poorly equipped and of mediocre size: they are not the giants that the Austrian gazettes so emphatically announced. The details which we are beginning to receive on the affairs which are taking place in Helvetia, prove that we have never fought so fiercely. 1500 Russians, hopelessly engaged in a defile, and surrounded by 6000 French, refused to surrender after four summonses; it was necessary to resolve to exterminate them. Our troops have already recaptured Winterthur and are driving the enemy before them everywhere. ... The military fund of the Russians has fallen into the hands of the French.[12]

During the capture of the city, Johann Lavater, a renowned Swiss poet and writer, sustained severe injuries. The episode was explained by Duthilt:

The next day, the 26th (4 Vendemiaire), Zurich was taken. The city was somewhat pillaged. The most deplorable accident was that of the famous Lavater, who had risked all dangers to bring help to the wounded of the three nations exposed to fire; a mortal blow was dealt to him, not by a French soldier, as calumny said at the time, but by a hand guided by personal vengeance, and which the fury of party spirit

12. *Journal de Toulouse, l'Observateur républicain, ou l'Anti-Royaliste*, 19 vendémiaire an 7, pp. 1–2.

> had long since raised on the philosopher's head. Lavater was struck down in one of the streets of his native town; he lived for another fifteen months, but languishing, suffering, working, writing and preaching as an evangelist minister, during this painful and slow agony, beautiful as virtue, good as the charity of which he was the apostle and model. This misfortune was deplored for a long time by the French army and by the entire population of Zurich.[13]

Sergeant Blanchet, who was promoted to captain during the campaign, participated in the battle and even sustained a bayonet wound:

> You thought I was dead, no doubt, my poor old chap, when you saw that in spite of my promise I had gone so long without writing to you; but rest assured, I am not even very ill, although I am writing to you from the hospital; it is the effect of a Russian bayonet that pierced my thigh at the battle of Zurich, and pinned me to a bed for a month. ... Soon the campaign began. Masséna had us invade the country of Grisons, occupied by the Austrians; we took Coire, the capital of this country, and there we captured an Austrian general named Aufenberg. Our company was detached to a small town or rather a small village called Stanz, where we stayed for nearly a fortnight. ... However, everything announced that we were going to have a tough battle. It was said that a Russian army, which had just beaten Moureau and Joubert in Italy, was going to fall on us with the intention of crushing us. Fortunately, these threats, with which certain people sought to frighten our conscripts, had little effect on them. In short, Masséna began the battle on the 3rd of this month of Vendémiaire, just twenty days ago today (25 September 1799), at five o'clock in the morning. I will not tell you anything about the dispositions and the plan of the battle; placed as I was to act on an isolated point, I saw nothing of it and understood nothing of it. All I know is that at dawn we were taken across the Limmat, near the village of Dietikon, in boats prepared in advance and in the greatest secrecy. The crossing took place in complete silence, while General Foy set up several batteries to protect our passage. There were about six hundred of us, who were the first to embark and reach the other shore. Immediately, we swooped down on the enemy skirmishers and dispersed them. But there were three Russian battalions with guns on the plateau. Our artillery, admirably directed, soon extinguished the Russian artillery fire, and protected the successive passage of our vanguard, for which we had been the first scouts. When General

13. Lévi, op. cit., pp. 76–97.

> Gazan, who commanded us, had gathered sufficient reinforcements, we marched on the three Russian battalions guarding the plateau called Closter-Fahr. These battalions had taken up residence in a wood and were defending themselves with the courage of despair. Gazan, by a skilful manoeuvre, enveloped them in such a way that not a man could escape. My captain was killed in this attack, and I, in charge of the company, was wounded in the right thigh by a bayonet blow that is still keeping me in hospital. Although surrounded on all sides, the Russians did not want to surrender; we had to kill them one by one to dislodge them. More than two thirds of them had already fallen to our bullets, when Tour d'Auvergne, sorry to see this useless shedding of blood, went forward to meet our men and signalled for them to cease firing; then he spoke a few words to the Russians in their language, and immediately these poor devils, who were all expecting to die, threw down their weapons and held out their hands to us as if to say that we should let them live. After that, I was taken to the ambulance, and I saw nothing more of the rest of the battle. I learned only that a bridge had been thrown up at the place where we had made the crossing, and that fifteen thousand men had crossed the river at this point, to go up the Limmat and bring themselves to the rear of Zurich. Other movements had been made on other points with equal success, and Korsakoff, the Russian general, found himself trapped in Zurich. The next day, the battle began again with renewed ferocity; but Masséna's dispositions had been so well taken that nowhere could the Russians resist, and after a fierce battle, the most complete victory remained with the French.[14]

The second battle of Zurich signified the failure of the Russian expedition in the area. Suvorov was compelled to flee as he could not breach the French defences, resulting in a loss of up to 5,000 soldiers during the retreat. On 15 October the Helvetic Republic was liberated from the presence of allied troops. Although the commander-in-chief was not personally defeated, he was forced to return to his country with his troops, while Russia withdrew from the coalition.

The Anglo-Russian invasion of Holland

During their operations in Switzerland, Czar Paul I dispatched a group of troops to fight alongside the British led by the Duke of York in the Batavian Republic on the north Holland peninsula, with the aim of promoting an uprising against the Republic and neutralising the Batavian fleet. Under Lieutenant General Sir Ralph Abercromby, the British landed on the Dutch coast and

14. Just-Étienne Roy, *La Tour d'Auvergne dit le premier grenadier de France*, Tours, 1870, pp. 163–74.

won the battle of Callantsoog on 27 August 1799. Despite being scheduled to meet their ally early, the Russians were delayed. Abercromby also beat Generals Brune and Dandels at the battle of Krabbendam on 10 September 1799, an attempt by the French and Batavians to dislodge the British from their bridgehead. Initially, the situation appeared favourable for the British, yet the French soon demonstrated their military prowess. On 19 September 1799 the Anglo-Russian armies attempted to strike a decisive blow against their adversaries, confident in their numerical superiority. However, the French general Guillaume Brune, alongside General Daendels, emerged victorious in the battle of Bergen on the same day. On the third supplementary day of the year 7 (19 September 1799), Brune reported his success to the Minister of War:

> Citizen Minister, since the action of Slaperdijk (on the 24th of Fructidor) the English had returned to their entrenchments in the Zyp, and there had been only light skirmishes, small attacks on posts. Reinforced by 14,000 Russians, who landed successively for the last five days, they made today at five o'clock in the morning, a sharp attack on the whole line. The main attack was on the French troops forming the division on the left under General Vandamme; it was made with a very considerable body of Russian troops and an English division in the rear. The Battalion division holding the centre, under the orders of General Dumonceau, was also seriously attacked by an Anglo-Russian corps, while a dummy was directed against the division on the right, commanded by General Dandels. Our brave French led by Generals Vandamme and Gouvion, ... soon overcame all the obstacles by pushing the enemy with such impetuosity that without their weariness, they would have entered with the fugitives into the English entrenchments. The fields were littered with the dead. The Dandels division had been pushed back for a moment; it soon recovered all its positions by a counter-movement which gave it back the battalions which had been detached from it. The battle lasted from five in the morning until four in the afternoon. General Dumonceau was wounded at the beginning of the action. ... The result of the action is 1000 prisoners, more than 3000 dead and wounded, 25 pieces of cannon and five flags, including those of the regiments of Fersen and Suvorov. General Hermann, commander in chief of the Russian troops, is among the prisoners. ... The enemy army was 39,000 strong, including 14,000 Russians and 25,000 English. The French and Batavian troops did not exceed 20,000 men. Our loss is 50 dead and 300 wounded. The calculation does not seem believable, but it is exact.[15]

15. *Journal de Toulouse, l'Observateur républicain, ou l'Anti-Royaliste*, 9 vendémiaire an 8 (1 October 1799), pp. 2–3.

The *Journal de Toulouse*, which published Brune's letter, also reproduced the writing of an officer who signed his report only 'M':

> Alkmaar, the third supplementary [Republican calendar]
>
> 2500 prisoners, 30 pieces of cannon, if it is pleasant, my dear, to arrive the day before a battle, it is very sweet to be able to announce a victory; the Russians and the English are beaten; 3000 men killed or wounded, 2500 prisoners, 30 pieces of cannon, 25 flags, 26 officers in our power among whom the general in chief of the Russians: such are the results of this day. I will give you some particular details on the battle of Bergen, which will make you know how important it is for the French Republic. The Russians had been disembarked for 36 hours, when the English put them forward; the Russians joined the English, forming an army of 35,000 men. They attacked with superior forces the French division which was only of 7000 combatants; their project was to destroy this division which it regarded as the greatest obstacle to the invasion of the *roulante* [Holland]. General Brune, who had guessed this movement, gave the order to the French troops to withdraw successively, in order to draw the enemy out of his entrenchments and to be able to profit from ground advantage. The light artillery formed an avant-garde, and as the Russians advanced in columns, it did not cease to strike them with grapeshot: at midday, all the ammunition was exhausted, there was not a shot of cannon which had not riddled the Russians at half range. New ammunition arrived; the French beat the charge. A Battalion brigade detached from the central division took the enemy in flank; the fusillade was terrible for a moment and decided the victory. The Russians and the English were pursued with bayonets in their backs, and if the troops had not been harassed and the day very advanced, they would have been followed in their entrenchments.
>
> Their cannon, their ambulance, everything was abandoned: they committed horrors, they dared to kill old men and women; they set fire to the villages; finally, the first fruits of their brigandage were found in the pockets of the killed. May the courage of the brave French armies preserve us, my dear, from the visit of these barbarians, they only know how to be killed: the French have learned to know them and no longer fear them. They were told before the battle that if they surrendered, the French would cut off their heads. I have seen these unfortunate men who were expecting this ordeal kneel down to undergo it, and get up again, kissing our clothes and our hands, when they were told that they had nothing to fear. Would you believe that these Russian grenadiers, so highly praised, that these soldiers of the proud Emperor

> of all the Russias, are covered with uniform rags strewn with pieces and fragments. The contempt which the Russians have for the English is in no way inferior to that which we have for these soldiers. I saw the Russian officers, caught at the beginning of the affair, refuse to be confused with them in the same room at Alkmaar, and beat them by telling them that they were cowards and traitors. The ground from Berghem to the enemy's entrenchments was covered with killed and wounded; these French soldiers, who had not yet eaten at seven o'clock in the evening, were carrying wounded Englishmen on their shoulders for more than half a mile. One man said to them, 'Why, soldiers, are you amusing yourselves by picking up these people? It is time to go and eat soup.' I heard this reply, which is worthy of a Frenchman: 'Are we hungry when there are still good deeds to do? And are we not doing two at once, by preserving the lives of wounded Englishmen? We are fulfilling the duties of humanity, and we are taking out of England's prisons one of her best comrades.'[16]

The military campaign was not yet over. The Duke of York secured a victory at Egmond-Aan-Zee on 2 October 1799. However, four days later, on 6 October 1799, Brune and his troops numbering 24,000 overpowered the Anglo-Russians, comprising 11,000 Russians and 21,000 British, at Castricum.[17] The battle at Castricum was a violent confrontation, resulting in numerous casualties on both sides. The town was seized and surrendered repeatedly before the signing of the Convention of Alkmaar on 18 October 1799. Following Brune's agreement, the Duke of York and his troops retreated. Although the ill-fated expedition was not considered a failure in Britain, its outcome was viewed differently in Russia. The Czar was deeply dismayed by the poor performance of his soldiers, resulting in their dishonour. The Duke of York was compelled to exonerate a number of Russian regiments that had exhibited bravery. Similarly, Paul I expressed dissatisfaction with the conduct of his Austrian and British allies during the operations. He therefore left the coalition in 1799.

Relations between Russia and its allies were strained. In 1798, despite being the leader of the Russian Orthodox Church, the Czar had proclaimed himself Grand Master of the Sovereign Order of Malta, to which he had offered asylum in St Petersburg after Bonaparte had taken the island on his way to Egypt. The surrender of the French garrison on 5 September 1800 to Captain Alexander Ball made Malta a British possession, which London refused to return to the Order of Malta. Consequently, it provoked the Emperor of Russia's anger.

16. *Journal de Toulouse, l'Observateur républicain, ou l'Anti-Royaliste*, 9 vendémiaire an 8 (1 October 1799), pp. 2–3.
17. It should be noted that these figures vary greatly from one source to another.

On 16 December 1800 Denmark, Russia, Prussia and Sweden signed a treaty of armed neutrality. However, the United Kingdom disapproved of it, leading to a ban on ships from the signatory powers' ports and the bombing of Copenhagen. On 20 January 1801 Paul I initiated a rapprochement with the French Republic by expelling King Louis XVIII, then living in exile in Mitau. On 30 January he requested Prussia to close the Elbe, Ems and Weser rivers to British vessels. On 9 March 1801 First Consul Bonaparte liberated 5,000 Russian prisoners held by France without any ransom being paid. The Czar even planned to attack British possessions in India, but this project was abandoned after a group of officers, with the tacit approval of his son, who became the new emperor Alexander I, assassinated Paul I on 23 March 1801. Despite the murder, a flurry of diplomatic activity ensued, culminating in the preliminary agreement to the Peace of Amiens being signed on 1 October 1801. A week later, on 8 October 1801, the Treaty of Paris was signed by France and Russia, formally ending the Russo-French hostilities in the war of the Second Coalition. A secret convention was also signed two day later by Talleyrand and Morkov. Russia and France were resolved to find a balance within the Holy Roman Empire.

Chapter 2

The road to Austerlitz

From Boulogne to the east

Peace in Europe was short-lived. France continued to occupy Holland, which was expected to have been evacuated by 1801, as well as Naples and Rome. Napoleon's interventions in Switzerland and Germany were also poorly received. Following the breakdown of the treaty of Amiens on 23 May 1803, Britain reached out to its allies on the continent, with the concentration of the Grande Armée aimed at invading Britain from the French coast being particularly worrying. For a century Russia had been trying to intervene in European politics: 'the question of Russia's entry into the Western concert was a matter of common interest, no one wanted to hear about it; Russian diplomats logically deduced that, in order to be European, to finally play a role in the affairs of the continent, their country had to enter into conflict with France, a sort of enemy of all, which would make their intervention tolerable and would allow them, after victory, to better negotiate their place in the new Europe'.[18] Czar Alexander, who had proclaimed himself the protector of the King of Sardinia, was highly displeased by the incorporation of Piedmont into the French Republic on 11 September 1802. With its own designs on the Mediterranean Sea, where it held joint sovereignty with the Septinsular Republic, Russia deployed an army of 150,000 men to Moldavia and Wallachia on 25 January 1805. A potential conflict loomed large.

Negotiations between Britain and Russia resulted in an agreement. It was decided that Russia would mediate in the conflict between Britain and the French Republic, according to terms already discussed by both parties. If Napoleon refused, a declaration of war would follow. Afterwards, Austria, Prussia, Sweden, the German principalities and the Kingdom of the Two Sicilies would be invited to join the alliance. On 11 April 1805 Russian and British officials signed an Act of Coalition against France in St Petersburg. The aim was 'to restore the peace of Europe, and to give it back the independence

18. Thierry Lentz, 'La formation de la troisième coalition. Un grand succès de la diplomatie anglaise', in: *Revue du Souvenir Napoléon*, n° 459, July–August 2005, pp. 7–12.

of which it is deprived by the ambition of the French government. These powers undertook to gather forces to obtain the evacuation of Hanover and northern Germany, the independence of the republics of Holland and Switzerland, the re-establishment of the King of Sardinia in Piedmont, the independence of the Kingdom of Naples, the evacuation of Italy, even of the island of Elba, and finally the establishment in Europe of an order of things which could stop new usurpations. Austria must provide 250,000 men, Russia 150,000, independently of the levies made in Albania, Greece, etc., and the remainder will be provided by Naples, Sardinia, Hanover and other states. The contracting parties will make common cause against the powers which will unite with France.'[19]

Napoleon also endeavoured to form an alliance of friendly states. Holland, the Kingdom of Italy, Spain, the Grand Duchy of Baden, Bavaria and the Grand Duchy of Württemberg joined forces with him. Conversely, Prussia, which was also cautious of Russian ambitions regarding Poland, gained for Prussia in the territorial divisions of the previous century, chose to remain neutral in this conflict in exchange for the occupation of the electorate of Hanover, in French hands since June 1803.[20]

On 27 August 1805 the Boulogne camp was disbanded, and the Grande Armée, located along the Channel coast, began its march towards Germany. The troops stationed in Holland and Hanover force-marched to the Rhine's banks, leaving only the French garrison in the city of Hameln. On 7 September the Austrian army had infiltrated and conquered Bavaria, which was promptly recaptured by French troops. On 17 October Napoleon achieved a remarkable triumph at Ulm, with relatively little combat, capturing the Austrian commander Mack, as well as 17 generals and 20,000 soldiers. Meanwhile the Russian army gathered in Wilna, accommodating Emperor Alexander and his commanders on 30 September. On 19 October Kutuzov, leading the Russians, linked up with the Austrians near the town of Branau on the Inn.

After capturing Ulm, the French encountered the Russians for the first time during the campaign. On 31 October there took place a preliminary combat in front of Lambach, on the Traun. Two days later[21] Lieutenant François[22] noted in his diary:

---

19. Buret de Longchamps, *Les fastes universels, ou tableau historique chronologique et géographique contenant siècle par siècle depuis les temps les plus reculés jusqu'à nos jours*, t. 10, Brussels, 1827, pp. 97–8.

20. George III was also Duke and Prince-elector of Hanover.

21. Digby Smith, *Napoleonic Wars Data Book*, London, 1998, p. 212, does not mention this battle on 2 November. It is probably the battle of Amstetten on 5 November, on a wider front that also included Austrian troops.

22. The author, Charles-François François, born in Guinchy (Somme) on 19 June 1775, enlisted on 5 September 1792 in the 9th demi-brigade, took part in the battle of Valmy, in the Egyptian campaign,

> Prince Murat ... made us form an attack column. We marched on the Russians, who put up a stubborn resistance (The Russians are holding on well). Our general Oudinot, seeing the stubbornness of the Russians, made us rush the whole division with bayonets. We pushed them back on all points, killing at least 500 Russians, and taking 300 prisoners; we lost a hundred men, killed and wounded. We named this battle Enns, being not far away. The hussars of the 9th and 10th pursued the Russians in their rout. This failure accelerated the retreat of the Russians ... whom we pursued. The bridges cut by them on the Inns river were promptly repaired by us. The pursuit lasted four days.[23]

Several minor skirmishes took place between the French army and the opposing forces under General Kutuzov's command. The violent confrontation resulted in heavy casualties. On 11 November Marshal Mortier's corps, comprising approximately 14,000 soldiers, engaged in combat with the 24,000-strong army of Russians and Austrians led by General Schmidt near Dürenstein. The French sustained approximately 4,000 casualties with the loss of 47 officers, 895 soldiers and five cannon. The Russian and Austrian armies lost 4,000 soldiers wounded or dead. Both parties claimed victory. Despite the loss of their general-in-chief, the Austro-Russians kept retreating. On 14 November Napoleon arrived in the Austrian capital. As the allies were forced to retreat from the French, numerous conflicts occurred between the coalition's rearguard and the pursuing French; these conflicts predominantly involved soldiers from the Grande Armée and Austrian troops, due to the disposition of the retreating armies. While the Austrians performed admirably, the same cannot be said for the Russians:

> The Russians committed great disorder in all the places where they passed in retreat. These excesses drew upon them the curse of the inhabitants of Upper Austria, astonished to see allied troops treating them with more inhumanity than the French, whom they had endeavoured to represent as barbarians and devastators.[24]

After his visit to Berlin in an attempt to persuade the King of Prussia to join the hostilities against France, Czar Alexander returned and assumed command of

---

where he was taken prisoner by the Turks in 1800. Released in 1803, he returned to the 9th Line as a second lieutenant. Made lieutenant in 1807, he was taken prisoner in Spain and sent to the pontoons of Cadiz. He escaped in 1810 and remained active. He received the Legion of Honour in October 1812. Dismissed in September 1815, he again joined a departmental legion where he received the rank of captain until his retirement in 1824. He died in Nantes on 24 April 1853.

23. Charles-François François, *Journal du capitaine François*, Tours, 1913, p. 484.

24. *Victoires, conquêtes, désastres, revers et guerres civiles des Français*... t. 15, p. 190.

his retreating army. On 18 November he joined the Emperor of Austria: 'it was on 18 November that the Emperor of Russia had his first interview at Olmutz with the Emperor of Austria; the next day he sent his deputy general Prince Dolgorukov to Berlin; it is said that the Emperor Alexander will not return to Petersburg as had been announced and that he has resolved to put himself at the head of his troops. He has ordered the generals Kutuzov, Michelsohn and Boeswilen to unite their corps and form a single army.'[25] According to the *Journal de l'Empire* of 18 December 1805, 'The Russian emperor arrived in Olmutz, where he was received to the sound of cannon fire and the cheers of the Austrians, who regarded him as a liberator.'

On 24 November Jean Gheerbrant, an NCO of the 10th Hussars, arrived in the small town of Wischau:

> I was at a soap maker near the Olmutz gate ... this gentleman spoke good German. That same evening he told us that the hills around the town were held by Austrian-Russian light cavalry; that the two emperors, Francis II of Austria and Alexander I of Russia, had passed through the town; that there was an imposing Austro-Russian force not far from us, at Prosnitz and Kremsier, two towns 5 leagues from Wischau; that the Russians were going to receive a very large reinforcement; that their vanguard had already arrived at Olmutz, a very strong town, 10 leagues away.[26]

The Cossacks managed to penetrate Prince Murat's outposts and encircled the town. Gheerbrant, who was on guard that night, described an endeavour made by the Cossacks to capture the town:

> We heard that the enemy horsemen must have been very numerous and that they were spreading out on our left to surround the town and thus cut off our retreat; they began to fire at the town with two cannons and a howitzer, which must have been in battery near the city; by the glow of the fire from the cannons, I could make out the pavements and behind them, the pieces that cavalry were piling up next to each other. Behind us, in the town, we could hear the sound to gather 'horses'; As soon as my men heard this ringing they were anxious to leave their post and go back into the town, arguing that they should not be left alone to be chopped up for others (they were not altogether wrong) but ... I felt that if we abandoned our post we were putting the salvation of our men in

25. *Journal de l'Empire*, 11 décembre 1805, p. 1.
26. Bernard Wilkin, René Wilkin and Christian Remy, *Mémoires des campagnes de Jean Gheerbrant*, Brussels, 2021.

> the town in jeopardy as the enemy would soon find out and rush into the town, causing carnage and perhaps even the annihilation of the Brigade. At first, I had to use all my powers of persuasion to keep them in place, which they eventually accepted. The enemy, who had heard the bell, certainly understood. They approached their battery to the bridge, from where they began to fire at the door in front of which we were standing ... we had nothing to fear from the fire itself; Nevertheless my men were very afraid; I had to show them even more restraint than before by explaining to them that the Biscayans could not reach us; moreover, the first one who would have abandoned his post, I would have slashed him through the body with my sword ...[27]

Following a fierce battle, the town remained unconquered by the Russian forces. On 25 November a significant confrontation occurred between four French hussar and dragoon regiments and the Russian cavalry led by Prince Bagration.[28] General Kutuzov reported to the Czar regarding the event:

> Prince Bagration marched on 14 November in three divisions on Vischau, which was occupied by four regiments of enemy cavalry. The enemy, seeing that Prince Bagration had the design to envelop him in Wischau, abandoned this city at once. Four squadrons of hussars and Cossack regiments were ordered to attack the enemy, who withdrew in great haste, although almost all the cavalry came to his aid and he was far superior to us in strength. The enemy garrison, which was in Vischau, prevented the march of the first division which followed the main road. Prince Bagration gave the adjutant-general Prince Dolgoruki the order to seize the town with a battalion of the sixth regiment of chasseurs and the regiment of musketeers from Pskovitch. This was carried out after some resistance and the 100 soldiers and four officers who were there were all taken prisoner.[29]

Unsurprisingly, the propaganda newspaper *Le Journal de l'Empire* had a different take on the same event:

> On the 7th ... at 9 o'clock in the morning, a group of Cossacks, supported by the Russian cavalry, made the outposts of Prince Murat

27. Bernard Wilkin, René Wilkin and Christian Remy, op. cit., Brussels, 2021.
28. Digby Smith, op. cit., p. 215.
29. *Campagne de la Grande Armée et de l'Armée d'Italie, Supplément, Relation officielle de la bataille d'Austerlitz, présenté à l'empereur Alexandre par le général Kutusow, et observations d'un officier français,* Paris, 1806, pp. 93–4.

> bend, surrounded Vischau and took 50 men on foot of the 6th regiment of dragoons. During the day, the Russian emperor went to Vischau, and the whole Russian army took position behind this city.[30]

The Czar arrived in the city, and this minor triumph elevated the Russian officers and provided them with a false sense of security, which would cost them a few days later. Napoleon, skilled in playing psychological games, feigned fear of the opposing army. He requested an audience with the Emperor of all Russia. The latter sent Prince Dolgorukov, his aide-de-camp, who observed a despondent and demoralised French army:

> This aide-de-camp could see that everything in the French army's demeanour was reserved and timid. The placement of the large guards, the fortifications that were being hastily built, everything showed the Russian officer a half-beaten army.

The author of the account, no doubt Napoleon himself, also remarked:

> The Russian officer wanted to start political questions. He decided above all with an impatience difficult to imagine: he was in the most absolute ignorance of the interests of Europe, and of the situation of the continent. He was, in a word, a young trumpeter of England. He spoke to the Emperor as one speaks to Russian officers, whom he has long since outraged by his haughtiness and ill manners.[31]

The triumph of Austerlitz

On 1 December Emperor Alexander endeavoured to position his army advantageously against the French. The right side of his army was safeguarded by a wood and marshes. Napoleon, however, managed to manoeuvre the Russians out of their chosen positions. As a result, the Russian troops made a flanking movement to turn the French right. Both sides had their troops in place for what would become the most renowned victory of the French emperor, Austerlitz, also known as the 'Battle of the Three Emperors'. One side, under the command in chief of Napoleon, comprised the following troops:

- The Imperial Guard under the orders of Marshals Mortier and Bessières and the 3rd, 4th and 5th corps of the Grande Armée, commanded by Marshals Bernadotte, Davout, Soult, Lannes and Ney.
- In total, 50,000 infantrymen, 15,000 cavalrymen and 282 cannon.

30. *Journal de l'Empire*, 17 December 1805.
31. *30th Bulletin de la Grande Armée*, Austerlitz, 3 December 1805 (12 frimaire an 14).

The Austrian and Russian armies, commanded by Emperors Francis II and Alexander I, had the following personnel:

- The Russian Imperial Guard commanded by Prince Constantine;
- The vanguard under the command of the Russian Kutuzov;
- The troops commanded by General Buxhoeveden;
- The Austrians of Feldmarschall Graf von Kolowrat-Krakowsky;
- The cavalry corps of Feldmarschall Moritz, Prince of Liechtenstein; and
- The right wing commanded by the Russian Prince Bagration.
- In total, 69,460 infantrymen, 16,565 cavalrymen and 252 cannon.

At the beginning of the attack, Napoleon made a short but energetic harangue to the troops surrounding him: 'Soldiers, remember that this battle must be a fight of giants. We must end this campaign with a thunderbolt that will confound the pride of our enemies, and finally teach the world that we have no rivals.'[32] Marshal Soult, on leaving the Emperor, had gone to the village of Kobelnitz, in the rear of which was the St-Hilaire division, under arms; the Marshal passing in front of each regiment excited their ardour and enthusiasm; stopping in front of the 10th regiment of light infantry he said: 'Remember that you beat the Russians for us in Switzerland.' 'We have not forgotten it,' replied the latter, 'even less today than ever.'[33]

Lieutenant François, who observed the battle of Austerlitz as a spectator, documented in his diary the events of the day's fighting:

> On the night of the 1st to the 2nd, General Savary, aide-de-camp to the Emperor, returned from the headquarters of the two emperors having obtained nothing from them, and told the Emperor, as well as many generals and officers, that nothing equalled the jactance of the Russian officers, jeering at the Austrian generals over their defeat. These boasters were ignorant of the genius of our emperor, the skill of our generals and our valour.
>
> The army, towards half past four, took up arms and saw towards five o'clock the Russian army in movement descending the heights of Pratzen in the plain of Antos on Telnitz, marching towards ponds on the right of this village, and other columns on a castle where there are also ponds on the right and left of the roadway. Near a cabaret was the vanguard of the Russians commanded by general Bagration, supported by a numerous artillery; prince Constantine marched on the village of Austerlitz and general-in-chief Kutuzov, in the centre of his columns.

32. *Victoires, conquêtes*, t. 15, p. 243.
33. *Victoires, conquêtes*, t. 15, p. 244.

The Emperor, towards six o'clock, put his army corps in movement. We, the reserve army, saw the movements of the two armies ... From this moment the attack began with the skirmishers on the line. Towards eight o'clock the cannon on both sides thundered, but at nine o'clock the action was almost general, and the fusillade and cannonade were heard on all points and lasted for several hours without advantage on either side. At about noon, Marshal Soult took the position of Pratzen, which was the key to the Russians, and routed them, and all the other enemy lines were shaken. Our people, whom we saw, we, the reserve army, fired only at 100, 80 and 60 paces from the enemy, and overthrew the ranks; we heard the cheers of the Russians, charging on our people, but their cries and their bayonets could not stop the ardour of the soldiers, who, with the bayonet at their backs, made themselves masters of the heights of Pratzen, and of all the artillery which was there. I, like my comrades, saw our battalions mixed up with the Russians, fighting with the bayonet. The Friant division completely beat the Russians on its side, and pushed them back towards an icy pond, which they tried to cross; towards one o'clock, the Emperor made us advance to support the St-Hilaire and Vandamme divisions, which marched in front. As for us, the Emperor made us remain in position; enraged at not being able to fire or use our bayonets, we only manoeuvred, often changing position, hoping that the Emperor would give us the opportunity to show ourselves worthy of our reputation. Bored with doing nothing, several grenadiers and voltigeurs asked the Emperor, when he passed in front of the division, for the honour of sharing the glory of their comrades. 'Rejoice,' he replied, 'in doing nothing, I am keeping you in reserve. So much the better if you are not needed today.'

Towards two o'clock we saw, from our position, near a chapel, the St-Hilaire division push the enemy back to the pond of Sokolnice where the troops that General Friant had knocked down were already halfway through. Some battalions passed over the ice of the pond; but the ice, giving way under the weight of the men, broke, and several thousand officers and soldiers were drowned, and those who escaped, about 6,000 in number, surrounded on the plain of Sokolnice, were taken prisoners; finally we saw these poor Russians in the greatest disorder. A few moments after this event, I saw a park composed of at least 50 pieces of cannon, with their caissons, wanting to pass the icy lake of Aujerzd; when it was in the middle, the place broke, and men, horses, cannons and caissons were swallowed up, as well as four battalions which escorted this park; a similar scene took place on the lake of Moënitz, which general Vandamme experienced. Towards four o'clock in the evening, one saw the two emperors taking great pains to

> gather the debris of their army and to withdraw behind Austerlitz; we lay down on the position which the Russian army, defeated the previous night, had occupied. The allies had more than 40,000 men out of action: 18,000 Russians and 6,000 Austrians were killed or drowned, the rest were wounded and taken prisoner, and among the latter, 15 generals and more than 400 officers, who were less boastful than the day before. I saw them. We, our loss amounted to 2000 dead and 5000 wounded, including eight generals.[34]

The triumphant soldiers had no grounds to grumble about the Emperor's appreciation. Allowances were bestowed upon the widows of the generals, officers and soldiers who had perished in this battle. He took guardianship of their offspring, oversaw their schooling, the progression of sons and the dowries of daughters. All the injured were provided with a gratuity of three months' remuneration, and the Legion of Honour was awarded to those who had demonstrated their talents the most. Finally, Napoleon issued the following proclamation on 3 December to express his great satisfaction with the army's recent performance:

> Soldiers!
>
> I am happy with you. You have, on the day of Austerlitz, justified all that I expected of your intrepidity; you have decorated your eagles with an immortal glory: an army of 100,000 men, commanded by the Emperors of Russia and Austria, was in less than four hours either cut off or dispersed; what escaped your fire drowned in the two lakes. 40 flags, the standards of the Imperial Guard of Russia, 120 pieces of cannon, 20 generals, more than 30,000 prisoners, are the result of this forever famous day. This much vaunted infantry, and in superior numbers, could not resist your shock, and henceforth you have no more rivals to fear; thus, in two months, this third coalition has been defeated and dissolved ...

The Russian army had lost forty-five flags and nearly all the standards of the Imperial Guard. On the French side only the 4th line infantry regiment had lost its eagle. Following the battle Napoleon, stopping during the review, approached the men of the 4th and said to them: 'Soldiers, what have you done with the eagle that I had entrusted to you? You swore that it would serve as a rallying point and that you would defend it at the risk of your

34. Charles-François François, op. cit., pp. 490–2. In reality the French losses were 14 generals, 80 staff officers, 514 officers killed and wounded, and about 10,000 soldiers killed and wounded; the eagle and flag of the 1st battalion of the 4th line infantry regiment were taken.

lives. How did you keep your promise?' Major Bigarré,[35] who commanded the regiment, replied that the flag-bearer had been surrounded and killed and that they had not noticed his fall because of the smoke; that it was only a long time afterwards that he had noticed the loss of his eagle. The first battalion, wishing to repair this loss, had then rushed upon two Russian battalions and taken from them two flags, with which the soldiers paid homage to the Emperor, hoping that Napoleon would give them another eagle in exchange. The French emperor had hesitated for a moment before saying: 'Officers and soldiers, do you swear that none of you noticed the loss of your eagle, and that, if you had noticed, you would have rushed to take it back, or you would have perished on the battlefield, for a soldier who has lost his eagle has lost everything?' Immediately the soldiers replied: 'We swear it, and we also swear to defend the eagles which you will give us, with the same intrepidity as we have put into removing the two flags which we are presenting to you.' Napoleon replied, 'I will therefore give you back your eagle.'[36]

The 33rd *Bulletin de la Grande Armée* of 7 December contained the following remark on one of the enemies confronted on the battlefield: 'The Russian troops are brave, but much less brave than the French troops. Their generals are so inexperienced and the soldiers so ignorant and heavy-handed that their armies are, in truth, not very formidable. And besides, supposing the Russians to win, it would have been necessary to depopulate Russia in order to achieve the insane goal which the London oligarchs had prescribed for them.'

At dawn, the day after the battle, the German emperor Francis II dispatched Prince John of Liechtenstein to request an audience with Napoleon. The French emperor agreed to the meeting on 4 September, whilst the Austro-Russian army retreated. Czar Alexander I took residence in Holitsch, whilst Emperor Francis II was at Czeitsch. Upon arriving at the outposts, Napoleon was greeted by Emperor Francis II. The two monarchs reached an armistice agreement and established the primary terms for peace, which would be immediately negotiated. Additionally, François II requested a truce for the remnants of the Russian army. However, Napoleon reminded him that the Russians were completely encircled: 'But in order to do something agreeable to my brother the Emperor Alexander, I agree to stop the march of my columns and to let this troop pass; but does your majesty promise me that this army will return to Russia and evacuate Germany, Austria, Prussia and Poland?' The reply came: 'This is the intention of the Emperor Alexander, I can assure you; you can moreover convince yourself of it, by sending one of your officers to this prince.' General Savary was immediately sent to Czar

35. Auguste Julien Bigarré (1775–1838), second lieutenant in 1793, distinguished himself in various campaigns under the command of Generals Brune and Drouet.

36. *Journal de l'Empire*, 5 January 1806, pp. 1–2; *Victoires, conquêtes*, t. 15, p. 272.

Alexander; the latter received him at once and said to the general: 'Tell your Master that he has worked miracles; that the day of the 2nd [December] has increased my admiration for him; that I look upon him as predestined, and that my army needs a hundred years to equal his, but may I retire with safety?' General Savary assured the Czar that his troops would be free to withdraw. He immediately set off for Josephsdorf, where Marshal Davout was, to whom he gave the order to let the Russian army go.

The convention which was signed between the French and Austrians included a paragraph concerning Russia: 'The Russian army will evacuate the states of Austria, as well as Austrian Poland, namely, Moravia and Hungary within 15 days, and Galicia within a month. The order of route of the Russian army will be traced, so that it will always be known where it is, as well as to avoid any misunderstanding.' On 7 December the Russian emperor departed from Holitsch for St Petersburg. All the prisoners of the Russian noble guard and Prince Repnin, the colonel of the Chevaliers Guards, were returned by Napoleon without any exchange. The Russian army left in three columns. Pressburg witnessed the signing of the peace treaty between France and Austria on 26 December 1805. The news of this victory disseminated rapidly, chiefly through the letters of the participants. Two days after the battle of Austerlitz, a soldier named Isidore Masuy, stationed in Vienna, sent a letter to his family containing news of the event. The language used within the letter was not of a high standard:

> Vienna, 4 December of the year 14, of the Empire of France, King of Italy.
>
> I will tell you again that we are in Vienna that we do not expect to stay there much time, because we were given cartridges much these days. We are waiting to join the army in Hungary that is pursuing the Russians and Austrians. And we had a big battle before arriving in Vienna, that we lost half of our regiment. In this battle, we had a lot of work to do to defend our lives; there were twenty-five thousand Russians and only five thousand French. And in Hungary they fought again: the battle of the three emperors of France, Austria and Russia. It was the French emperor who beat the other two, the Austrian and the Russian. They had fifteen thousand men killed and wounded and fifteen thousand taken prisoner and the rest, one does not know where it is any more: one seeks to find everywhere. I will tell you again that everything is very expensive, that a pound of butter costs six pounds fifteen cents and it is very difficult to live in that country.

Another soldier, a horseman named Toussaint Walthéry, wrote as soon as he could to his family about the victory of Austerlitz:

Brenne 5 nivosse year 14 [26 December 1805]

My very dear father

I take the liberty of writing this letter to know how you are. I am very well, thank God and I hope to find you the same as well as my brothers and sisters, parents and friends. Since the last time I wrote to you, I left Calais to join the army of the Rhine. We did not give a moment of rest to the Austrian army, which we chased from all of its strongholds and even from its capital. We have fought hard since the crossing of the Danud [Danube] where twenty thousand people died and at Oumes [Ulm, Baden-Württemberg, Germany] where another thirty to thirty-five thousand soldiers were killed. I will not give you details about the battles of Bath, Bille, Branaux and Passeaux and also Linzes, Lixze, which were all very hard. They did not want to leave their capital and as a result forty-five to fifty thousand men died on both sides. At the battle of Bonne, we lost so many people because of the river. But I want to talk about the battle of Desterlix [Austerlitz], the biggest fight ever heard of. The three emperors were there: the Emperor of Russia, the Emperor of Vienna [Austria] and the Emperor of the French. We began firing at six in the morning. The Russians and the Austrians answered five minutes after. The fire was so intense that it was impossible to see anything six feet in front of you. We retreated three times but the fourth time we managed to rout the Russians and the Austrians. We fought against the Imperial Guard of Russia; they were very strong but we beat them. My horse was killed during the battle of Desterlix and I almost died but I fortunately took the horse of another dragoon who had just been cut in two by a cannonball. Forty thousand French, seventy thousand Russian and thirty-five thousand Austrians were killed at Desterlix. For Bresse, I do not know the losses. Dead bodies were buried for fifteen days but it is such a glory for me to have fought in so many battles and to have my horse killed without being killed. I have not received the postal order of 12 frans [francs] but I hope to have it soon so we do not worry. I end this letter by kissing you one thousand times with all my heart. I am forever your son Toussain Waltery. My address

To mister Toussain Waltery Dragon 13th rgt [regiment] 8th compe [company] great army of the Rhine in Moravia.

The bloodshed of the battlefield was not the only memorable fact that Walthéry chose to document. He ended his letter by commenting on local women, a source of curiosity and amusement:

> Many greetings to Hubert Oroge of Angleur [Belgium].[37] Give me news of the country, especially of those who have been conscripted, and of everything in general. I will tell you that I am in a country where they do not speak German or French. Women have the faces of monkeys, the arms of dogs and the feet of camels. They are so beautiful that I want to bring one home. This is it, I am done. I salute you. We are 400 miles from Liege [Liège].[38]

News was sometimes slow to reach the country. Here, for example, is a letter which, five months after the end of the campaign, recounts the events of 1805. It was written by Pierre Sironval, soldier in the 92nd line infantry regiment:

> From Sividal Venetia 9 May 1806
>
> My dear father and dear mother,
>
> I write to enquire about your health. Mine is good at the moment and I hope to find you well. It is all we can hope for each other. I apologise for taking so long to write about myself. The current campaign is responsible and I have not written earlier because we left from Nijmegen to embark. We stayed for a month on a ship and during the month the war was declared with the Austrians and we left right away for the army of the Rhine. When we were in front of the enemy, we fought several battles. God preserved me and I thank him for that. So, we had several big battles, which you probably heard of. Our first battle was the blockade of Ulm where we did good. We took 25 thousand men prisoners and killed five thousand. The weather was unfavourable to us because it was raining a lot and we stayed for six days on site without being able to take cover. When we defeated the Austrian armies, we marched on Vienna and fought several battles. It is not useful to indicate how many men we killed or took prisoner. I just need to tell you that when we arrived in Vienna, there were 160,000 men killed or wounded and we carried on. Moravia was where we fought the biggest battle of the campaign [Austerlitz] and we won the war. I cannot tell you how many men were killed on the battlefield but we put out of action at least 50,000 men, killed or wounded and prisoners, and we took several cannons and ammunition. I cannot give you more details because for two months convoys left for France and you can believe that the battle was cruel and led by

37. Angleur, now a suburb of Liège, Belgium.
38. AEL: FFP 1044. Toussaint Walthéry to his father, 9 October 1805.

> three emperors. There was the one of France, the one from Austria and the one from Russia. The two emperors of Russia and Austria were almost captured. They took advantage of the night to run away and after all of that we were based in Astirie for a month and we rested. Then, we came to Venice and it was really too hot and on one side we have mountains and snow all the time. We crossed the mountains and walked 560 miles. Nothing else, please send my regards to Marie Catherine Palatte and her family. I kiss her with all my heart. Tell mother Michot that he [her son] is not serving France anymore. He deserted to the Austrians. He passed me a message stating that he was well and he salutes you.[39]

The first information disseminated in the French capital appeared in the quasi-official newspaper *La Gazette nationale ou le Moniteur universel* of 12 December 1805: 'Mr. Colonel Lebrun, aide-de-camp of the Emperor, dispatched by His Majesty at the end of the battle which took place, on Friday 11, between Brunn and Olmutz, announced the following results: 40,000 prisoners; 70 cannons; the guard of the Emperor of Russia routed and a part taken, as well as several officers and a colonel; the two emperors of Russia and Austria on the point of being taken, and fleeing in all haste to Olmutz; several general officers taken, among others a prince Galitsin; the remainder of the Russian army in the rout no longer complete; the battle called, by the soldiers, the battle of the three emperors. The French army lost little.' It was not until 14 December 1805 that the Parisian press said more about the course of the battle, without yet giving too many details or even mentioning the name Austerlitz. The *Journal de l'Empire* commented on the second page: 'All the Russian troops were united, the remnants of the Austrian armies increased their forces. The leaders of the two empires of Austria and Russia were at the head of the armies. Grand Duke Constantine had just brought in reinforcements: masters of the field, of the moment, they themselves presented the battle to the French army, much inferior in number, and their rout was complete; if the negotiations continue, it is not known what language the Emperor Alexander will use; but there is reason to believe that the Emperor of Germany will entirely separate his cause from that of such a dangerous ally. The particular letters leave no doubt as to the arrogance with which the Russians treated the Austrians before they had learned from the event that one can be beaten by the French, let 40,000 prisoners be taken, without however deserving the contempt of the other nations of Europe. Remembering that Alexander did not want to recognise the Emperor of the French, we say to ourselves that he has at least

39. AEL: FFP 1043. Pierre Sironval to his parents, 9 May 1806.

learnt to know him, and some jokers are holding him harmless today from all recognition.'

It was not until 17 December and the arrival of the 30th *Bulletin de la Grande Armée* that the public, which until then had had to make do with news of the days preceding 2 December, was finally informed of the progress of the fighting and the victory at Austerlitz. The following day the *Journal de l'Empire* published the 31st and 32nd *Bulletins de la Grande Armée*, both dated Austerlitz, 15 Frimaire (5 December), as well as the text of the armistice concluded between the Austrian and French emperors. The enthusiasm was at its height. A *Te Deum* was sung at Notre-Dame in the presence of all the princes of the imperial family and the various orders of the State on 22 December.

Czar Alexander had not signed an agreement with the French, so in principle he remained at war with Napoleon. The Russian soldiers taken prisoner during the campaign and not released early therefore remained in the hands of the victors and were sent to France. A dispatch sent from Bamberg on 25 December states that: 'the number of Russian prisoners taken by the French is so considerable that it is more difficult to keep them all than it was to seize them ... Russians who manage to escape cross our town without stockings, without shoes, without money;[40] in a word, in such a terrible state of destitution that it is impossible not to be touched. They all ask for the way to Dresden; it is to this city that they are heading.'

The Czar set off to return to his capital. A dispatch from Berlin dated 22 December stated: 'Emperor Alexander has left for Petersburg with all speed. There is much talk of a new campaign; but if peace is concluded with Austria where will Russia be able to wage war against France?'[41]

The victory of Austerlitz was the occasion for new attacks on Britain in the French newspapers. In a long article published by the *Journal de l'Empire* on 19 December, it was written: 'it is doubtful, moreover, that the English people will at first be deeply moved by the shame of Russia and the disorder of Austria; they are too ignorant to guess the consequences of the campaign which has just ended, and too vain not to believe themselves capable of extending and holding on to their domination: they will find it easier to accuse their allies than to admire the courage of the French. Fear will begin with the educated people capable of reflection and it is from there that it will spread to the people.'

In Paris on 1 January 1806 the Tribunate, to the accompaniment of cannon firing, escorted by troops and by members of various bodies of the administration, went to the senate in order to deposit there fifty-four flags conquered during the

40. Prisoners of war were regularly robbed by their captors.

41. *Journal de l'Empire*, 2 January 1896, p. 1.

campaign of 1805, all carried by veterans. The crowds invaded the streets and shouted as the procession passed: 'Long live the Emperor! Long live the Great Army! Victory! Victory! Long live the Emperor!'; the houses were decorated with tapestries, hangings and various ornaments. Everywhere were inscribed the words: Napoleon, Ulm, Vienna, Austerlitz.

Napoleon returned to Paris on 28 January 1806, more powerful than ever.

Chapter 3

War and peace

The Fourth Coalition

Following the battle at Austerlitz and the retreat of the Russian military, there remained a significant threat that, without a formal peace agreement with the Czarist empire, Alexander would prolong the war. Consequently, Napoleon endeavoured to divert the Russian emperor's focus by provoking tensions with the Ottoman empire under Sultan Selim III. This strategy proved advantageous. In January 1806, at the urging of Russia, uprisings in Bosnia were initiated by Montenegrin and Serbian forces, which resulted in widespread destruction. On 27 February the region's vizier and his entire retinue were captured. On 11 March the Turks were ousted from Sarajevo by the Serbs and Montenegrins. The revolt in Serbia expanded to Bulgaria. On 28 March the Serbian rebels captured Belgrade. A Turkish army crossed the Drina but suffered defeat on 26 April at the hands of the Serbs, who were joined by 3,000 Montenegrins. On 20 June 1806 Napoleon corresponded with Sultan Selim III: 'if your Highness wishes to allow us to finish with a piece of advice, we will tell him that the true interests of his empire require that she does not allow any foreign power to intervene in her discussions with the Serbs; that she must use the most vigorous means to subdue these rebels, who are excited and encouraged by Russia; the request she has made to grant them independence proves this enough. As for Moldavia and Wallachia,[42] if your Highness does not want these provinces to escape her, she must seize every favourable opportunity to recall the old houses there; the Greek princes who govern them at present are the agents of the Russians; to these measures you must add that of preventing Russian vessels from passing the Bosphorus ...'[43]

During the early months of 1806 there were discussions between representatives from France and Russia. On 20 July 1806 a peace treaty was signed in Paris by the French general Clarke and the Czar's adviser, d'Oubril, on behalf of the respective powers. The document was subsequently taken to St Petersburg by d'Oubril for ratification by Alexander I. However, on

42. The two Romanian-speaking provinces of the Ottoman Empire.
43. Napoléon Bonaparte, *Correspondance générale*, t. 6, p. 534.

15 August the Czar not only refused to ratify the document but also disowned and discredited the negotiator. As a result, France and Russia remained at war. In response to this, Napoleon wrote a letter to his brother, Joseph, addressing the matter: 'The treaty concluded on 20 July with M. d'Oubril was not ratified. The only reason that the Emperor of Russia could give is that he did not want to make peace without the British.'[44]

It will be recalled that since the time of Czar Paul I, the court of St Petersburg had had its sights set on the Mediterranean Sea. Despite a failed attempt to gain a foothold on the island of Malta, the Russians controlled the Septinsular Republic opposite the Albanian coast. Taking advantage of the fact that the treaty of Pressburg ceded Venice and its possessions, including the Republic of Ragusa (Dubrovnik, Croatia today), to the French on 4 March 1806, the Russians took control of Cattaro (present-day Kotor, Montenegro) with support from the Republic of Ragusa (currently Dubrovnik, Croatia), before the Austrians surrendered the province to the French. General Lauriston was instructed by Napoleon to send troops to occupy Ragusa on 27 May 1806. Negotiations between Russia and France for a peace treaty were announced, leading to a pause in military operations. However, as the negotiations failed to reach an agreement, the situation changed.[45] The *Journal de l'Empire* explained:

> In the course of September, the Russians, having received notice that the peace treaty had not been ratified by their sovereign, continued to stir up the inhabitants of Montenegro and those of Cattaro. They succeeded in forming a corps of 9,000 armed peasants and joined them with about 6,000 Russians whom they had brought from Corfu. This army was commanded by general Pantakolof, with prince Wasminskoï under his orders, who had recently arrived in Corfu with some reinforcements. General-in-chief Marmont, pretending to avoid combat, made a retrograde march of two days, in the hope of drawing the enemy out of his entrenchments. Indeed, the Russians took this manoeuvre for a retreat, and on the morning of 29 September they came to camp on the mountain of Kilibrick. At the same time General Marmont, at the head of 6,000 men, advanced to attack them. The combat began at 10 o'clock, and after a lively fusillade, the Montenegrins were driven out of their jurisdiction and forced to retreat precipitately, to be able to join the Russians who had placed themselves only in second line. General Marmont had the abandoned posts occupied and resumed the attack the next day at dawn, near Castelnovo (Herceg Novi, Montenegro today). This time the Russians could be reached. Our soldiers attacked the

44. Napoléon Bonaparte, *Correspondance*, t. 6, p. 788.
45. Buret de Longchamps, op. cit., pp. 120–2.

> enemy with the bayonet. Although both sides fought extremely hard, the victory was not undecided. The Russians withdrew in great disorder, leaving the battlefield covered with dead and wounded. The suburbs of Castelnovo were set on fire with the provisions which the Russians had amassed there; the result of these two days was for the enemy the loss of 850 men killed, among whom 550 Russians, more than 1,000 wounded and several hundred prisoners; the French army had only 25 men killed and 150 wounded.[46]

Beaten on land by the French, the Russians still ruled the sea, a fact admitted by the main French propaganda newspaper: 'Trieste, 6 October. The Russians blocked the Istrian coast tightly, so that no production can reach us by water. There is a 74-gun Russian ship of the line in our harbour.'[47] On 23 November Russia declared war on the Ottoman empire. General Kutusov and Prince Dolgoruky took Choczin and Iassy (Moldavia). On 27 December General Michelson took Bucharest.

During the War of the Third Coalition, Prussia resisted the temptation to align with Austria against the French in exchange for the cession of Hanover, which belonged to King George III of England. Therefore, Prussia did not participate in the conflict. On 11 June 1806 the United Kingdom declared war on Prussia. Napoleon was aware of the unreliability of the Berlin government, which had taken a threatening attitude at the end of the conflict. At King Friedrich Wilhelm III's court, a significant faction, led by Queen Louise, exerted pressure on the monarch to declare war against France. While Britain was in the process of negotiating a peace treaty with France, it notified Prussia of the potential return of Silesia to Austria and the evacuation of Hanover, resulting from a diplomatic agreement between France and Russia. Consequently, on 21 August the Prussian army began retreating from the electorate of Hanover. Following Fox's demise, the British cabinet endeavoured to incite the collapse of the negotiations, laying the blame on the French. Meanwhile, Napoleon, who remained convinced of his military superiority, attempted to form an alliance with Prussia, but to no avail.

As early as 26 August 1806 the Prussian court was informed of Alexander's refusal to ratify the treaty negotiated in Paris.[48] On 30 August the Czar published a manifesto announcing the rupture with France. In spite of prolonged deliberation, the King of Prussia finally elected to align himself with anti-French forces, buoyed by the legacy of Frederic II's formidable but ancient campaigns. Without awaiting the arrival of Russian troops, an

46. *Journal de l'Empire*, 27 October 1806, p. 1.
47. *Journal de l'Empire*, 26 October 1806, p. 1.
48. Louis Madelin, *Histoire du Consulat et de l'Empire*, t. 2, Paris, 2003, p. 388.

ultimatum was issued to the French sovereign on 25 September. The French emperor was asked to stop putting obstacles in the way of the formation of a Northern League, which would bring together the German states that were not part of the Germanic Confederation, and to allow all French troops present in Germany to cross the Rhine again. The Prussian ultimatum expired on 8 October. The *Journal de l'Empire* reported: 'Berlin, October 4 [1806]. For a few days, there has been a succession of distinguished Russians arriving in this capital ... We are told that a considerable army of Russians is on the march under the orders of Field Marshal Kamensky and Generals Kutuzov and Prince Bagration; but it is not said when this army will be brought to the theatre of war. However, time is short.'

Napoleon, alerted by his new enemy's military preparations, had immediately entered the campaign. He wrote from Bamberg to Talleyrand, his minister of foreign relations, on 7 October: 'you will find enclosed the letter of the King of Prussia. I read it only very lightly ... What there is pleasant in all this, it is that the Prussians give me their ultimatum on the 8th, and that I, without knowing it, had entered the country of Bayreuth on the 7th, and that I had begun my movements. I hope that great events will take place within a month, and that the King will realise that the advice of women is fatal. The King of Württemberg announces that a courier has left for St Petersburg with a political memorandum and a letter from the Queen of Prussia asking for 100,000 men from her lover.'[49]

The French army advanced rapidly, and on 14 October the battles of Jena and Auerstedt occurred simultaneously. These engagements proved disastrous for the Prussian forces, resulting in the near-complete annihilation of their army in a single day. Consequently, the King and what remained of his troops were compelled to retreat to East Prussia and face the Russians, under pursuit by Napoleon. The Prussian fortresses were besieged and surrendered successively: Erfurt on 16 October; Spandau on 25 October; Prenzlau on 28 October; Pasewalck and Stettin on 29 October; Boldekow on 30 October; Anklam and Küstrin on 1 November; Wolgast on 3 November; Wismar on 5 November; Lübeck on 6 November; Ratkau on 7 November; Magdeburg on 11 November; Boizenburg on 12 November; Hameln on 22 November; Plassenburg on 25 November; Nienburg on 26 November; Glogau on 2 December; Bierzun on 23 December; and Soldau on 25 December.

Napoleon entered Berlin on 27 October. From this city he wrote on 30 October to the King of Wurttemberg: 'Until this hour, I do not hear of the Russians. I admit to Your Majesty that I would be very happy to meet them to give them a good and severe lesson, which would make them repent of the

49. Napoléon Bonaparte, *Correspondance générale*, t. 6, p. 988.

little memory and recognition they have retained of the good behaviour I had towards them at Austerlitz.'[50]

The French were hot on the Prussians' heels. A series of battles took place between pursuers and pursued: Halle on 17 October; Zehdenick on 26 October; Waren and Nossentin on 1 November; Criwitz on 3 November; Schwartau on 6 November; Bierzun on 23 December; and Soldau on 25 December. The *Bulletin de la Grande Armée* of 5 December 1806 stated that 'the Russians having refused the battle in front of Warsaw have crossed the Vistula again. The Grand Duke of Berg has passed it after them … He is pursuing them on the Bug.' Two days later the second *Bulletin* reported that 'the Russian army, commanded by General Bennigsen, has evacuated the Vistula and seems determined to push inland'.

Czar Alexander had sent a new general-in-chief, Kamensky, who decided to go on the offensive. The first French encounter with the Russians took place on 11 December: 'at six o'clock in the morning, the cannonade was heard on the Bug side. Marshal Davoust had made Brigadier General Gauthier cross this river at the mouth of the Wrka, opposite the village of Okunin. The 23rd Line and the 89th had passed ... when a Russian division presented itself to take this village. It made only useless efforts, was repulsed and lost many people. We had twenty men killed or wounded.'[51] The pursuit continued and on 23 December 1806 at Czarnowo, 30 km north of Warsaw, Napoleon with 8,500 men defeated 15,000 Russians, who lost 3 generals, 38 officers and 1,360 soldiers, killed, wounded or taken prisoner.

On 26 December two battles were fought simultaneously by the French against retreating Russian troops. The first, at Pultusk, was described by Jean Gheerbrant, sergeant of the 10th Hussars:

> From our position we were able to see the fighters' locations, the surroundings of the town of Pultusk. This was the place where the enemy had their masses; a great part of their cavalry was divided on the extremity of their flanks and a strong artillery in front, which cannonaded. One saw no reserve, unless it should have been in the city; they had for all retreat only the bridge. Also, in my opinion, their position was bold, it is true very tight on the height overlooking the plain; but if the road had been practicable and if we had charged their positions to seize the bridge, they should have surrendered at the discretion of the conqueror of the bridge.
>
> The French army was breaking through on several points in the vicinity of this plain; their extent was great; there were two main

50. Napoléon Bonaparte, *Correspondance générale*, t. 6, pp. 1059–60.
51. *Bulletin de la Grande Armée*, 14 December 1806.

points by which the great force was to go to the place of combat. Unfortunately, it could not arrive at the main outlet, because in general the approaches were so bogged down and impassable that within living memory, nothing of the kind had ever been seen. At about four o'clock I saw, dumbfounded, on the main road, at the outlet of a wood, by which a French Corps should have gone, up to 16 to 20 horses harnessed to a four-gauge gun, and it was still impossible to drag it. This plain, so vast and well-cultivated, now had the appearance of a swamp, equally impassable to the manoeuvres of a cannon, and for men and horses impossible to get out of it; finally the best horses only knew how to go at a walk and even then, slowly.

Having only recently taken position, our regiment was in reserve behind the 9th and 21st, which were threatened by a charge from a large group of Cossacks, infinitely superior in number. The Brigade went forward at a walk in this mud and stopped to wait for them firmly, a little before a shallow valley in this plain. The Cossacks came up to the said shallow valley, which served as a barrier between the two lines. The distance between the two was within pistol range; having remained two or three minutes examining our brigade and the mud of the shallows from which they could not have escaped, they withdrew and returned towards the town. The brigade retrograded a few paces and our regiment returned to the position it had previously occupied.

Back on the rise we saw this poor French Infantry, in spite of the greasy mud, sinking to half a leg, spread out and extend their flanks under fire and within range of the enemy guns. On our side we could only see two or three guns bogged down at the beginning of the plain, which could only fire in the direction they were facing, without being able to manoeuvre. We saw General Claparède's division arrive in the mud, which had come to place itself in front of the 9th and 21st. The 17th Light sent its voltigeurs as skirmishers forward, and they slowly followed their impulse; another regiment of *chasseurs à pied* followed them. These were deployed between the road we were on and the Narew.

The enemy sent a strong line of skirmishers to oppose these Regiments. The enemy did not cease to cannonade our lines; it is true that their fire was not deadly, for all the cannonballs that hit the ground sank into the mud without ricocheting. At that moment I saw a strange move which proves that danger, combined with fear, makes one make efforts. A *Chasseur à Pied* found himself wounded in the line, two of his comrades led him back, each holding an arm. The one on the left got up first without looking back and, full of mud, began to run towards us with all his speed; the one in the middle also got up, previously he had to be supported, in addition he was doing a thousand contortions, but then he knew how to run so well that the other, the third, remained lying down for good.

Not long afterwards the same aide-de-camp who had placed us in ambush, arrived at the regiment; he carried orders to close on our brigade pending further orders from our commanding general. The brigade pressed to the left, approached the wood and the outlet, through which the 5th Corps arrived and placed itself in second line. To give an idea of the slime and mud that lay on the ground at the exit of the wood: the ground at this point was lower than the plateau; the road or path was very wide, the ground greasy from the trampling of men and horses, and the ditches that bordered it, formed one level, and so kneaded that the whole formed one mortar. Even when one reached the plateau one did not recognise the place of the ditches; so men and horses, who missed the road, fell above the kidneys into the ditches which always formed the greatest floods. I saw a horse being pulled which, despite its strength and vigour, would not have got out of it on its own and would have stayed there. Ahead, 100 paces across the plain and level with the first line, on the left of the road, there was an eight-gauge gun in battery in the mud. It could not move and could only fire in the one direction in which it was placed, so the gunners were quite on the lookout and only fired when the enemy moved in the right direction.

The position of the 5th Corps: the Claparède Division in the centre and on the right of the road, the Suchet Division; the other Division, on the left of the road, formerly commanded by General Gazan and at the moment, I believe, by General Cafarelli; a division of dragoons behind them. On our side the plain was surrounded by a wood. The centre of the French army and the left wing cannoned the enemy from afar, but they could not move towards the town, which became inaccessible because of the mud. So the enemy, surrounded by three quarters of a victorious army of one hundred thousand men against their weak forces of forty-five thousand men, owed their salvation only to time and not to their success.

Towards three o'clock a thick cloud covered the whole horizon. By a darkness that took away all clarity and an impetuous wind blowing at the same time, the fog caused the heavy hum of the gun to cease. A calm reigned for a few minutes, when all of a sudden, we heard shouts, a few rifle shots on our left and further forward than our lines; we judged well that it was a surprise made in the darkness, without knowing what it was made of; the noise calmed down for a few minutes and then started again as strongly as before; finally all this was a mystery to us! Shortly afterwards the cloud was unloaded by the snow which fell in large flakes. Chased by the weather, it blinded us; the light reappeared

> a little, but the snow continued to fall well into the evening. According to what was said the next day, it was the two Battalions of the 88th and 64th Regiments of our country who wanted to take advantage of the darkness and rushed, with energetic courage, on a Russian Corps in battle not far from them. With bayonets they massacred a large part of them and took the rest prisoner. As they were bringing the latter back, they were charged by the enemy cavalry, who had been warned by some escaped prisoners …
>
> After the heavy frost had cleared, the Infantry withdrew into the woods and we were ordered to leave a picket of twenty-four men per Regiment and go and occupy a village in the rear. At the entry of the village there was a bridge and a water mill; the General Staff stopped there and the accountants of the regiments were asked to help; I was obliged to stop. From then on, after having taken note of the order, I left with my quartermaster to seek shelter among the congestion. All the houses were full. We pushed on to the end where we found a barn to take refuge in with our horses; no sooner had our horses been tied up, than fire broke out by accident in the house or thatched cottage opposite the barn on the other side of the street; a fire caused by a candle that a wounded infantryman carried into the house, while searching in the attic. By the strong wind the thatched cottage, covered with straw, was entirely engulfed in flames, and as it blew in the direction of the village the fire spread with such celerity and impetuosity that any help was too late, because the French ambulance was occupied at the first house and horses had to be withdrawn; all the houses and barns were set ablaze and everything fell prey to the flames, with the exception of our own barn and two others further on our side. The next day, at daylight, we saw the rest of the thatched cottages smoking, the unfortunate inhabitants wandering around with their families. …
>
> [The brigade] set out for the battlefield. On the way we learned that the enemy, during the night, had evacuated the town and had blown up the bridge behind him.[52]

A letter published without giving the author's name by the *Journal de l'Empire*, dated from Pultusk on 18 January 1807, stated: 'On our way to arrive here, we only encountered abandoned Russian cannons and equipment; the generals left their carriages to the first people who wanted to seize them, and the prisoners are going to be used to bury their fellow citizens. Every day prisoners are brought in from the other side of the Narew: the regiments flee,

52. Bernard Wilkin, René Wilkin and Christian Remy, op. cit., pp. 200–6.

leaving their baggage and their sick behind; but, unfortunately, the season is an insurmountable obstacle. In order to advance, you need a terrain, and there is none here. The foot sinks where it is placed, and our guns would be lost in the mud.'[53]

The battle of Pultusk, which saw two armies fighting fiercely, was presented to the Czar by the Russian general Bennigsen as a victory over part of the French army. The clergy celebrated this so-called success in all the churches of Russia.[54]

The other battle on 26 December, that at Golymin, was reported by Jean-Nicolas Curély,[55] a lieutenant at the time:

> The brigade crossed the Vistula on 15 December at Warsaw, remained until the 21st at Gradeffki, moved forward on the 22nd and crossed the Bug on the 23rd, despite the resistance of the Russians; they killed men and horses and took prisoners. We continued to march on the 24th and in the evening at the bivouac we met the enemy. On the 25th, the brigade was strongly cannonaded after having passed a long and narrow pond. It lost some men and was forced to retreat. It arrived in front of Golymin on the 26th of December at about 10 o'clock in the morning and found a quarter of a league or so beyond this village, the cuirassiers of the Russian guard and dragoons, forming a total of about 1000 men with 8 or 10 pieces in battery, the whole ranged in a plain, the left supported on a point. The Russian army coming from Pultusk marched on the road through Golymin to Machow. The roads were terrible, especially for the French army, which had only the crossings at its disposal. In my opinion, the aim of the French army was to block the road to the Russians at Golymin, to throw them into the marshes of the river Orezyc which flowed to their right, and to make them lay down their arms; both things could be done at least in part, if the generals commanding on this point had agreed. The Lasalle brigade waited for three hours for the orders of the Grand Duke of Berg; they arrived very slowly with very little infantry and only one cannon which, not being able to reach the line, – on the enemy's side

53. *Journal de l'Empire*, 29 January 1807, p. 1.

54. The text of Bennigsen's proclamation is reproduced in the 14th *Bulletin de la Grande Armée* of 14 January 1807. Digby Smith, op. cit., p. 235, gives the following losses in this battle: 5 generals, 140 officers killed and wounded, 3,200 men killed and wounded, 700 taken prisoner by the French. On the Russian side 3,500 killed and wounded, 1,500 taken prisoner, 12 cannon lost.

55. Jean-Nicolas Curély (1774–1827) volunteered in the 8th Hussars in 1793. He successively rose through the ranks and was appointed colonel in 1813 and general after the battle of Château-Thierry on 12 February 1814. Louis XVIII appointed him *maréchal de camp*. He rallied to Napoleon during the Hundred Days, without returning to active service.

> without reaching it. On the left of Murat's corps came to place Marshal Augereau with almost all his infantry, which he formed in square and in mass in the middle of the plain, within cannon range of the road on which the Russians marched, who presented their left flank to us. Murat had thrown what little infantry he had into the wood which was on the right of his corps and on the left of the Russians. Towards two o'clock in the afternoon, the attack was ordered; our line of cavalry had its right supported in the wood; the brigade of Lasalle formed the extreme left and was to charge on the Russian artillery. No sooner had this brigade taken 20 steps forward to charge than it heard the cry: Halt! Halt! And this cry was repeated throughout the line. The enemy did not fire a cannon shot, and yet the two regiments turned around and built a retreat; they could not be rallied until after half a quarter of an hour. What was absolutely inconceivable; there was neither a cavalryman nor an infantryman in front of our brigade; there were indeed eight or ten cannon, but which might not have had time to fire if the charge had been rapid, which in any case would certainly have been taken after the first salvo. The cavalry which was on our right was not stopped in its movement; it tumbled the enemy, who on his side charged on it, and it took from him a quantity of men and horses as well as two standards … As soon as the brigade was rallied, General Lasalle sent for the elite company of the seventh hussars, which had remained alone and without incurring the least danger on the ground thus abandoned in disorder. Then the general led his two regiments under the enemy cannon, and they remained there until midnight without moving. To give an idea of the loss which this brigade suffered from the fire of the cannon as a punishment for its retrograde movement, it will suffice for me to say that the general who stood in front had two horses killed under him. Men and horses were falling at every moment, no one moved, and not even a murmur was heard.[56]

It seems that Napoleon, after these victories, thought the campaign was over. The 10th *Bulletin de la Grande Armée*, dated Pultusk on 30 December, stated: 'The battle of Czarnowo, that of Nasiesk, that of Kursomb, the cavalry battle of Lopaczin, were followed by those of Golymin and Pulstuk, and the entire and precipitous retreat of the Russian army ended the year and the campaign.' Napoleon displayed his successes over the Russian army to the inhabitants of Warsaw:

56. Jean-Nicolas Curély, *Itinéraire d'un cavalier léger de la Grande Armée (1795–1815), publié d'après un manuscrit authentique par le général Thoumas*, Paris, 1887, pp. 199–203.

> 99 pieces of cannon, taken from the Russians, are ranged in the square of the Palace of the Republic in Warsaw. … In the countries occupied by the army, there are several hospitals containing a large number of wounded and sick Russians. 5,000 prisoners were evacuated to France, 2,000 escaped in the first movement of the disorder, and 1,500 entered the Polish troops. Thus the fighting against the Russians cost them a large part of their artillery, all their baggage, and 25 or 30,000 men both killed and wounded or prisoners.[57]

Despite Napoleon's belief, the campaign was far from over. On 25 January 1807 a battle, known as the battle of Mohrüngen, was fought in Prussia between Marshal Bernadotte's 12,000 troops and General Markov's 9,000 soldiers. Around 1,100 French troops were lost, with the Russians suffering 1,400 casualties and retreating to Liebstadt.[58]

A bloody draw

On 7 February 1807 the Russians chose to halt their retreat and engage Napoleon in battle. The French army was exhausted from the extended marches in pursuit of the enemy amidst the harsh cold weather, and numbered between 55,000 and 60,000 men. They consisted of 15,000 from the third corps (Davout), 16,500 from the fourth (Soult), 6,500 from the seventh (Augereau), 6,000 from the Imperial Guard, and 10,000 from the cavalry reserve (Murat). The arrival of the sixth corps, with 9,000 to 10,000 men (Ney), which had been pursuing a Prussian corps, was long-anticipated. The number of artillery pieces did not exceed 200. With a smaller force of 40,000 men facing 60,000 Russians, the Emperor had to rely on the modest town of Eylau and reserve troops to pin down the enemy whilst waiting for reinforcements from Davout and Ney. As a result, only the fourth corps was deployed in the front line, with the seventh held in reserve. The guard and cavalry, under the command of Klein, Grouchy and d'Hautpoul, were positioned at the rear. The left flank was covered by the light cavalry of the corps, as well as the Bruyère and Colbert brigades. All available artillery was positioned at the front. The initial imbalance of the French front, which occupied only 3km while the Russian front occupied 1.4km more, dictated the battle plan of the opponents.

The Russian general-in-chief, Bennigsen, had hoped that Lestocq's Prussian corps, consisting of 10,000 men, would join him during the day. He chose a suitable position for the cavalry's action, but his plan had a major flaw: only the centre received adequate support. In his memoirs, he explained that he had intended to provoke the French into directing their efforts towards his centre by

57. 54th *Bulletin de la Grande Armée*, 27 January 1807.
58. D. Smith, op. cit., pp. 239–40.

allowing them to occupy Eylau. His primary formation consisted, from right to left, of the Tuczov, Essen, Sacken and Ostermann divisions, complemented by 170 artillery pieces. The cavalry was positioned on the wings and behind the centre with an additional reserve of horse artillery comprising 70 pieces. The reserve consisted of the Somo, Dokhturov and Kamensky divisions, which extended the right wing, while Markov's mixed corps was behind the first line. On the left side Serpalen was occupied by Barclay de Tolly's corps. This formation created a 4km front, 1km east of Eylau.

Both armies were situated on terrain that contained multiple ponds, but these went unnoticed due to the snow covering them. Bennigsen was aware of the possibility that the French right wing could receive reinforcements from Davout and therefore launched an attack with his own right wing to envelop his opponent. In response, Napoleon exerted all efforts to speed up Davout's arrival, instructing him to target the enemy's left without any concern for their envelopment attempt, anticipating Ney's arrival to put a halt to their efforts.

Between 7 and 8 o'clock in the morning an intense artillery bombardment commenced upon the town of Eylau and the St-Hilaire division. The attack set fire to Eylau and Rothnen. The Russian right flank began to move, advancing in columns and firing at half range with each shot finding its mark. For a brief moment, they appeared eager to advance and overwhelm the French left. Nevertheless, the Leval division was able to repel the attack, although they did not pursue the enemy. At that precise moment, Marshal Davout's skirmishers announced their arrival at the enemy's rear. Simultaneously, Marshal Augereau's corps emerged in columns, advancing towards the enemy centre, thus dividing his attention and preventing him from attacking Marshal Davout's corps in its entirety. The Friant division successfully pushed back Baggovout and overran the enemy's left flank. Meanwhile, the Morand division continued the offensive and occupied the vacated position. By 10 o'clock the Emperor deemed it opportune to launch an attack, given the weakened state of the enemy's left. He instructed Augereau to move in a column towards the south of Eylau, aiming for the Russian centre. The initial first line was formed by Soult's corps, with the St-Hilaire division leading the right flank of the charge. Their main objective was to move forward without leaving any gaps between Augereau's and Davout's corps. The French right was thus to pivot around Eylau. Marshal Augereau, who was suffering from illness, had himself fastened to his horse and led his divisions south of the cemetery, with Desjardins on the left and Heudelet on the right. The artillery, which had been positioned near the cemetery since morning, advanced 400m to provide support to the infantry. However, at that moment a snow blizzard became so heavy that visibility was reduced to only two steps, affecting both armies. The snowstorm was driven towards the French by a strong easterly wind, and, as a result, they lost direction. The darkness lasted for thirty minutes. Augereau's divisions were blinded and deviated to the left. Instead of facing the Russians directly, they marched in front of the Russian centre, exposing their flank. The Russian cavalry drove them into complete disorder after being hit at close range by seventy-two pieces of artillery. Captain Marbot, an eyewitness to the battle, wrote the following passage in his memoirs:

> The heavy guns which were in a semicircle round Augereau belched forth such a hail of grape and canister as had never been seen within human memory. In one instant our two divisions were rent to pieces by the storm of iron. General Desjardins was killed, General Heudelet dangerously wounded. Still they held their ground, until the army corps being almost entirely destroyed, its fragments had perforce to be recalled to the neighbourhood of the cemetery of Eylau; always excepting the 14th, who, wholly surrounded by the enemy, remained on the little hill which it had occupied.[59]

The situation was critical: to the south of Eylau, where Napoleon was, a gap had opened between the St-Hilaire division and Davout's corps on one side and the rest of the army on the other. The Russian cavalry initiated a counterattack, causing disarray within the St-Hilaire division, and the French line was in danger of collapsing entirely. In a last-ditch effort, Napoleon commanded Murat to lead all of his cavalry in a charge against the Russians. The dragoons of Grouchy led the charge, followed by the grenadiers of Hautpoul and the dragoons of Milhaud. Despite the artillery firing indiscriminately at both sides, the first Russian line was overcome, and the second line was pushed back, but ultimately held out. The French cavalry was taken by surprise as the first line reformed and attacked in reverse. Upon witnessing this, the Emperor commanded Colonel Lepic to lead the six squadrons of grenadiers of the guard in a charge, followed by General Dahlmann leading the chasseurs. The guard squadrons then crossed the enemy army twice. Two lines of Russian infantry were defeated, while a third line managed to hold its ground with the protection of some wooden cover. Despite being considerably weakened, the French cavalry succeeded in halting the Russian offensive as intended, and then regrouped in the rear of Eylau. It was during this engagement that both General d'Hautpoul and General Dahlmann sustained serious injuries. Ultimately, both succumbed to their wounds.

Meanwhile, a column of 4,000 Russian grenadiers marched straight ahead and reached the cemetery where the Emperor stood. General Dorset led a battalion of grenadiers of the guard to attack the column from the front using bayonets and without firing a shot. The squadron of chasseurs on duty charged

59. Marcellin Marbot, op. cit., pp. 204–5.

the column from the flank, while the Bruyère brigade attacked it from the rear. As a result, most of the 4,000 Russians were either captured or killed and the enemy centre was now shaken. A decisive counterattack could have secured the victory, but Napoleon only had eight battalions of the foot guard in reserve and needed to keep them to hold off Lestoc's Prussians who were on the verge of breaking through at any moment. It was necessary to maintain the point of support at Eylau and assign Davout with the task of inciting the decision on the right flank. After encountering a near-disaster, the situation improved. The St-Hilaire division had to retreat, left to fend for itself after the catastrophe of the seventh corps. Morand himself was discovered. Klein, who had just charged alongside Murat, recognised the situation, and ordered one of his brigades to attack. Davout personally came to rally the Morand division. With the help of Milhaud's cavalry, the remainder of the third corps was able to regain the offensive.

At this point, Lestoc's 8,000 Prussians, who had escaped the pursuit of Marshal Ney, arrived in front of Davout's men after having bypassed the rear of the Russian army. Davout once again demonstrated his leadership ability and successfully held his corps' position for three hours, allowing Ney, who had finally reached them, to push through on the Russian right flank. Ney's arrival, combined with the apprehension of Bernadotte's potential interference, convinced Bennigsen, who was wary of his communication lines being severed, to order a retreat.

The French were left in control of the battlefield, but the question of victory remains disputed. According to reports released by the French, the casualty count was relatively low. Both sides asserted their success in the battle. The *Bulletins de la Grande Armée* stated there were 1,900 deceased and 5,700 wounded French soldiers, while the retreating Russians left behind 7,000 dead bodies and many wounded. However, these figures were proven to be inaccurate. Napoleon, who frequently wrote the *Bulletins*, minimised the number of French casualties in the battle to reduce the impact on public opinion. Of the 60,000 French soldiers thrown into battle, witnesses estimate that about 20,000 men were put out of action. Generals Binot, d'Hautpoul, Desjardins, Corbineau, Lochet, Dahlmann, Bonnet and Varé were either killed or mortally wounded during the battle. The French lost a total of six eagles or flags. Napoleon was well aware of the potential damage to public opinion if the results of the battle were to be widely disseminated in France and Europe, as they could be interpreted as a partial victory and thus would subsequently tarnish the reputation of the victor of Austerlitz. He spent an unusually lengthy eight days on the battlefield from 8 to 16 February, and his reasons for doing so were directly tied to the severity of the casualties sustained. The French emperor was appalled by the battlefield scene when he visited after the fighting. He took special measures to evacuate the injured soldiers and to ensure that no trophies were left behind for the enemy to claim. These efforts were made to strengthen the victory in the people's minds. According to French propaganda, the army that retained authority over the terrain won the battle. The Emperor wrote on 12 February that 'a father who loses his children has no taste for victory. When the heart speaks, even glory has no more illusions.' The 'victory' was so bitter this time that no *Te Deum* was sung in its honour.

During a period of inactivity, Napoleon wrote the official battle report. The booklet which appeared shortly afterwards contained not only the text of the *Bulletins* but also a so-called 'relation of the battle of Eylau by an eyewitness, translated from German', of which the Emperor was the author. The military operations were suspended temporarily, although the French forces had failed to eliminate the enemy entirely. Was this the result of a Pyrrhic victory? Resumption of hostilities against the Russians and Prussians occurred only on 4 June, after the French army received reinforcements from France restoring its military power.

If the battle of Preussich-Eylau on 7 and 8 February 1807 was the bloodiest of this campaign, it was far from decisive. Despite their heavy losses, the Russian and Prussian armies withdrew in good order and even proclaimed victory. The French soldiers were hardly triumphant. Thus Alexandre Coudreux, sub-lieutenant in the 15th line infantry regiment, wrote to his brother:

> Nagladen, April 8, 1807, ... Gentlemen the Russians give us trouble, but woe to them if we beat them again! ... These rascals fight like mad and hold firm; but besides, they are brute beasts whose spirit is even rougher and more repulsive than their body and who are really not capable of this noble enthusiasm which makes us such good soldiers. The famous Cossacks of whom so much was said at first are also miserable scoundrels who tremble before our bayonets when they are not drunk on schnick. They will also be beaten to a pulp.[60]

Coudreux wrote again on 10 May, while the Grande Armée was still licking its wounds: 'The battle of Eylau cost a lot of people: almost no prisoners were taken. The enemy fought with incredible intrepidity; they held out until 10 o'clock in the evening; they did not abandon the battlefield until the Sixth Corps arrived. The Russian artillery wreaked appalling havoc; almost all the squares were broken up by grapeshot and the 14th line regiment lost thirty-two officers in two hours. Judge the rest. The French dragoons, known since then as 'la *dragonaille*' [a wordplay mixing *dragon* and *mitraille*, grapeshot in French], generally did their job very badly.'[61]

60. Gustave Schlumberger, *Lettres du Commandant Coudreux*, Paris, 1908, pp. 79–80.
61. Gustave Schlumberger, op. cit., pp. 84–5.

The decisive victory of Friedland

Napoleon persisted with his quest for a definitive battle. On 14 June the opposing armies confronted each other afresh at Friedland. Captain François was present on the battlefield:

> Around three o'clock in the morning, we saw the Russian army, on the right bank of the Alle, emerge on the Friedland bridge and attack us, Marshal Lannes' corps ... The Russians made great efforts to overwhelm us, seeing only two army corps in front of them, but we managed to hold our ground without retreating a step. However, the enemy passed the village of Posthneen. Our cavalry near this village captured four cannons. Around half past three, two army corps and the guard arrived at our point and rekindled our ardour. Marshal Ney was on the right with a division of dragoons commanded by General Latour-Maubourg. We, the division of the reunited and the army corps of Marshal Lannes in the centre, having for reserve a division of dragoons and the Saxon cuirassiers commanded by General Lahoussaye, had on our left the army corps of Marshal Mortier with a division of dragoons and one of cuirassiers commanded by General Grouchy. The reserve was General Victor's division and the guard ...
>
> The Emperor, having recognised the position by scanning these lines like lightning, ordered Marshal Ney to take the town of Friedland immediately, and the attack began on the right. At about six o'clock Marshal Ney struck the Russian left on the side of the Sortlac wood which covered it. At that moment, swarms of Cossacks charged General Latour-Maubourg's cavalry, shouting, but Marshal Ney's artillery thundered down on them and all the cheering and demonstrations the Russians wanted to make were useless. The Russian general-in-chief, wanting to hold the important point of Friedland, had his troops make an effort to push us back, but they were bayoneted by us, and we knocked his columns into the Alle, where several thousand men were drowned and few of them swam away. At that moment Marshal Ney took advantage of our charge and advanced towards a ravine surrounding Friedland. The [Russian] imperial guard on foot and on horseback that emerged caused some confusion in Marshal Ney's corps, but having received reinforcements, he attacked the guard and made a great slaughter of them, as we saw in the evening. We, the Oudinot division, bayoneted a Russian column on the Alle and made a horrible carnage of it. More than half of them were pierced by our bayonets, stained to the sockets with blood, others drowned and few escaped. Despite this horrific charge, the division had few men killed or wounded ... I escaped with

a few scratches and a slight bayonet wound to the right thigh which did not prevent me from staying with my company, more than half of whom had their clothes torn. The failure of the Russian imperial guard did not prevent the general-in-chief from sending new reinforcements to Friedland. This beaten guard was quickly repulsed between the river Alle and a stream. And the enemy's left was cornered on Friedland, crushed by our artillery, which forced them to retreat in disorder into the town, whose streets were littered with their corpses. The town I saw in the evening was an appalling spectacle of the horrors of war; the dead and wounded, not yet collected, were piled one on top of the other. Those who had escaped from the city with bayonets crossed it in the greatest disorder, especially the Friedland bridge to reach the right bank of the Alle. The entrance and exit of the bridge were clogged with men who had choked on it. Almost all the artillery of this army remained in our power, as well as a large number of prisoners. While Marshal Ney on the right entered Friedland, Marshal Lannes' corps ... had returned and was attacked, but the Russians were vigorously received by us, the Oudinot division and General Verdier's division of the same corps. It was in vain that the Russians, with infantry and cavalry charges, tried to stop the momentum of the brave men of Marshal Lannes' army corps, especially Generals Oudinot and Verdier, and their worthy soldiers, whom nothing had been able to shake. Not since the Egyptian campaigns had I found myself in such carnage; the division suffered greatly. Marshal Mortier, on our left, when he saw that we, in the centre, were working as well as the Russians by pushing them back at the double, followed us, supported by a regiment of fusiliers from the guard commanded by Colonel Curial. The Russians, although strongly repulsed by us, only gave way foot by foot. However, the general under his command, seeing our victorious columns coming down on him, made his move on Friedland where he thought he had a way through. But Marshal Ney was inside, having passed through on the left, and we, Marshal Lannes' corps, in the centre. The Russian general, seeing the town on fire, thought he had no choice but to lay down his arms, but these runners found a ford on the Alle, and these troops went there in droves, but pushed by us. This crossing was carried out in such disorder that many of them were drowned or taken prisoner. However, the enemy managed to pass a few cannons on the right bank of the Alle; the rest, both in the countryside and in this river, remained in our power, as did the caissons and carriages. At 11 o'clock in the evening, victory was ours; although the fusiliers of the guard and two divisions of the first corps had not been engaged, at least 15,000 Russians covered the

> battlefield, 70 cannons, a large number of caissons, several flags and several thousand prisoners were the trophies of this memorable day. The Russian cavalry suffered immense losses: 25 generals and a large number of officers of all ranks were killed, wounded or taken prisoner. Our loss was at least 6,000 men killed and wounded, which will seem incredible given the charges made by the infantry and cavalry, but it will be believed when it is known that our positions were covered, whereas the Russians, on the contrary, were exposed for a long time to the deadly fire of a large and well-directed artillery ... I suffered nothing, only my hat, like many others in the melee, was lost.[62]

The campaign against the Russians and Prussians continued. Nevertheless, the allied forces were fatigued. The Prussian army was nearly non-existent and, despite their tenacity, the Russians were willing to settle with Napoleon. The French emperor, who had been campaigning for nine months and feared becoming trapped in the vast Russian empire with a weary army, agreed to meet with the two opposing sovereigns. This was the Tilsit meeting. The last days of the campaign were briefly recounted by Commandant Coudreux in a letter to his brother written two weeks later:

> On 5 June, the enemy army attacked the Sixth Corps at Guttstadt and pushed it back as far as Dreppen. On the sixth, at noon, the entire French army was reunited and stopped the bold march of the Russians; on the seventh, we crossed the Passarge under the fire of their batteries; we beat them at Guttstadt, and entered the town; On the eighth we were masters of their formidable redoubts at Heilsberg, and the positions at Preuss-Eylau were turned; the fourth and third corps were at Königsberg on the 14th, and the rest of our army struck down the debris of the coalition army on the vast plains of Friedland the same day. Finally, on the 16th, we had arrived on the banks of the Niemen, we had taken Tilsitt, and we were about to strike the final blow, when the first cries of peace were heard. On 25 June, the two emperors met in the middle of the river. The next day, Alexander and Frederick entered the city, where they were received by Napoleon the Great at the head of his victorious army! From that moment on, there was no more war or fighting! Everyone wants peace, and there is every reason to believe that it has already been signed as I write. The Russian and French Imperial Guards and the Prussian Guard are currently garrisoned at Tilsit. The three monarchs see each other every day, and we no longer take up arms except to show off our

62. Charles-François François, op. cit., pp. 530–2. In writing this, the author was obviously inspired by the 79th *Bulletin de la Grande Armée*, dated Wehlau, 17 June 1807.

> fine dress and the precision of our manoeuvres to those who feared us so much a fortnight ago. Our camp is filled from morning to night with foreign officers, who come to visit the French officers; we go with them to the other side of the river, and all the days are spent in continuous festivities. These gentlemen are generally very well-mannered; almost all of them speak French. Yesterday, the three imperial and royal guards got together for a banquet given by our emperor; after the meal, they changed weapons and clothes, and these brave and proud grenadiers roamed the town and the surrounding area to the 1,000 repeated cries of 'Long live Napoleon! Long live Alexander! Long live Frederick! Long live the grenadiers of the Imperial and Royal Guards!'[63]

Prussia was treated harshly by Napoleon, although, thanks perhaps to Alexander's protection, it avoided being completely wiped off the map. The territories between the Rhine and Elbe were taken from it and given to Jérôme Bonaparte, King of Westphalia, while the Prussian part of Poland and Posnania formed the Grand Duchy of Warsaw, created in favour of the King of Saxony, with the exception of a province offered to Alexander. Although Napoleon was determined to punish Prussia for its policy, which he described as treacherous, he did try to seduce the young Russian sovereign and make him an ally by imposing conditions that were much less harsh than he could have demanded. The Russians not only kept their piece of Poland, but were also given the province of Bialystok, taken from the Prussians. Alexander agreed to evacuate the Danube provinces, return the mouths of Cattaro and give back to France the Seven Islands which the Russians had seized in 1799. Corfu, an important strategic port, was thus returned to Napoleon's control. The Russian fleet was to evacuate the Mediterranean. Alexander also undertook to mediate between the French empire and the United Kingdom. If the British refused this mediation, the Czar would declare war. While the armistice concluded on 21 June, before the talks scheduled for 24 June, news arrived from Constantinople of the fall of Sultan Selim III, whom Napoleon had pushed against the Russians. He therefore felt free to come to an agreement with Russia, a long-standing enemy of the Ottoman sultans. In return for Alexander's mediation with England, Napoleon undertook to mediate with the Sublime Porte. If the latter refused, the Russians and French would agree to wrest 'the European provinces of the Ottoman empire, except Constantinople, from the barbarism of the Turks'. Once the peace treaty had been signed on 8 July, the Czar of Russia and the Emperor of France parted on the best of terms, both happy with what they had achieved.

---

63. Gustave Schlumberger, op. cit., pp. 91–2.

Chapter 4

Invading Russia

The collapse of peace

After the Tilsit Agreement, Napoleon urged Russia to focus on Finland and Turkey's Danube provinces. This would enable him to confront Spain without the risk of battles on multiple fronts. In a letter written from Paris to the Emperor of Austria, Metternich wrote: 'the end of the war between Russia and the Ottomans does not suit him; the prolongation of a quarrel in which the Russians used great means ... the moment has arrived when he will have a Russian army, formerly occupied, placed on points threatening him; he must fear that with the feeling of strength does not revive in Russia that of independence ...'[64]

At the 1808 Congress of Erfurt, Napoleon attempted unsuccessfully to enlist the Russian empire in a prospective war with Austria. Russia was the sole continental power to have avoided any losses in its confrontations with the French empire. The Emperor recognised that Russia was a potential threat. While attempting to convince General de Caulaincourt, whom he knew enjoyed Alexander's esteem, to become his ambassador to the St Petersburg court, he told him: 'The affairs of the world are there ... General peace is in Petersburg. We must leave.'[65]

During their talks in Erfurt, the French emperor discussed a matter close to his heart with Czar Alexander: the possibility of a marriage with a Russian archduchess following his divorce from Empress Josephine. However, the Czar did not provide a response, stalling for time. In addition, Alexander refused to recognise Napoleon's brother Joseph as the King of Spain. The Erfurt meeting proved to be a failure for Napoleon's diplomacy in every aspect. A proposal to wed the Grand Duchess Anne, Alexander's 15-year-old sister, was officially made in December 1809. Alexander hesitated before responding, concerned that his refusal might lead to war and the reconstitution of Poland.

---

64. Clemens von Metternich, *Mémoires du Prince de Metternich, Chancelier de Cour et d'État*, t. 2, Paris, 1880, p. 367.

65. Armand de Caulaincourt, *Mémoires du général de Caulaincourt, duc de Vicence, grand écuyer de l'empereur*, t. I, Paris, 1933, p. 242.

Napoleon learned of Russia's reticence and favoured an Austrian marriage before receiving a response to his proposal. While the war the Czar feared did not occur immediately, the failed proposal left a bitter taste. The following year, as diplomatic tensions intensified, Napoleon informed Caulaincourt that: 'it is the wedding with Austria that set us apart. Emperor Alexander was angry about the fact that I did not wed his sister.' Caulincourt added: 'I had to remind the Emperor that Russia at the time did not care about the wedding, that the Emperor would have had to concede several things, but that religion would have been a major issue. Had the Emperor received her mother's agreement, he would have waited a whole year. There was never a positive agreement and people were rather happy than angry when they had heard of a wedding with Austria.'[66]

The problems arising from Napoleon's wedding did not represent the only challenges between the two empires. From the Russian perspective, the alliance between France and the Polish Kingdom was a source of worry. The establishment of the Grand-Duchy of Warsaw in 1807, which incorporated Polish land taken from Prussia, received little consideration in St Petersburg. However, the expansion of the Duchy in 1809 resembled a potential restoration of the Polish Kingdom, posing a threat to the Polish territories annexed by Russia during the reign of Catherine the Great. Alexander tried to convince Napoleon to sign a treaty stating that 'the Kingdom of Poland will never be restored' but failed.[67]

Russia experienced economic problems due to the adherence to Napoleon's continental blockade, leading to discontent. Initially, declaring war on Britain had benefited Czar Alexander's plans as it had allowed him to enter Finland, which was part of the Kingdom of Sweden, a British ally. Military operations were favourable to the Russians, as the troops the British had planned to use to rescue the Swedish allies were redirected towards the Iberian Peninsula. The triumph of Czar Alexander's army allowed him to establish Finland as a Grand Duchy, where he was declared the ruler in a personal capacity on 17 September 1809.[68] Napoleon acknowledged the increasing frustration of the St Petersburg court. French ambassador Armand de Caulaincourt, in office since December 1807 and held in high esteem by the Czar, attempted to allay the Emperor of Russia's concerns. In August 1809 Napoleon corresponded with the goal of bolstering the alliance with Russia: 'the feelings I have for Your Majesty, as well as the political considerations of my empire, make me desire more and

66. Armand de Caulaincourt, op. cit., p. 296.

67. Michel Kerautret, 'Napoléon et le mirage récurrent de l'alliance russe', in: M.-P. Rey and T. Lentz, *1812, La campagne de Russie*, Paris 2012, p. 34.

68. A situation that lasted until the Russian revolution of 1917.

more the continuation and permanence of the alliance we have contracted. For my part, it is impervious to any change or event.'[69]

Another factor impacting relations between France and Russia was the political instability in the Kingdom of Sweden. The reign of the new king, Charles XIII, was challenged by a series of crises. Being heirless and in poor health, Charles XIII was effectively unable to rule. On 6 January 1810 peace was established between France and Sweden, and Napoleon returned Pomerania to the Swedes. In addition, Napoleon's new allies announced the closure of their ports to British ships. The Parliament, which was then controlled by those in favour of an alliance with France, extended an invitation to the French marshal Bernadotte to assume the position of Crown Prince of Sweden. Bernadotte had been married to Désirée Clary, Napoleon's sister-in-law.[70] The Swedes regarded the marshal as a leader who could facilitate their military campaign to retake Finland. Despite Napoleon's antipathy towards Bernadotte, he granted his approval. King Charles XIII formally adopted Bernadotte in November 1811. In Russia, the announcement of the marshal's election as Prince Royal of Sweden caused a significant shift in the cabinet in St Petersburg. A detachment of Russian troops made ready to advance towards the borders of Poland, while British vessels returned to Russian ports as Russia distanced itself from the continental system.

The announcement of Bernadotte's appointment promptly sparked rumours of conflict, which the respective governments sought to quell through press releases. The *Journal de l'Empire* of 22 November 1810 stated that: 'The election of the royal prince of Sweden ... equally unexpected for the two emperors of France and Russia, far from opening up any prospect of war in the north, was only done out of hatred of the English and the English party; that Russia and France are in the best understanding, and that Finland remains united to the Russian empire.'

In July and August 1810 Napoleon reinforced measures to block imports of British goods. The extensive expropriation and destruction of English products in all French-controlled or allied countries created severe economic hardship in the British Isles. The London government sent a significant convoy of illicit goods to the Baltic Sea, disguised as neutral ships. Russian ports allowed six hundred of these ships to enter. Napoleon was informed of the situation and requested that the Czar seize the ships and dispose of their cargoes. However, the government in St Petersburg declined to comply. On 12 November 1810 Napoleon was notified of this decision. Consequently, on the following day it was decided to annex the Hanseatic cities and the Grand Duchy of Oldenburg,

69. Napoléon Bonaparte, *Correspondance générale*, t. 10, p. 581.
70. Joseph Bonaparte, the elder brother of Napoléon, had married Julie Clary in 1794. In 1810 she was the queen of Spain.

whose sovereign was closely related to the Russian emperor through marriage. The Duke of Oldenburg declined the proposed exchange of his hereditary states for the Duchy of Erfurt, which was slated to be part of the Confederation of the Rhine. He sought sanctuary with his nephew Alexander, who strongly objected to Napoleon's offer. Napoleon declined to reverse his decision. The Czar, on 11 October 1810, issued a decree to carry out a significant conscription to reinforce the imperial army. The diverse territories were required to enlist three men for every five hundred residents.[71]

On 13 December 1810 Napoleon also made the decision to conscript new soldiers. This was the largest conscription since he had come to power, with a total of 120,000 men being drafted. In February 1811 an additional 46,965 men were called up, with another 25,000 in July. Another 129,000 were called up between August and December. On 24 December 1810 Napoleon informed General Foy: 'I have just called up 120,000 conscripts. I could do without them; Emperor Alexander wants peace, the Russian nation, although it has many enemies, wants peace, but it is possible that it will go to war without wanting it.'[72] On 31 December 1810 a decree was issued authorising imports by sea, with the exception of British products, and imposing heavy taxes on imports by land. The violation of the ban on British ships entering Russian ports further resisted the treaty of Tilsit. The new policy significantly weakened the continental blockade enforced by Napoleon. In January 1811 five of the nine divisions of the Russian army departed from the Danube towards Poland. Because of the tensions caused by the annexation of the Duchy of Oldenburg, the Grand Duchy of Warsaw feared that these divisions would be directed against it. At the same time Russia protested against France's conquests and annexations.[73] On 20 February 1811 Napoleon requested that Russia provide an explanation for its military actions and encouraged the King of Saxony to concentrate the Grand Duchy of Warsaw's troops on the Vistula river. The move was aimed at safeguarding the troops from any unforeseen attacks and placing them within the range of support from the Confederation of the Rhine's troops. As tension between the two powers increased, Napoleon sent a lengthy letter to Czar Alexander on 28 February 1811 in which he outlined his complaints against Russia:

> Your Majesty's latest decree, in substance but above all in form, is directed specifically against France. At other times, before taking such a measure against my trade, Your Majesty would have made it known to me, and I might have been able to suggest means which, while fulfilling

71. *Journal de l'Empire*, 22 November 1810, p. 1.
72. Albert Vandal, *Napoléon et Alexandre Ier*, Paris, 1896, p. 522.
73. Buret de Longchamps, op. cit., p. 282.

> its main purpose, would nevertheless have prevented it from appearing to France to be a change of system. All of Europe has seen it this way; and already our alliance no longer exists in the opinion of England and Europe: even if it were as complete in Your Majesty's heart as it is in mine, this general opinion would still be a great evil. … Under the Treaty of Tilsit, he was to return Moldavia and Wallachia to Turkey; however, instead of returning these provinces, Your Majesty has united them to his empire. Wallachia and Moldavia are a third of the Turkey of Europe; it is an immense acquisition, which, by supporting Your Majesty's vast empire on the Danube, deprives Turkey of all strength and, one might even say, annihilates this empire, my oldest ally. However, instead of holding out for the execution of the Treaty of Tilsitt, in the most disinterested manner and out of pure friendship for Your Majesty, I recognised the reunion of this beautiful and rich region; but without my confidence in the continuation of her friendship, several very unfortunate campaigns could not have led France to see her former ally stripped in this way. In Sweden, at the time that I restored the conquests I had made over this power, I consented to Your Majesty keeping Finland, which is a third of Sweden, and which is such an important province for Your Majesty that it can be said that since this reunion there is no longer any Sweden, since Stockholm is now at the outposts of the kingdom. However, Sweden, despite the false policy of its king, was also one of France's old friends. … Your Majesty abandoning the alliance once and burning the conventions of Tilsit, it would be obvious that war would ensue a few months earlier or a few months later.

Napoleon's letter appeared conciliatory, but its ending threatened war if Alexander refused to comply with the master of Europe's wishes. The Czar was unmoved. In April, knowing that the French empire was unprepared for war, Napoleon instructed his foreign relations minister, Champagny, to direct his new envoy, Count de Lauriston, on what to convey to St Petersburg: 'ask permission to reply frankly, using the formula: this is how they see it in Paris. I will not wage war on behalf of Poland, although I do not wish to suffer any encroachment on the Grand Duchy, nor any harm done to it. I will not go to war over the customs tariff, even though the latest decree is contrary to the Treaty of Tilsit, and the idea of burning the goods of a friendly and allied power seems to imply a contradiction with the ideas of friendship and alliance; but however serious these grievances may be, I will only go to war if Russia wants something other than the left bank of the Danube, or if this power, tearing up the Treaty of Tilsit, makes peace with England.'

Upon the return of his previous ambassador to St Petersburg, Napoleon met with Count de Caulaincourt in an audience that lasted for more than seven hours, during which they thoroughly discussed the issue of a potential war with Russia. The diplomat was convinced that Napoleon's mind was made up: he would attack Russia. The conscription of December 1810 appeared to contribute to the spiking tensions within the Czar's empire.

While all the elements needed to start the war were being put in place, some good news reached St Petersburg: the victorious outcome of the war against Turkey: 'On 25 May, just as the resumption of hostilities was expected, the Turkish and Russian plenipotentiaries signed the preliminaries of peace in Bucharest and, according to the conditions of this inconceivable treaty, the new limits of the two empires were to be the Prut. Thus, the Porte ceded to Russia a considerable part of Moldavia and Bessarabia. The Russians, to make it easier for the Sublime Porte to ratify the preliminaries, had made their troops move backwards, as they had been ordered to move northwards.'[74] Thus, one month before the war with France began, the Russian empire was able to move its army, occupied by the war against the Ottomans, back to the Danube regions ready for the confrontation that was about to begin. The news of this event would not reach Paris until July and was therefore unknown to Napoleon at the time when he was to go on the offensive.

Preparing the invasion

The idea of war with Russia was not new in the ranks of the army. In a letter sent from Spain in November 1810, a conscript from the region of Liège (today's Belgium) named Ferdinand Chantraine discussed the fact that Russia had declared war on France:[75]

> Madrid, 3rd November 1810.
>
> It is said here that Russia is declaring war on France, and you will let me know something about this in your reply to this letter. Don't worry that it's badly written, because I'm in too much of a hurry. Tell me news of the country, I am five hundred leagues away and will soon be seven hundred.[76]

From the spring of 1811 to the spring of 1812 Napoleon, although he had not yet decided to declare war on Russia, was nevertheless actively preparing a campaign by bringing together troops scattered throughout Europe. His plan was made. The army of Italy would be the first to take up position after crossing the Tyrolean Alps and crossing Bavaria. It would take station between the Rhine and the Elbe, south of the Erfurt region. It would then move north-

74. *Journal de l'Empire*, 11 July 1812, p. 2.
75. Ferdinand Chantraine, born on 2 June 1790 in Wasseige, served in the 3rd horse artillery regiment.
76. AEL, FFP, 1042–1044, letter of Ferdinand Chantraine.

east towards the lower Oder. The second and third corps, under the command of Marshals Oudinot and Ney, would march on the Elbe and then on the Oder; the sixth corps, composed of the Bavarians, the seventh of the Saxons and the eighth of the Westphalians would all move to its left. They too would advance towards the river; the first corps, led by Davout, would wait for them there to prevent a possible surprise attack by the Russians. Indeed, since the alert in April 1811 Napoleon had feared a Russian attack in Prussia and Poland. While he assembled enormous military forces along the border, the Emperor pretended to still want to negotiate with the court in St Petersburg. He agreed to receive Nesselrode, the Czar's envoy, in Paris and instructed his ambassador Lauriston to impress upon Czar Alexander his desire for peace.

Although the final decision to attack Russia had not yet been taken, rumours were circulating among the population and the army. In a letter to his brother, Commandant Coudreux wrote on 12 July 1811: 'There is much talk of war with Russia. We would not be at all displeased to wage a new campaign.'[77] In another letter written less than a month before the start of the war, the same officer talked about the preparations for the expedition to Russia:

> Danzig, 26 May 1812.
>
> We always expect from one moment to the next to make some large movements. We have 50 cartridges per man in the cartridge box and three pairs of shoes in the bag. If war breaks out, we will certainly go a long way without stopping. It is said here that His Majesty the Emperor and King passed through Dresden, where he stayed for only two hours. The King of Westphalia is in Poznan and the King of Naples in Warsaw.[78] It is said that the latter is to take command of all the cavalry ... a battalion of a singular kind has just been formed in our army corps. It is made up of 1,000 oxen and 500 wagons, all driven by a number of pikemen. The wagons will be used for transporting the corps, and if necessary, the oxen will be put on spits. This is a pleasant battalion; it promises to be doubly useful. It is likely that each corps will have its own.[79]

Although well-informed people feared this new expedition towards the vast Russian empire, the soldiers were sometimes quite relieved to be directed towards Russia rather than Spain, which had a terrible reputation. Here, for

---

77. Gustave Schlumberger, op. cit., p. 200.
78. The King of Westphalia was Jérôme, brother of Napoleon, and the King of Naples was Joachim Murat, step-brother of the Emperor.
79. Gustave Schlumberger, op. cit., pp. 208–9.

example, is a letter sent to his family by a conscript named Quirin Jamar, who said he was relieved not to return to Spain, where he had already fought:

> Written in Toul on 22 February 1812
>
> My dear father and mother
>
> My dear father, the news I have to give you is to tell you that after staying three months in Bayonne on the borders of Spain, I was waiting from day to day for orders to enter Spain. It was quite the opposite. We got to return to the depot in Metz and since the 1st of the year we have been on the road and we have not yet arrived, we will only arrive on the 24th of this month, which is why I am in a hurry to write to you in order to receive news from you sooner, because we are not staying in Metz for perhaps eight days before we leave to go to Russia or Prussia. So I hope as soon as this arrives, my dear father, you will not delay in sending me news of the country and of this year's Conscription here and of all my relatives; If I have taken a little longer than usual to write to you, that is because I was waiting until the time came to enter Spain, and when I saw that we were returning to Metz I was patient because the port would not cost you so much, Finally, my dear father, I have nothing else to tell you other than that on the roads we have travelled, we have found everything expensive, and a lot of cold and bad weather that we have endured, but we are very happy to leave that country. We prefer to experience other countries.[80]

Jean-François Chalseche, a soldier in the Imperial Guard, was also relieved to be out of Spain and was wondering if his next fight would be in either Russia or Turkey:

> Orléans, 2 April 1812
>
> Dear father and mother
>
> I will tell you that the service had been so hard on me that on returning to France I had been obliged to enter the hospital in Dax where the hot fountain is, and after 12 days of rest I came out well, thank God, I hope that this letter finds you the same way; but dear father and mother, if I show you even a little of the misery that it will not hurt you because it is as much on your side as on mine. For I do believe that we are all soldiers, for in these countries the last five classes are taken.

80. AEL, FFP, 1042–1044, letter of Quirin Jamar.

> Is it the same with us? Of course, there is a lot of talk about Turkey and Russia.[81]

Sergeant Bourgogne, who had fought in Spain with the Imperial Guard, recounted at the beginning of his memoirs, without any apparent qualms of mind, the beginning of the Russian campaign:

> It was in March 1812, when we were at Almeida in Portugal, fighting against the English army commanded by Wellington, that we received the order to leave for Russia. We crossed Spain, where each day's march was marked by a battle, and sometimes two. It was in this way that we arrived at Bayonne, the first town in France. Leaving this town, we took the post and arrived in Paris, where we thought we would rest. But, after a stay of 48 hours, the Emperor reviewed us, and judging that rest was unworthy of us, made us turn around and march in columns, by platoons, along the boulevards, then turn left into the rue St-Martin, cross the Villette where we found several hundred carriages and other cars waiting for us. We were made to stop, then four of us got into the same carriage and, whip coachman! To Meaux, then on wagons to the Rhine, walking day and night. We stayed in Mainz, then crossed the Rhine, then walked through the Grand Duchy of Frankfurt, Franconia, Saxony, Prussia and Poland. We crossed the Vistula at Marienwerder, where we entered Pomerania, and on the morning of 23 June, in fine weather, not dreadful weather, as Monsieur de Ségur says,[82] we crossed the Niemen on several boat bridges that had just been built, and entered Lithuania, the first province of Russia.[83]

According to Thoran Pagan, author of memoirs on the Spanish campaign and his captivity in Russia, the expedition began in a climate of general pessimism: 'I think it is common knowledge that the Emperor alone was confident about this war, which was so horribly disastrous. Already, in France, there were very bad forecasts, but it was still very different that we heard about it, as soon as we found ourselves on the other side of the Rhine. Not one of those who spoke to us about it stopped saying that our loss was certain.'[84] Pagan

81. AEL, FFP, 1042–1044, letter of Jean-François Chalseche.
82. Philippe de Ségur, *Histoire de Napoléon et de la Grande Armée*, t. 1, Paris, 1826, pp. 144–5.
83. Adrien Bourgogne, *Mémoires du sergent Bourgogne (1812–1813)*, Paris, 1910, pp. 1–2. Adrien Bourgogne (1785–1867) joined the imperial guard in 1806. He was appointed sergeant in April 1812. He took part in the Russian campaign. He was appointed second lieutenant in the 145th line and taken prisoner in 1813.
84. Thoran Pagan, *Mémoires d'un prisonnier en Russie, par M. Pagan, ancien chef d'escadron*, Lyon, 1843, pp. 68–9.

was not the only one to speak of the climate of pessimism that surrounded the early days of the expedition. A German doctor, Heinrich Roos, on his way with his regiment to the concentration of troops forming near the Niemen, reported that:

> Everything led him to believe that our future fate would not be a happy one. The good man could read the future clearly. He painted a dark picture of the terrible winter we would have to endure in the depths of Russia, and the hardships that awaited us there. In advance, he sympathised with our fate: 'You are numerous, you will surely be victorious at first. The Russians will let you into the heart of their immense empire. But then you'll be weakened and you'll have to fight against the weather and with deprivation. That's when the Russians will start waging war energetically. You will be tired, thrown out of Russia and few of you will return.' These words offended one person, made another laugh and a third grumble. Personally, I like to hear people with experience talk.[85]

Those who knew the Russian empire were also reticent. Thus, in February 1812 Heinrich de Brandt, a Polish officer in the service of France, then fighting in Spain, recounted:[86]

> I met, by chance, an aide-de-camp of Chlopicki. He told me that an order had just been received to send the Vistula regiments to France immediately, as they were apparently destined to be used in a very imminent war against Russia. This order was carried out with remarkable speed ... This time, we were leaving Spain never to return. I have to say that the prospect of this new war did not smile very much on our soldiers, who were so patient and so brave. Some of them, born in the vicinity of Pultusk and Ostroleka, told their comrades that in their country they had seen thousands of wounded dying abandoned in the mud, during the terrible winter campaign of 1807. Chlopicki, who had once served in Suvorov's army against the Turks, then fought against the Russians in a Polish insurrection in 1794, and later in Italy, considered this new

85. Heinrich Roos, *Avec Napoléon en Russie, Souvenirs de la campagne de 1812*, Paris, 1913, pp. 14–15. Roos was part of the contingent from the Kingdom of Württemberg. At the end of the campaign, taken prisoner by the Russians, he agreed to change sides. He remained in Russia for a long time, where he accumulated rewards and honours.

86. Heinrich de Brandt served in Spain, Russia and Germany in the Vistula Regiment. After the fall of the French Empire, he entered the service of Prussia, ending his career as an infantry general in the service of that power.

complication to be very serious. 'Napoleon', he said, 'is burning the candle at both ends; he'll end up burning his fingers!'[87]

In November 1811, before the war had been decided, Napoleon concentrated his troops in Poland. The soldiers on their way to their assembly points tried to guess the reason for these concentrations near the Russian empire's border. François Paquay, an artillery man, understood on his own that they were about to fight:

Minden, 12 November 1811

My dearest father and mother, I am writing you this little note to ask you of the state of your health ...

I would say to you that we made a convoy of 15 days, I left it to the hospital of Munster in Germany. As for me, thank God I've always been well. I arrived at Minden in Prussia, in Westphalia. My dear cousin ... you tell me that you hope to see me in a few days, but I tell you that I will see the Russians sooner than you ...[88]

Soldiers were getting ready for the campaign. The mood in the army did not seem particularly happy, as can be seen in this letter started in one place and finished in another by Louis Puybusque:

My dearest father and mother

I would say to you that we passed to Thorn in Poland, I would say to you that we are in old Prussia on the border of Russia and we hope to fight from day to day with the Russian or with the Turk, but I hope that God would keep me as well in battle as at home. I would say to you that we are to drive the gun we have driven since Minden, that it took 8 horses and up to ten to drive them. When you write to me again, please be good enough to tell me who has left and in which regiment they are ...

Mainz, 25th May 1812

I am sorry to tell you that I have learnt nothing here which might indicate to me against whom this terrible outcry is directed; if it is still a secret for the Senate which usually received official communications in such circumstances; if these Gentlemen who had the right to ask for

87. Henrich de Brandt, *Souvenirs d'un officier polonais, Scènes de la vie militaire en Espagne et en Russie, 1808–1812*, Paris, 1877, pp. 206–7.
88. AEL, FFP, 1042–1044, letter of François Paquay.

> them in the name of the Nation, have learnt nothing: this secret, rest assured, will be kept until the moment when the first cannon shots will bring the news of the beginning of hostilities to the banks of the Seine.[89]

Although some people still pretended not to know against whom Napoleon's gigantic army was to be directed, the same was certainly not true of the court in St Petersburg. The newspapers announced that at the end of May, Czar Alexander had left to inspect his troops in the Grodno and Wilma regions of Russian Poland, where a few days later the regiments of the Grande Armée were to advance.[90]

One word: forward!

At the beginning of June 1812, on the eve of going on the offensive, Napoleon was in a more martial mood than ever. According to Henri de Brandt: 'Napoleon spent the night of 3 to 4 June at Thorn. Around one o'clock in the morning, the officers on duty were not a little surprised to hear him coming and going for quite a long time in his room, singing at the top of his voice this stanza from Méhul's hymn (*Le Chant du départ*): And from north to south the war trumpet, has sounded the hour of battle! Tremble, enemies of France ... etc.'[91]

The Grande Armée never bore its name better than in the spring of 1812. Never before in the history of Europe had such a large number of soldiers been brought together under the command of one general. All the nationalities of the empire and its allies were represented. Most of the troops were French (450,000 men).

The masses crossing the Dnieper were not made up solely of soldiers. Many civilians accompanied the army. The doctor Heinrich Roos noted in his memoirs: 'I was extremely surprised to see a considerable number of talkative women, some in carriages, others on horseback and even on foot, some of whom were said to be destined to care for the sick and wounded in the hospitals. I also saw a large number of doctors, most of whom were very young men being reproached and admonished by a veteran in command.'[92]

Many officers were accompanied by at least one servant. In a letter sent after the campaign, Colonel Pierre Lejeune, who at the end of the campaign was bemoaning the loss of his possessions, wrote: 'I saved with me only what I had on my body: horses, carriages, equipment and servants, all remained. Of

89. Louis-Guillaume Puybusque, *Lettres sur la guerre de Russie en 1812, sur la ville de Saint-Pétersbourg, sur les mœurs et les usages des habitants de Russie et de Pologne*, Paris, 1816, p. 9.
90. *Journal de l'Empire*, 5 July 1812, p. 1.
91. Henrich de Brandt, op. cit., p. 233.
92. Heinrich Roos, op. cit., p. 22.

nine people, both servants and others who were attached to me and followed me.'[93] There is no record of all these civilians, so we have no idea how many there were. Their presence undoubtedly increased the difficulties of supply and the mobility of the Grande Armée. This mass of people was accompanied by numerous wagons intended to feed the army. Squadron Leader Pierre Dupuy noted at the end of the year, during the retreat:

> Good measures had been taken at the beginning of the campaign to ensure our subsistence. Companies of oxen had been organised in the vicinity of Königsberg; non-commissioned officers had been drawn from our regiments to lead them, with the rank of second lieutenant. The companies were made up of 100 oxen and about twenty drivers; each ox was harnessed to a cart, known as a 'comet cart', made of clinkered wicker, tightly closed and containing a certain quantity of biscuits. A regiment could therefore be given a cart with a harness; the biscuit was shared, the ox was killed and distributed, and the wood from the cart helped to cook it.[94]

Napoleon watched the great army pass over Russian soil. An anonymous witness, a doctor by profession, described the Emperor at this moment:

> Napoleon, from the top of the hill where his tent was located, contemplated this spectacle with the help of his spyglass, which he held in his right hand, while his left arm was folded behind his slightly stooped back, an attitude that was familiar to him and that can be found in many portraits of this prince. The sight of this beautiful army, the ease with which it crossed the border without the enemy seeming to think of making the slightest resistance, caused him a joy that was painted on his face, which was usually impassive. Several times he was even heard humming the new air from Roland played by the Guard. Finally, when a certain number of regiments had crossed the river, he dismounted and also wanted to set foot on Russian territory. After crossing the bridge, he stood for some time on the riverbank, encouraging the soldiers with his gaze. They all greeted him enthusiastically with their customary shouts. Then, having crossed, he and his guard headed for Kowno.[95]

93. Emile Fairon and Henri Heuse, *Lettres de Grognards*, Paris, 1936, p. 285.
94. Victor Dupuy, *Souvenirs militaires de Victor Dupuy, chef d'escadron, 1794–1816*, Paris, 1892, pp. 211–12.
95. Just Roy, *Les Français en Russie*, Paris, 1886, pp. 20–1.

In the face of this gigantic army, Russia's strength seemed very limited. According to the Prussian strategist Karl von Clausewitz (who fought in the Russian campaign of 1812):

> The Russian forces on the empire's western frontier consisted of the 1st and 2nd Armies of the West and a reserve army. The 1st Army could count 90,000 men; the 2nd, 50,000 men; the 3rd, 30,000 men. This made a total of 170,000 men, to which 10,000 Cossacks had to be added. The 1st Army was under the command of General Barclay, who was also Minister of War. It was positioned along the bed of the Niemen. The Second Army, under the command of Prince Bagration, was in southern Lithuania. The reserve army, under Tormazov, was in Wolynia. In the second line, there were around 30,000 depot men or recruits along the Dnieper and Duna rivers.[96]

Russian forces were not, of course, limited to the army facing Napoleon. Clausewitz drew up a table of the troops available at the beginning of 1812:

> On the border with Prussia and Poland 180,000 men. On the Duna and Dnieper, depots and new formations 30,000. In Finland 20,000. In Moldavia 60,000. On the eastern border 30,000. Inland, depots and new formations 50,000. Garrison troops 50,000.
>
> Total 420,000.[97]

The two Russian generals facing the main body commanded by Emperor Napoleon had completely opposite views on the strategy to follow. The commander of the 1st Army, Barclay de Tolly, was in favour of a retreat, which would aim to stretch the enemy's lines of communication in order to weaken them. The commander of the 2nd Army, Bagration, was strongly in favour of going on the offensive against the French. Supreme command was exercised by Emperor Alexander, accompanied by the Prussian general Phull. The latter advocated a plan based on Wellington's experience in Portugal: that is, a retreat of the Russian army before the superior forces of the French, until, having drawn Napoleon away from his bases, the Russians would halt in a powerful entrenched camp, such as Drissa, where the French would use up their forces, while other armed groups would attack them on the flanks. However, this plan soon proved unworkable and was abandoned. Alexander, realising his inability to command in the field, withdrew and left the supreme command to General Barclay de Tolly.

---

96. Karl von Clausewitz, *La campagne de 1812 en Russie*, Paris, 1987, pp. 4, 5.
97. Karl von Clausewitz, op. cit., p. 9.

At the beginning of June 1812 the French soldiers were eager to move. General Compans wrote to his young wife from Brandenburg in Prussia in June 1812:

> I am here in an old village; my headquarters have never been so bad. I hope it will not be long before I leave it and lodge under the stars. In three short marches, I'll be close enough to the Russians to send them bullets and cannonballs if they want them; I'll march with my head on. … The weather has changed completely; the temperature is now very mild; but, if it does not rain soon, we'll have finished the dry and we will not have the green ... this was the serious problem that so preoccupied Napoleon. In his mind, the war had been decided months ago, but in order to wage it under the least adverse conditions, it was necessary at all costs to reach the time when the state of the vegetation would make it possible to live in the country. To this end, Napoleon used every diplomatic expedient and delayed the opening of hostilities as long as he could.[98]

The campaign began on 22 June 1812 when Napoleon read out a proclamation to his army announcing the start of hostilities against Russia. The troops were soon in motion, but conditions were difficult. Aubry de Vildé, a second lieutenant in the 46th line infantry regiment, wrote to his father on 18 July:[99]

> We have no bread and live on meat alone, like wild beasts; lying in bivouac, as the weather permits, we spend the nights on the ground, and during the day we keep chasing after those cursed Russians who run away from us as fast as we chase them. We have not yet fought, but I hope that this happy moment will come soon.[100]

While the bulk of the troops intended to fight the Russians were already on the other side of the Niemen, others, intended to reinforce them, were still on the march. The letters sent to their families during a day of rest bear witness to this:

> Berlin, 29 July 1812
>
> We have travelled a long way from Chambéry, we have reached Berlin and we hope to go from there into Russia. We hope to stay in

98. Jean Compans, *Général Compans (1769–1845), d'après ses notes de campagne et sa correspondance (1812–1845)*, Paris, 1912, pp. 147–8.

99. Jean Aubry de Vildé was later killed at the battle of Borodino.

100. Jacques Olivier Boudon, *Lettres de la campagne de Russie*, Paris, 2012, pp. 43–4.

Berlin for a while. Since we crossed the Rhine, we have not received any pay. We've been living with the bourgeois.

Jean Gilissen, 5th line, 4th battalion.[101]

Berlin, 30th July 1812

We departed from Brégançon. We left to go to Russia. We passed through Strasbourg, Mainz and Frankfurt, where we were fed by the bourgeois, for whom we have no pay. We are 1,810 thousand men, both French and Prussian, and we are going to Russia to begin the campaign. We don't know if we'll have the good fortune to see each other again, but I'm not losing heart.[102]

There are many soldiers' accounts of the early days of the 1812 campaign. Here is one written by Alexandre Picard in his journal. He was fighting in the 12th line infantry regiment:

We set off from Eylau to begin the campaign. Six leagues away, we slept more than 100 men per house. The next day, we were in bivouacs on the plains between two bridges. We were given meat, but no bread. We did have eight pounds of flour in our sacks, but we were forbidden to touch it. We stayed in bivouacs for two days, four leagues from the Niemen, waiting for the pontoons to be made and placed. We crossed the Niemen on Midsummer's Day at nine in the morning. On the pontoon, the Emperor passed in front of our regiment. The two battalions on the left shouted 'Long live the Emperor!', but the three battalions on the right started shouting 'Let him give us bread! That would be better.'

The Emperor asked 'Which regiment is that?'

'The 12th,' we replied. Then the Emperor waved his hand and said: 'My children, don't be sad! You'll have your fill this evening.'

There were three pontoons: one for the infantry, one for the cavalry and another for the artillery. We saw the troops coming from all sides. There was nothing so beautiful!

We had our weapons loaded and the Second Division of the First Corps marched past. We bivouacked there, and some of us went marauding. The Cossacks were all around us. We could not get out of the way. The Russians were in the woods. After two hours, they made us take up our weapons and leave. We marched for four days and four nights, without respite, until we were two leagues from Vilna. We went marauding, two leagues from our bivouac, in a large village where there

101. AEL, FFP, 1042–1044, letter of Jean Gilissen.

102. AEL, FFP, 1042–1044, letter of Martin Léonard. He served in the 5th line infantry regiment.

was a baron. His castle was devastated. The windows were broken, the cupboards smashed. We went down into a cellar that was full of milk and we each drank a good glass. But it did not fill our bellies properly, because we were short of bread. At a mill below the Château, we searched everywhere and found nothing but coarse flour with bran in it. We each made a load and were ready to leave when a comrade saw a capon enter through a window that went under the mill. We could not take it, but when we looked for it we found some boxes full of things. Inside were a bottle of liqueur, another of brandy, 15 large hams and a pig weighing over 300 pounds. To take all this away, we took a horse from a peasant, who started shouting and called twenty other peasants to him. But there were seven of us and four cuirassiers, and the peasants beat a hasty retreat.

That same evening, as it was my turn to make the soup, it began to rain during the night and throughout the next day was a heavy downpour. I asked the sergeant if he wanted to take care of the soup, because I wanted to get some sleep and I could not have walked if I'd had to do a long march. I lay down in the hut and started to sleep. I hear the 'terror' beating in the bivouac and everyone takes up arms. I was shaking because I'd slept in the water due to the cold. I took my rifle to run to the fire and I wanted to throw the soup that was boiling in the pot, but I thought better of it and let it go where it was. I went to line up with the others; roll call was taken, and we were told that we would be leaving in half an hour. We had time to eat the soup and you can believe how happy I was not to have thrown it away. The Vilna plain was worse than a battlefield: the night's flood had killed thousands of horses. To take the town of Vilna, it only cost the French two cannon shots.[103]

The French troops advanced rapidly. Murat with his cavalry, followed by Davout and Napoleon with the Imperial Guard, marched towards Vilnius (Vilna, Wilna), where the Emperor entered on 28 June. He expressed surprise and regret that the Russians had not offered him a battle. Baron Pierre-Paul Denniée was at Napoleon's side when he entered Vilnius. Right from the start of the campaign, he saw how difficult it was going to be to feed the enormous forces that had just entered Russia.[104] He recounted the following:

No regular distribution could be made in Vilna. When the Russians left, they had ravaged everything; the mills had been destroyed, the storage facilities demolished and the warehouses devastated, to such an extent

103. Alexandre Picard, *Le journal de route d'un soldat de la Grande Armée*, Gilly, 1946, pp. 22–6.
104. Pierre Denniée (1781–1848) was an income inspector of the French Army.

> that we had no other resource than to give the troops who went forward some flour and, in order to provide bread for the Guard and the officers, to have some made by the Jews who lived in the suburb and who all had small ovens in their garrets. The march from Kowno to Vilna, through the forests, across shifting sands, in oppressive and continuous heat, had resulted in considerable losses of men and horses. In fact, 5,000 horses perished in a journey of less than 25 leagues;[105] it is true that this enormous loss was due in particular to the need to feed the horses with the green rye that the horsemen were going to cut far into the countryside; but this sad result nonetheless showed how difficult, not to say impossible, it was to sustain a large army, especially in a country without resources, when movements were too rapid.[106]

At the beginning of 1812, Captain François, a witness we have already met, was in Hamburg. In January, he wrote in his diary: 'For a long time, there had been talk of war and of Russia. As I will not go into the details of the struggle between two rival powers, I will confine myself to following the progress of the First Corps of the Morand Division, of which I was a member'. On 27th February he wrote: 'The regiment received the order to leave, as did those of the division and even of the army corps, to move towards the Oder.' Day after day he listed the milestones of the 30th line infantry regiment. On 23 June the invasion of Russia began and Captain François was one of the first soldiers of the Grande Armée to enter the Czar's empire. This was the beginning of what Russian historians call 'the Great Patriotic War'. François wrote in his diary:

> Corps movements. The first corps, of which I was part of the first division, met near the towns of Shawtdy and Pissa, where the Emperor reviewed it. This general movement was to prepare the army to cross the Niemen, and the Emperor, at two o'clock in the morning, visited the outposts near Kowno [Kaunas, Lithuania], where I was with a piquet of Polish light horses. The Emperor took the capote and bonnet of one of the horsemen and rode along the left bank of the river with General of Engineers Haxo. My post was facing a small Russian corps posted on the right bank. This corps was commanded by General Baggowout. Towards eight o'clock in the evening, the whole army moved again and went between Kowno and Keidani, where I went to head the division of the first corps, having been designated to cross the Niemen with my voltigeurs. The bridge crews, under the orders of General Éblé,

105. 111km.

106. Pierre Paul Denniée, *Itinéraire de l'Empereur Napoléon pendant la campagne de 1812*, Paris, 1842, pp. 21–2.

> approached the point where we had gathered, and three bridges were established.
>
> 24th June. Around 10 o'clock in the morning, three companies of voltigeurs from the 30th (I commanded the first) embarked on boats and I was the first to land on the right bank of the Niemen, without encountering any obstacles. The other companies followed me. We advanced in line, firing a few shots at some Russian cavalrymen who were in front of us in the brush. We chased them away. While the voltigeurs formed a line in front, three bridges were thrown over the Niemen and established in less than an hour. At 11 o'clock, the First Corps passed in three columns, one on each bridge. At noon, General Pajot entered Kowno, which the Russians had evacuated. As the First Corps spread out across the plain, we voltigeurs advanced as the Russian cavalrymen retreated. In the evening, we got together with our regiments and learned that the headquarters of the First Corps was at Roumchiky, that of the Emperor at Kovno, and that of the King of Naples, who commanded the vanguard cavalry, at Eketanoui ... The army marched over the bridges from 11 o'clock on the 24th until the evening of the 25th. Then to the artillery and the crews.
>
> 26th June. The division left at four o'clock in the morning, entered the plain of Wilna and bivouacked on the road, about 10 leagues from this town. In the evening, the first corps, joined to King Murat's cavalry, invaded the entire plain of Wilna following the corps of the Russian general Barclay. Our cavalry extended as far as Zamozsa, chasing the Russian light troops on all sides.[107]

The first letters from soldiers in the field to arrive back home painted a picture of a Russian army with low fighting spirit. For example, Jean-François Monsez, a soldier in the Young Guard, wrote from hospital in Kovno on 7 August:

> I'm in the hospital in Cofinoga, Russia, recovering from an injury to my foot caused by tiredness on the road. As we were heavily laden, it caused us a lot of pain but, thank God, it's fine now. I'll tell you that our troop is marching. We are taking a lot of prisoners. We are only 40 leagues from St Petersburg, the capital of Russia. But as far as I'm concerned, I'm fine for the time being.[108]

Faced with the enemy's enormous numerical superiority, the Russians would not accept combat. Their army withdrew in front of Napoleon. On 27 June the

---

107. Charles-François François, op. cit., pp. 643–4.
108. AEL, FFP, 1042–1044, letter of Jean-François Monsez.

French saw for the first time a spectacle that would be repeated many times during the first part of this campaign: the destruction by the Russian army of everything that could supply the enemy:

> We, the First Division, crossed Wilna and went to bivouac above it, about half a league away, on sandy mounds. Wilna looked like a town taken by storm. All the shops were on fire and the inhabitants had shut themselves up in their homes, except for the Jews, who are in large numbers in this town and were busy removing from the river the weapons that the Russians had thrown in there.

The 4th *Bulletin de la Grande Armée* gave a few details:

> The Russians redeployed everywhere. After exchanging a few cannon shots, they hurried back across the Vilia, burnt the wooden bridge at Wilna, and set fire to huge shops valued at several million roubles: more than 150,000 quintals of flour, a huge supply of fodder and oats, and a considerable mass of clothing were burnt. A large quantity of weapons, which Russia generally lacks, and munitions of war were destroyed and thrown into the Vilia.

In their hasty retreat, the two main Russian armies had drifted apart, but Bagration and Barclay de Tolly had to join forces to avoid finding themselves in a difficult situation. Marshal Davout, trying to prevent the two Russian armies from reuniting, had thrown his force between them. Napoleon realised that Barclay seemed to be waiting for him at Drissa and sent his younger brother Jérôme, King of Westphalia, to support Davout. The young king was at the head of a large contingent: under his command were Poniatowski's 40,000 Poles, 20,000 Westphalians and 24,000 Saxons, making a total of 84,000 men. Jérôme's orders were to head straight for the Dnieper and attack Bagration from the flank, while Davout would attack him to the north of the town of Minsk. The Russian general would then be crushed under the pressure of the two armies. Jérôme, despite his good opinion of himself, unfortunately did not have his brother's military qualities. He lacked authority, decisiveness and the most elementary strategic sense. The crossing of the Niemen was very slow. Bagration took advantage of the enemy's deficiencies to get ahead. Jérôme demanded great efforts from the troops under his command, while the spring was scorching, forcing the soldiers to drink from every available water source. Dysentery ravaged his army. Demoralisation set in. In addition, the King of Westphalia did not communicate his movements to Napoleon or Marshal Davout. As a result of his imprudence, Jérôme almost had his cavalry corps destroyed by the Russian rearguard. Davout then approached the Emperor to inform him of the situation. As a result, on 10 July Napoleon decided that Jérôme would henceforth be under the orders of the marshal. Jérôme, furious that as the Emperor's brother he had to obey Davout, decided to return to Cassel without authorisation, entrusting the army corps he commanded to his chief of staff. It is probable that it was this event which saved Bagration's army. The new general-in-chief of this portion of the troops might still have engaged in combat with the Russian army he was pursuing, were it not for the fact that before leaving, Jérôme had ordered his men to retreat.

News from the front eventually began to arrive in France. The slowness of communications and the difficulty of writing while on the move meant that it was not until almost a month after the beginning of operations that families were able to receive the first letters sent by soldiers of the Grande Armée. Captain Coudreux told his brother about the latest events:

> At the bivouac near Braslav on 17 July 1812.
>
> . . . the Morand division and that of General Friand, of which my regiment is a member, have been under the orders of the King of Naples since the crossing of the Niemen. We form the vanguard with the cavalry. The light cavalry led the way and the infantry marched with the cuirassiers and mounted riflemen. Up to now, we have not had any serious engagements; but as we arrive tomorrow on the banks of the Duna, we expect to use our cartridges and bayonets.
>
> We have just learned that Marshal Ney's corps had an engagement with the Russians the day before yesterday.[109]

Napoleon's advance on Vilnius had been so rapid that it was necessary to remain there for a fortnight to allow the large number of stragglers and troops left behind to rejoin the main body of the army and to remount large numbers of cavalry, owing to the deaths of a large number of horses along the route followed by Murat, as well as the exhaustion of the remaining horses, which had suffered greatly from the forced march to Vilnius and the lack of food. According to General Antoine de Jomini, the fifteen days lost at Vilnius were Napoleon's first serious mistake of the Russian campaign:

> The Emperor had stayed 15 days in Wilna, in a state of expectation that was reproached to him as a serious fault; it seems constant that if he had displayed here the fearsome activity that had presided over this fine campaign of Ulm and Regensburg, the war might have taken a different turn. ... In spite of all these reasons, one cannot conceal the fatal influence exerted by this long stay, since it became the cause of

109. Gustave Schlumberger, op. cit., pp. 209–10.

> the junction of the two Russian armies at Smolensk and of the bloody days that took place around this town.[110]

At this point, Napoleon thought that the 1812 campaign was coming to an end. As proof of this, Jomini related the following anecdote:

> Napoleon, having finished his administrative work, and his presence in Wilna no longer being useful in closing off any escape route for Bagration's army, finally prepared to leave this town on 16 July to march against Barclay. A few days before this departure, he invited General Jomini to dine with the Polish deputies Wibicki and Alexander Potocki. In the middle of the dinner, the Emperor asked Wibicki, who had been taken prisoner in Moscow after the Kociousko uprising in 1794, 'How many leagues are there from Wilna to Moscow?' – Wibicki searched his memory and hesitated to answer. 'Is it not 250 leagues?' – 'Ah, yes, Sire, 125 miles of Germany; that's it.' – 'Then we can get there in six weeks, at the rate of six leagues a day: it's a game for my soldiers!' – 'Oh, certainly; Your Majesty could easily be in Moscow in even less time.' At these words the Emperor, against his custom, burst out laughing and replied to the Polish conqueror: 'I'd much rather go in two years. It is easy for politicians to cross spaces like that. If Monsieur Barclay thinks that I want to chase him as far as the Volga, he is very much mistaken; we shall follow him as far as Smolensk and the Duina, where a good battle will allow us to encamp; I shall return here, to Vilna, with my headquarters to spend the winter; I shall bring a troupe of opera singers and a French theatre company. Then, next May, we will complete the good work, if we do not make peace during the winter. That is better, I think, than running to Moscow. What do you say, Mr Tactician?' (addressing General Jomini, seated opposite him, next to Grand Marshal Duroc). It is clear that, flattery aside, the general's reply could only be affirmative. Was Napoleon sincere in this statement, or did he just want to give the impression that he was thinking, as was his wont? No one can say for sure.[111]

As can be seen from this text, Napoleon seems to have been aware of the dangers of the Russian winter and envisaged conducting his campaign over two years. Unfortunately for him, this was not to be. The Grande Armée marched relentlessly in pursuit of the Russians. During the rare days of rest

---

110. Antoine de Jomini, *Précis politique et militaire des années 1812–1814*, Lausanne, 1868, p. 70.
111. Antoine de Jomini, op. cit., pp. 71–2.

the soldiers, such as Jean-Henri Lemaye of the 4th line infantry regiment, wrote to their families to give them news:

> Liozna, 4 August 1812
>
> We have arrived in Russia. We are camped in Liozna for a few days. We had a very hard time, because we could not find food where we wanted and we travelled fifteen to twenty leagues a day in pursuit of the enemy. We left the country six months ago. We've always walked.
>
> Jean-Henri Lemaye, 4th line, 2nd battalion, 2nd division, 3rd corps.[112]

Jean Chalsèche, serving in the Old Guard, wrote the following letter. He was to disappear in Russia less than four months later:

> Vitebsk, 4 August 1812
>
> Dear father and mother
>
> I am writing you these words in reply to your letter dated 11 May which reached me on 1 August and which gave me great pleasure to see that you are well. As for me, thank God I am still in good health, I hope that this letter finds you the same way; I will tell you that we entered Russia on 30 July. We fought for 3 days. The 1st line was all damaged, but the Guard did not give because the Russians did not hold out. We are still 800 leagues from Paris. We've been sleeping in the bivouac for 40 days now, so we're not doing too well with food. I will tell you that we had a good time passing through Germany and Saxony. We were fed by the bourgeois. We had bread, meat, beer, plenty of rice and other vegetables. Germany is a country that must be respected as one of the most beautiful and abundant, apart from wine. I believe that the wood that takes from the Rhine goes all the way to Russia, depending on how abundant the wood is, there are some very beautiful woods. The climate of the country is similar to ours. What I will tell you is that on St John's Day, it does not get dark. It's 17 hours past sunny, but the day does not disappear. I'll also tell you that we marched for ten to twelve hours, barely able to pass for the horses that died on the road from fatigue and misery. We are five army corps, not counting the Imperial Guard, which have gone over to the Russian 1st, 2nd, 3rd, 4th and 6th Corps.[113]

As can be seen, the morale of the troops was quite high. The soldiers' letters at the start of the campaign reflected cautious optimism. Confidence in Napoleon

112. AEL, FFP, 1042–1044, letter of Jean-Henri Lemaye.
113. AEL, FFP, 1042–1044, letter of Jean-François Calsèche.

was total. It is true that we have a few letters from men of the Imperial Guard who, whether young or old, enjoyed a more favourable regime than the line troops: better food, better medical care than the rest of the army, higher pay. The Old Guard was sent into battle less often and its soldiers therefore had a better chance of survival. If it were not for the long journeys, when the first shots had only just been fired, the soldier, whether in the Guard or in the line, would have little to complain about compared with other theatres of operation, such as Spain. It is also true that some were better off than others, even if they were not really aware of it. Here, for example, is a letter from a soldier garrisoned on an island in the Baltic Sea, who complained about his stay and looked forward to marching with the Grande Armée into Russia:

> Nehrung-lez-Pillau, 6 August 1812
>
> We left Wesel on 27 May, heading for Pillau. On 15 August, we arrived at the island of Pillau. It was a march of 300 leagues. We stayed one day in Pillau and then moved on to the island of Nerung where we are camped. We work every day in the batteries. Our life there is very bleak. Straw is our bed and the sky our roof. Our food consists of a pound and a half of bread, half a pound of meat and a few potatoes. There is no grass on this island, only sand and water. It is bordered on one side by the Baltic Sea and on the other by a river 300 paces wide. So you can imagine how pleasant it is to be garrisoned there. It is always cold. Sometimes the water is so rough that you cannot navigate it to bring supplies to Pillau. We've been on the march for 50 days, sometimes with tough stages, sometimes walking through mountains and woods. We're close to the Grande Armée and fortunately we will not be staying long in Pillau. The Grande Armée is in Russia and things are going well for us. Our emperor has promised to celebrate his patron saint's day, 15 August, in St Petersburg, the capital of Russia. During the march, the peasants provided the food. There was always brandy and beer on the table and good food. They had to give us everything, because we had no pay. The troops are full of enthusiasm and are rushing to victory over Russia. Dear father and mother, we are very far apart and will be even further apart. We will not see each other again in the New Year, but I do hope to see my homeland again. This is God's will and there is nothing we can do to change it. Let us hope that God will be our guide, that he will bless our weapons and put an end to the war, and that he will make us return triumphant to our homeland.
>
> Jean-Henri Rompen, 9th foot artillery regiment, 9th company.[114]

114. AEL, FFP, 1042–1044, letter of Jean-Henri Rompen.

Marshal Oudinot had been tasked with a diversionary manoeuvre on the road leading to St Petersburg. From 30 July to 1 August small battles pitted his men at Klyatitsy against Russian troops commanded by Marshal Count Wittgenstein. The Russians had the advantage, but losses were very light on both sides. Having retreated, Oudinot then joined up with the 6th corps of the Bavarian army, commanded by the French general Gouvion-St-Cyr. The 18,000 Franco-Bavarians took the town of Polotsk. Wittgenstein, with slightly larger forces (22,000 men), attacked the occupiers of the town. The battle began on 17 August beneath the walls of the stronghold. The two armies fought with equal courage. Marshal Oudinot was wounded in the shoulder but remained in command throughout. The two armies did not stop fighting until nightfall, when they began bivouacking. Oudinot thought it prudent to evacuate Polotsk and put the Dvina between himself and the Russians. Because of the pain caused by his wound, he handed over command of the army to General Gouvion-St-Cyr. Taking advantage of the night, the crews, cavalry and artillery crossed the river again.

The next morning Gouvion-St-Cyr pretended to retreat towards Vitebsk and, having succeeded in deceiving the enemy, returned to attack Wittgenstein by surprise. The Russian general, in difficulty, threw his cavalry on the attackers and managed to win the day. The Franco-Bavarians lost 6,000 men killed, wounded and missing, including two Bavarian generals. A large proportion of the wounded French and Bavarians died in the following days due to lack of medical care. The Russians suffered 5,500 killed, wounded and missing. Following this battle, the two armies remained face to face on both banks of the Dvina.

This success earned Wittgenstein the command of the Armée du Nord and the glory of being the man who had stopped the invaders on the road to St Petersburg. Thanks to this encounter, despite the defeat, Gouvion St-Cyr was promoted marshal by Napoleon. The 14th *Bulletin de la Grande Armée* of 23 August presented the defeat at Polotsk as a victorious battle:

> On the 18th, at four o'clock in the afternoon, General Gouvion-St-Cyr, commanding the 2nd and 6th corps, opened up on the enemy, having the Bavarian division of Count de Wrede attack the right. The fight started on the whole line; the enemy was completely routed and pursued for two leagues, as far as the day allowed. 20 cannon and 1,000 prisoners remained in the hands of the French army. The Bavarian general Deroy was wounded.[115]

115. 14th *Bulletin de la Grande Armée*, 23 August 1812.

After various manoeuvres, the French troops were in position in front of Smolensk. The Russians had decided to defend the town. Captain François explained:

> 17 August. Around three o'clock in the morning, the army took up arms and manoeuvred. At four o'clock, the First Division of the First Vanguard Corps began firing with a line of skirmishers towards the left of the town, one of which was led by the Fourth Corps. The First Corps, of which I was a member, in the First Division, manoeuvred under fire from the town's artillery, packed by division, and lost many men and horses. These manoeuvres, under the town's cannons, made us impatient. We wanted to fight. Finally, after several hours of manoeuvring, still under the city's cannons, we took the Bulchowka plateau where the Emperor had a battery of 60 cannon established, which caused the Russian army a great deal of harm on the right bank of the Dnieper and forced it to evacuate this position, leaving many dead and wounded.
>
> We, the 30th of the 1st Division, of the 1st Corps, at about one o'clock, Marshal Davout ordered us to attack. We were in close columns by division, and we lost many men and horses. We were in battle under enemy cannon and in a cemetery, with the other corps of the division behind us. In less than half an hour, two eagle-bearers were killed, one had his head blown off by a cannonball. We fired only our artillery. At the same time as us, the Desaix division marched on the citadel: that of General Compans on the faubourg, behind Tzenizi; the Friand division on the western faubourg, the Gudin division behind us. Approximately 200 toises from the town, the suburbs were entrenched and defended by infantry and large-calibre cannon on which were the 13th Light and part of the 4th Corps. The regiment in battle, at a short distance from the town walls, was cannonaded by the guns of the ramparts and those of a tower, which caused us a great deal of harm, as well as to the lines behind us, to such an extent that our leaders made us take cover behind the counterscarp of a ditch that surrounded the cemetery, where the enemy dominated us and sent us cannonballs and shells with three holes, filled with inflammable fuel. Around two o'clock in the afternoon, one of these projectiles fell in front of a platoon, near Colonel Buquet, Major Hervé and Major Plèche. I rushed at the projectile, which was spewing flames from its holes. I burnt my hands and my hair, but I had the good fortune to throw it into a well a short distance behind my platoon. My leaders and the battalion witnessed my audacity and shouted: 'Bravo! Long live Captain François!' Without my presence of mind, two caissons which were on my left, between the distances of

the battalions, could have exploded and caused a lot of damage to the left of the first battalion and to the right of the second. Colonel Buquet, who was very fond of me, reported this to the Emperor on my behalf; but as usual, I was forgotten and my only reward was my satisfaction and the esteem of my leaders and comrades.

By nine o'clock, the guns were established along the whole line and were firing like hell. The Russians were pushed back by our bayonets until they reached a covered road, where the battle became decisive. Despite the terrible fire from the Russian artillery, we took the suburbs by bayoneting the Russians. While the Russians lost many men, we had to deplore the loss of 1,300 men. At about six o'clock three batteries of 12 from the Morand, Friand and Gudin divisions were established, while we continued the attack on the covered way. Once these batteries were established, they defeated the Russians and drove them away from the detours they were occupying, because the projectiles set fire to them and to the town. We, the infantry, did not cease our fire on the covered road, without much success, but the enfilade batteries made them abandon it, and the Russians were forced to return to the town.

Despite this success, the battle lasted all night. The three batteries I mentioned earlier fired actively; two companies of miners, supported by us, were employed in digging at the foot of the ramparts near which we were. At seven o'clock, we heard a lot of noise in the town, both from the troops and the inhabitants; the town was on fire. Around one o'clock in the morning, we heard that the Russians had withdrawn to the other bank of the Dnieper after having set fire in various places to the bridge and the ramparts ... Around two o'clock, the grenadiers of the Morand, Friand and Gudin divisions of the 1st corps entered the town, which was burning at all points and whose squares and streets were cluttered with dead and wounded.[116]

Alexandre Picard, an ordinary soldier, recounted the siege of Smolensk with a certain naivety:

We were sent from Vitebsk to Smolensk, where we arrived at nine in the morning on 16 August ... During the night of the 17th and 18th, we were on the ramparts, in skirmishes; bullets were whistling in our ears. The general had us stopped and assembled to wait for the division that was to enter the town first. We crossed the town in our turn, crossed a pontoon bridge and bivouacked a quarter of a league away. Before taking Smolensk, we had been placed in battle in front of a mountain

116. Charles-François François, op. cit., pp. 655–6.

> where the cannonballs could not reach us: but we had to go down to fetch water for soup at the bottom of the mountain. The cannonballs, bombs and shells fell like hail. You can believe that we did not enjoy smoking our pipes ... On the outskirts of Smolensk, on the 18th and 19th of August, we had no bread or brandy, only meat. I got the urge to go out and scavenge, and found some flour mixed with bran. When I came in, they took it from me at the door, along with some stationery, sealed wax and the pencil I had in my bag. Back in the faubourg, I had started to finish a pair of canvas trousers, and I was about to put them on, when the order came to leave to join the division. We had travelled almost three quarters of a league. Suddenly, we were ordered to halt. The cannon thundered. An aide-de-camp, running on horseback, came to tell the general to move the division forward: we were going to give! A league away, we were stopped on a mountain among the cannon. We were badly damaged. All the guns were firing at once, one shot would not wait for the next ... We went down the mountain and there the shells were flying over our heads. But a cannonball landed at the rear of the company, where one man was killed. A Biscayan cut off the big toe of the right foot of the man in front of me and the right arm of the man behind me.[117]

Julien Combe, then a second lieutenant in the 8th *chasseur à cheval*, rode through Smolensk and described the horrific spectacle of a city in flames:

> The Russian army, probably in the hope of a longer resistance, had evacuated to Smolensk the wounded from Krasnoe, Mohilow and all the previous battles. A dreadful sight then presented itself to our eyes. As the French army approached, all the wounded had been piled up in the old town. The vigour of the attack and the activity of the pursuit had given the enemy just enough time to cut the bridges, but not enough time to evacuate their wounded, and these unfortunate people, left to die a terrible death, lay in heaps of material, charred, shrunken, barely retaining their human form, amid smoking rubble and flaming beams. Many of them, after vain efforts to escape the terrible elements, lay in the streets, reduced to charcoal and in limb positions indicative of the atrocious tortures that must have preceded their deaths. I shuddered with horror at this sight, which will never fade from my memory, and we hurried out into the countryside, suffocated by the smoke and the heat, and agitated by this horrible tableau. I felt as if I'd been through hell. We quickly reached the Russian rearguard; a line of skirmishers

117. Alexandre Picard, op. cit., pp. 27–33.

> was formed across the main road from Smolensk to Moscow, and we harassed the enemy until nightfall, which put an end to the fighting.[118]

Most authors attribute the burning of Smolensk to the retreating Russian army. After the battle and the capture of the town, a wounded man, Captain Coudreux, who was luckier than others, gave news to his brother:

> Smolensk, 25 August 1812
>
> If you enjoy reading the bulletins, you must now know, much more exactly than I could tell you, what happened around Smolensk during the brilliant days of the 16th, 17th and 18th of this month. I will limit myself to telling you that my regiment had the honour of taking a very lively part in the affair of the 17th. My grenadiers behaved with dignity; we bayoneted the enemy for half an hour, and we went to bed under the walls of Smolensk, after having forced everything in front of us to seek salvation behind the ramparts. The next day, 18th, at four in the morning, we entered the town ... I was quite seriously wounded by two shots to the left arm; one of the two bullets only bruised my shoulder badly, but the second went through the whole length of my arm, from the wrist to the elbow. However, the surgeons think that I will not be crippled. To make matters worse, as I was climbing up the hill, I was hung up by a piece of palisade that hit me on the head and knocked me into the ditch.[119]

As an officer, Captain Coudreux seems to have been well looked after. The same was not true of all the wounded. Alexandre Picard, wounded in the attack on Smolensk, wrote in his diary how difficult it was for the lower ranks to receive treatment:

> On arriving at the ambulance, I went to find the regimental surgeon and told him to bandage me. 'My friend, tomorrow morning,' said the surgeon. 'I'll think of you tomorrow morning at four o'clock.' To get through the night, I unpacked my bag and my giberne and lay down with my head on the bag. In the morning I was bandaged up and set off straight away for Smolensk. We made soup in the suburbs, ate it and then went to ask to be admitted to hospital. 'There's no more room!' we were told. There were more wounded in the city than paving stones

118. Julien Combe, op. cit., p. 77.

119. Gustave Schlumberger, op. cit., pp. 211–12. After this letter, Coudreux gave no sign of life to his family, who thought he was dead, until July 1813, when they learned that he had been taken prisoner by the Russians.

in the street! We were put in a garden, and when night came, we went to bed, when towards morning, the house collapsed in our midst and nearly crushed me. It had not been set on fire. The bricks rolled right over my head. The next day we were told that the general was going to give a 20 Fr. Napoleon to each wounded man. We ran there but arrived too late: the distribution had been made. We were then given a ration of bread and a carriage to a castle where the surgeons were to think about the wounded. But the surgeons were no longer there. So we went further on, to a village where we spent the night. We set off again the next day and walked for another three days. I had gone six days without being bandaged. On the sixth day, we met a surgeon on the road. There were six of us and he dressed five of them. When it was my turn, he refused to treat me.

'Why do you not want to bandage me up?' He looked at my arm and said, 'Because I do not have any bandages big enough to hold your arm.' And he added that I had to go as far as the town, where there was a hospital. We got there and I asked the guard which way the hospital was. 'There isn't one,' I was told, 'but see our surgeon major. He'll be able to dress you well.' I went and showed him my arm. 'I cannot bandage it for you,' he said, 'because I do not have the ambulance van with the bandages and lint. I'll only bandage it if you can get some linen.' 'But I was wounded six days ago!' At last I found some linen, I brought it to him and he set to work. He undid the bandage and went to lift the compress, but it was so hard, because of the blood, that it took him well over an hour to remove it. When the arm was undone, the surgeon asked me the name of the man who had dressed me. 'He's our regimental surgeon.' 'He's an apprentice. It's obvious that your major surgeon, Mr Foucherre, hasn't been there. He would have split your arm in four. If there was a hospital here, I would put you in it, but we don't have one, and you have to march tomorrow.' 'I was in so much pain that I could not sleep for more than an hour a night. My arm was as big as my thigh and the colour of earth. With injuries like that, we were still walking eight and 10 miles a day, and for food we were like birds. We had to look for it in the fields. Everywhere we went, because we were so weak, the farmers did not want to give us anything. That's why we had to live in the fields, like the birds ... When I got to a small town where there was only a local commander, I went to his house to ask him to come to the hospital. 'There aren't any here,' he replied, 'but you'll find a Jew who dresses wounds' ... I took the Jew a note in the commandant's handwriting, but he told me he did not work on Saturdays. I begged him, and showed him my arm, which hadn't been treated for 10 days. He shrugged his shoulders, went into the next room and came back with a compress of ointments and a bandage as black as the heart of a chimney. He bandaged me up and, after six hours, my arm was half swollen. The second day, I got into the habit of bandaging myself: I cut up two shirts I had in my bag and used them to make lint, compresses and bandages. We arrived in another small town and asked the local commander to let us into the hospital. But the commander told us that there was no room for us. He did, however, give us half a pound of bread, a quarter of a pound of meat and some broth. We slept in a village 10 leagues away, and the next morning we set off. When we got to another town, the commander sent us to the hospital with a ticket, but unfortunately it was the same thing at the hospital: there was no room. We were made to sleep in small houses full of lice, on straw, and given a ration of bread. Early in the morning, a nurse came to get us and put 10 of us in a van, and sent us to Vilna, with meat, brandy and bread for two days ... From there, we were on our way to Minsk, where we thought we were going into hospital. Once again, we were sent to abandoned peasants' houses to sleep on straw. There were as many lice in the straw as there were strands. Every morning, at seven o'clock, we went to the hospital to be bandaged, and every other day we were given a pound of meat and a pound of bread, blacker than the heart of a chimney. To get vegetables in the soup, you had to go marauding. Anyone who could not go was left starving. One night, while we were digging up carrots in a garden, we heard a noise. It was a farmer running up with three big dogs. We only had time to jump over the fences and save ourselves. The next morning, when I was in hospital, the surgeon undid my arm, looked at it and said: 'The bullet is still in there.' I replied that it had gone through and that you could see the hole through which it had exited. 'There's something there, though, bones or a piece of clothing. Your arm is ugly. If the chief surgeon were here, he'd cut it off. We'll see in the morning.' But I did not go for three days. At the end of the fourth day, I went back, but without showing my arm, for fear that it would be cut off. All of a sudden, an order came to send away the people who did not have any wounds on their legs. Those with wounds on their hands, those missing fingers and those with minor wounds were to rejoin the regiment.[120]

The pursuit of the retreating Russians was no pleasure at all for infantrymen and cavalrymen alike. Lieutenant Combe remembered this episode:

---

120. Alexandre Picard, op. cit., pp. 37–43.

> It was the end of August. In this climate and at this time of year, the heat is unlike that of southern Europe. It wasn't just the heat of the sun that we had to endure, but even more so the roasted vapours of the earth. Our horses raised a cloud of burning sand under their steps, as fine as dust, and with which we were so covered that it would have been difficult to distinguish the colour of our uniforms. This sand, when it got into our eyes, caused excruciating pain. I could hardly breathe and, despite the devouring thirst produced by the combination of these circumstances, we could not stop to refresh ourselves and quench our thirst in the clear water of the few springs we passed. Our horses were happier, dipping their burning nostrils into the water with a sort of fury, but had neither the time nor the opportunity to drink with the mouthpiece in their mouths. Some of them would roll around in the water with delight, despite the feigned or real efforts of their riders, who were not displeased to have an excuse to do the same. Finally, I have never experienced such unbearable heat in Italy. Every evening the smoke from the bivouac increased the irritation produced by the day, and I do not know how I never lost my sight. However, we were still advancing with daily battles between the vanguard and the rearguard, and we realised that the enemy's resistance was becoming more and more stubborn.[121]

As the Grande Armée pushed further and further into Russia, reinforcements continued to pour in from the rear. The soldiers, unaware of the dark days ahead, took advantage of their days of rest to write to their families and share their news, often for the first time since leaving. François Falise, an artillery man, was obviously still optimistic:

> Königsberg, 11 August 1812
>
> I am going to do the Russian campaign and I have been on the road for three months. I left Metz on 8 May. I still have almost 150 leagues to go to join the great army. Don't grieve any more than I do, for I am the happiest man in the world, were it not for a hole in my purse, which means that it is not very fat. However, I've come a long way since we were fed by the farmer. Now all I have left is the ration, which is very light.[122]

In France, news poured in of troop concentrations and generals passing through, but the newspapers, unaware of Napoleon's real intentions, never

121. Julien Combe, op. cit., p. 78.
122. AEL, FFP, 1042–1044, letter of François Falise.

mentioned war. It took around two weeks for dispatches sent from the borders of the Grand Duchy of Warsaw to reach the capital. It was only on 7 July 1812 that war with Russia was announced in the press. The first news of the battle of Smolensk appeared in the newspapers on 1 September 1812. The *Journal de l'Empire* reported:

> Today we received several private letters from the Grande Armée; they announce that on the morning of the 18th our troops entered Smolensk. It seems that the Russians had initially taken up position to defend this place, which they had armed and fortified; but that the rapid arrival of the French army completely disconcerted their plans. We fell upon the enemy with such impetuosity, says one of these letters, that he did not have time to recognise himself, and that we entered the town at full gallop, while he was still there. He fled in such haste that he left all his artillery on the ramparts. We took many of his crews and considerable shops. Our troops are full of enthusiasm. The country they have just entered is one of the most fertile in Russia; it is covered with villages and offers great resources to the army.[123]

As can be seen, optimism reigned in Paris and in the army. However, the rest of the campaign was to prove a disaster of epic proportions.

123. *Le Journal de l'Empire*, 1 September 1812.

Chapter 5

Moscow

First battles

As demonstrated in the preceding chapter, cautious optimism prevailed in August 1812. The French pursued the Russians with confidence in their eventual victory. Following their occupation of Smolensk, the Borysthene river was crossed at various points, and the French recognised the two roads leading to Moscow and St Petersburg. On 19 August the French vanguard encountered Russian infantry on the Moscow road, approximately 8km from Smolensk, and Marshal Ney promptly joined forces with them. The enemy was driven out from Garbuonovo village and the march continued to Valutino. At that location 35,000 Russians were gathered, quickly forcing Marshal Ney onto the defensive. Initially assuming it was just a rearguard action, Napoleon was subsequently better informed and dispatched the Gudin division to support Ney. The 1st and 8th corps, comprising 41,000 soldiers, came up against General Tuchkov's 22,000 men. The battle was furious. The Russians, after fiercely defending their position, were forced to give way. In the middle of the battle General Gudin was killed and replaced by General Gérard. In this battle, the French lost 9,000 men killed, wounded and missing, while the Russians had 5,000 killed and wounded. Although the Russians had retreated, they could not be deemed as defeated during this battle as they did so in an orderly fashion, taking with them their baggage, artillery and wounded personnel. Additionally, it is worth mentioning that Marshal Junot, who was in charge of the 8th Corps, executed a series of rather clumsy manoeuvres, thus allowing the Russian army to escape.[124] The battle of Valutino had significant consequences for the French army, as it put them on the path to Moscow which would ultimately prove fatal. Following the battle, Napoleon ordered Murat to pursue the retreating Russians. However, the cavalry's pursuit proved futile as they only encountered a few Cossacks. Julien Combe, an officer in a light cavalry regiment, explained:

124. Digby Smith, op. cit., p. 388.

> However, the days of combat followed one another without interruption for us, the light cavalry of the vanguard. The enemy army withdrew in admirable order, leaving no wounded and few dead. Since crossing the Borysthene, we had already suffered great hardship due to the scarcity of food. Only one distribution had been made at Smolensk, but the further we advanced into this wild country, the more severe the shortages became. We were too weak to be able, like the infantry, to send supplies in large masses some distance from the road. If we came within range of a village or hamlet, we found it in flames; the Cossacks would not abandon it until they had set fire to it, devastated everything they could not take with them, and rammed in the barrels of beer or oat brandy called vodka, which is very common in the country. Not a sheep, not an animal that could serve us as food, except from time to time, a thin hen escaped from the general immigration, or a young foal too weak to follow its mother, and which neighed in the countryside. When we made this find, our Chasseurs put it in the ranks; it followed, willingly or not, the movements of the regiment, and we killed it on arriving at the bivouac to eat it as a steak, everything natural, that is to say without any kind of seasoning ... I made a good meal when I was happy enough to discover a hiding place of potatoes.[125]

More letters written during this period were now arriving in France. They presented a relatively optimistic picture of the situation. They mainly came from soldiers who had stayed behind the troops in pursuit of the Russians, as troops on the march never had time to send news. For example, Louis Geuget of the 9th cuirassiers regiment, had plenty of time to write as he was in the rear waiting for a replacement for his horse that had been killed in action. He submitted a report whose precision concerning the sequence of operations remains uncertain:

> 14 September 1812. My dear father and my very dear mother. … we left on 28 February to go to war in Russia and I have not yet received any news ... What worries me is to know if my brother has suffered the fate and if he has fallen in or out ... After passing through several countries, Westphalia and Prussia, Poland and the former Prussia, here we are on the Russian border. I am at the Insterbourg depot for my horse, which has been killed. The army is 300 leagues into Russia and they are still advancing every day, but they have lost a lot of people. And we are thinking of getting horses every day to leave for the regiment. They have taken shops and more than 100,000 Russian men as prisoners. And

125. Julien Combe, *Mémoires du colonel Combe*, Paris, 1896, pp. 96–7.

we're thinking that, once the war is over, we'll go back to France. But we're better off there than in France, even though they're bad countries. And I will not tell you any more today, my dear father and mother.[126]

During his time with the Imperial Guard, accompanying Napoleon, François Joseph Detiège had considerably more leisure time than the average soldier on campaign. Napoleon sometimes stayed in the same place for several days at a time, as was the case for this extended stopover when the Emperor stayed in Vitebsk from 31 July to 12 August:

Written on 4 August in Vilbac

My dearest father, mother and brother

I will tell you that we are in Russia in pursuit of the Russians. We are 650 leagues from Paris and we are still marching ahead. It is a bad country for marching when the weather is poor, the terrain is very bad. I can tell you that we're not doing too well for food. We have been very happy on the road, especially in Silesia and Saxony, we were at the discretion of the peasants, but as soon as the Emperor joined us we marched for a long day – that is all I have to tell you for now.[127]

Jean-François Monsez was also a soldier in the Imperial Guard, present at Kovno with Napoleon. Unlike his compatriot, he was in hospital recovering from the long marches he had made so far. He later disappeared in Russia:

Kovno, 7 August 1812

I am in the hospital at Kovno in Russia to heal a wound in my foot caused by fatigue on the road. As we were heavily burdened, it caused us a lot of pain but, thank God, it's fine now. I'll tell you that our troop is making good progress. We're taking a lot of prisoners. We are only 40 leagues from St Perisbourg [St Petersburg], the capital of Russia. But as far as I'm concerned, I'm very happy for the present.

Jean-François Monsez from Dison, 5th regiment of the guard.[128]

Here was another letter from a soldier on his way to Russia, unaware of what was happening there, even though the war had been going on for more than two months. He died in Russia during the winter:

126. AEL, FFP, 1042–1044, letter of Louis Geuget.
127. AEL, FFP, 1042–1044, letter of François Detiège.
128. AEL, FFP, 1042–1044, letter of Jean-François Monsez.

Kainiber 30 August 1812

My dearest father and mother, I am taking the liberty of putting pen to paper to inform myself of the state of your health. Mine is doing well, thank God. I hope the same of you my dearest father and mother and brother and sister. I do not have to tell you that we are far from home. I want you to know that we are 500 leagues from home and I want you to know that we have travelled all the wrong roads and I want you to know that we have travelled through Germany, Austria, the desert, Prussia, Poland and old Prussia and we are going to enter Russia because we hear the cannons firing at us every day because I want you to know that it is eight months since we entered any house. We are still sleeping in the countryside, my dearest father and mother and brother and sister.[129]

Louis-Joseph Debroux of the 30th Dragoons had not yet left for faraway Russia. He sent a last letter to his family from his regimental depot, announcing his imminent departure. There was no sign of fear at the thought. It is true that so far, the news arriving from Russia still suggested that the expedition was going to be a complete success:

Faverney 1st September 1812

My dearest father and mother,

I am writing you this letter to enquire about the state of your health while I, thank God, am doing quite well. I hope that this letter finds you the same.

I am surprised not to receive any news from you seeing that I wrote to you on 22 July last. I will tell you that I have changed regiment I am now in the 30th Dragoon Regiment. If you would like to have a certificate for my brother, I would ask you to send me 12 francs immediately as I cannot have it without this sum, and we are waiting for the order to leave for Russia. Once we have gone, I will not be able to send it to you; we are very badly off here; since we arrived we have not yet received a liard and it is as expensive to live as you will not believe, nothing else to mark you for the present.[130]

Since the early days of the French invasion, the Russian high command was split between those supporting two different approaches to fighting. Barclay de Tolly advised systematically withdrawing when confronted with the French

129. AEL, FFP, 1042–1044, letter of Jean-François Wilmart.
130. AEL, FFP, 1042–1044, letter of Louis Debroux.

army, whilst utilising a scorched earth strategy. In contrast, Kutuzov preferred direct combat with the French aggressors. A significant faction of the public supported the latter option, arguing that the security of the empire should not be entrusted to a foreign general. Russia's fate lay in the hands of a native, and fortunately a capable one was available: a student of Suvarov who was not given to craven retreats before the enemy, unlike Barclay. Emperor Alexander, seeking to unify his command structure and weary of the endless withdrawals in the face of the foe, named Field Marshal Kutuzov as the general-in-chief, entrusting him with the task of taking on Napoleon.

Kutuzov determined to impede the French advance on Moscow, despite being somewhat outnumbered, and positioned his forces in the vicinity of Borodino. Upon hearing this news, Napoleon experienced immense joy. He had been searching for a significant battle in Russia without success until now. His opponent would be old Kutuzov, whom he had previously met and overcome at Austerlitz. The French army promptly began preparing for battle. In anticipation of a decisive encounter, Napoleon allowed his troops two days' rest. On 5 September the cavalry led by Murat, King of Naples, encountered that of Count Konovnitsin, marking the prelude to the great battle. The French emerged victorious, causing the withdrawal of the Russian cavalry. Captain François provided a detailed account of his regiment's three-day stay from 5 to 7 September:

> 5 September. The army set off at dawn in four columns. Around two o'clock in the afternoon, we, the 1st Corps, 1st Division in the lead, saw the Russian army at a short distance from us, having an open position on uneven ground. We, the 1st Division, fired for several hours in order to take up our position. The captain of the grenadiers of the 1st Battalion was killed; two other officers were wounded.
>
> We saw the enemy's right positioned behind the village of Borodino, protected by the small river of Kologha [Koloch river], which flows through a ravine and empties into the Moscowa, a short distance from the main road to Moscow. In control of the position that had cost us 66 men, we saw the left of the Russian army commanded by General Bagration, supported by the Passarewo wood, covered by three redoubts on the front of its line, including one in front of the village of Seminskoe [Semenovskoe]. This village was destroyed and fortified with fortifications. The Russian centre was near Gorka [Gorki], where there were large batteries. This corps was commanded by General Benigsen, with whom was General-in-Chief Kutuzov. The Fifth Division of the First Corps captured the redoubt and defences of the village of Chewarino [Shevardino], after several battles in which the Russians were routed and lost 7 cannons; but this redoubt cost us more than 1,000 men.

6 September. At two o'clock in the morning the Emperor toured the Russian outposts which were on the other side of the ravine and in front of the village of Seminskoe, protected by batteries placed along their line. During his tour he reviewed several regiments, including the 61st, and asked the colonel what he had done with one of his battalions. The colonel replied: 'Sire, it is in the Chewarino Redoubt.' The Emperor answered nothing and went to review other corps. This was reported to me by officers of the 61st. The day was spent in reconnaissance and manoeuvres. The enemy was in position, making little movement, as we, the 30th of the First Division, skirmished along the line of the Russian outposts, uncovering the whole army. The Russians occupied the line of the ravine and we skirmished with them all afternoon until 11 p.m., without leaving our positions on either side. The battalions were relieved successively, and the 1st Battalion, of which I was a member, did not leave the line of skirmishers until four o'clock in the evening and rejoined the regiment after being relieved by the 13th Light Infantry, which was part of the Morand 1st Division of the 1st Corps.

On that day, the regiment lost 300 men, 67 of whom were killed. I was among the wounded. A bullet had gone through the underside of my left hock. I had received this wound around eight o'clock in the evening, and despite the pain and loss of blood, I remained at my post still firing with my company and did not return to the regiment until 11 o'clock, the moment the battalion was relieved and reunited with the regiment. I took roll call. I was short 23 men, including 16 killed. Then I went to be dressed by the regimental surgeon major, who passed a probe through the bullet hole and removed the projectile. While limping, I joined my comrades with whom I spent the rest of the night.

6 September. The other four divisions of the 1st Corps in position and we, the 1st, in the outposts along the ravine and forming the extreme right, our left linking up with the 3rd Corps, the 4th Cavalry in rear of the Shevardino Redoubt, the 4th Corps also in rear of this redoubt crowned by shoulders and strong batteries to protect it. It rained for part of the day. In the afternoon of that day, as skirmishers as I have said, I saw much more movement in the Russian battle lines. I heard that a proclamation was being read to the soldiers and that an image of St Sergius was being carried by priests along their lines. This saint, carried in front of the army under arms, is highly venerated in Russia. Every soldier wears it on his collar. For us, our scapular was our emperor, in whom we had complete confidence.

7 September. Around three o'clock in the morning, the army was in action. Although wounded, I was at my post on the right of my company, the regiment being in battle. My colonel and several comrades said to me: 'Withdraw, go to the ambulance or the eagle guard.' I replied: 'My wound is nothing; I want to share your glory.' At 3.30 a.m., we began our movements to cross the ravine. As we marched, we learned from the orders that the Emperor was in the same position as the day before and that he had said to the marshals who had come to take his orders: 'This cloudless sun is the sun of Austerlitz. The army accepts the omen.' At about 5.30 a.m., we, the 30th, halted halfway up the ravine, where, after beating a ban, we were read the following order of the day.

Around six o'clock, a cannon shot from the Guard artillery signalled the start of the battle. At the extreme right, 120 cannons began the action, and the army corps carried out their movements ... Marshal Davout had left the second division of his corps in reserve in front of Shevardino, and he marched with the fourth and fifth, on the front of the redoubt on the left of the Russians. Artillery general Pernetti, with 30 guns, took command of the 5th division of the 1st corps. Prince Poniatowski marched to turn the forest on our right. The Viceroy of Italy attacked Borodino with the Delzons division of his corps. We, the Morand division, the Gérard and Boursier divisions of the 4th corps, the Italian guard, crossed the Kologhas on the bridges built by the general of engineers Poitevin. The cavalry of the King of Naples was on the move. Cavalry General Nansouty followed Marshal Davout's movement. General Grouchy followed the Viceroy. The Fourth Corps followed the Third. The 8th, deployed on the right in two lines and commanded by General Foucher, was supported by 60 cannons. The Emperor was in the Shevardino redoubt, from where he could see the Russian line moving, the Old Guard behind the redoubt, the Young Guard and cavalry in front. During these movements, the 30th marched up and down the ravine in line of battle, a tiring and difficult march under shells bursting overhead which killed and wounded some men. The regimental eagles had remained at the bottom of the ravine with the *fouriers*; the voltigeurs flanked our right, and one captain, out of caution, went up slowly so as not to take part in the capture of the redoubt, about which I will speak later. During our march to the top of the ravine, the other corps and divisions of the 1st continued their march; the 5th, at about seven o'clock in the evening, was in front of the redoubt closest to Passarevo Wood and the 57th of this division received the order to take the fortress. The colonel turned to his soldiers and said: 'To the redoubt!'[131]

131. Jean-Louis Charrière (1765–1846), enlisted in 1782 and was colonel of the 57th of the line in 1808.

The regiment charged forward and took the redoubt but lost between 2,500 and 1,600 men. The colonel was appointed general on the spot. The Second Division took Seminskoe and its redoubts, inflicting considerable losses on the Russians. The 3rd corps advanced and occupied the Shevardino heights and linked up with the 5th corps. While this was happening on the right and in the centre, the Viceroy advanced on the left and, at around eight o'clock, just as we, the 30th, had climbed the eastern slope past the Kologha, the battle line was rallied and General Morand, after receiving the Viceroy's order to march on the big battery, passed this order on to General Bonamy, who commanded the regiment. General Morand walked along the regiment's line of battle, urging the soldiers to win. When he reached me, and saw that I was wounded, he said to me: 'Captain, you cannot keep up, withdraw to the eagle guard.' I said to him, 'General, this day is too attractive for me to hesitate to share in the glory that the regiment wants to achieve.' 'I recognise you,' replied the general. He touched my hand and walked through the regiment's battle line, where hundreds of cannonballs and shells were flying over our heads. When General Morand had finished going through the regiment's line, he went to General Bonamy and gave him the order to march. When we reached the crest of the ravine, halfway up to the large Russian battery, we were crushed by the grapeshot from this battery and others flanking it. Nothing stopped us. We jumped to let the Biscayans roll by. Whole lines of half platoons fell, leaving large gaps. General Bonamy made me stop despite the grapeshot. He had the lines tightened and the regiment continued to march at full speed, with General Bonamy in the lead, towards the redoubt that we took, crossing it and overtaking it by 40 to 60 paces. But not being followed by the other regiments of the division, except for the 1st Battalion of the 13th light, the regiment was three-quarters destroyed. We could not hold on, and we withdrew in disorder, mixed up among the Russians, and went to regroup behind the redoubt, still under enemy grapeshot. We attempted a second charge, but were unable, given our numbers, to take the redoubt. The regiment withdrew to the rear of this fatal redoubt, with 11 officers and 257 non-commissioned officers and soldiers; the rest were killed and wounded, both in front of the redoubt and inside it, left to the wolves that were around it.

7 September. The brave General Bonamy, who commanded the regiment, was wounded in the Redoubt and taken prisoner by the Russians.[132] He

132. Charles-Auguste Bonamy (1764–1830), who enlisted in 1791 and became a brigadier general in 1798, is best known for the capture of the Moscova redoubt. He was seriously wounded there, being

had received 15 wounds. During our charge on the redoubt the rest of the division was in position on the plateau opposite, busy repelling the efforts of the Russians; it was therefore unable to come to our aid.

As we marched at full tilt on the large Russian battery, we fired a regimental fire on a Russian line in battle, which was on the flanks with skirmishers placed in the wolf holes. This line fell; we passed over it and entered the redoubt. We passed through the embrasures and were received by the enemy gunners with blows from levers and ramrods. Several of them even got caught in the snare. I was passing through an embrasure a few seconds after the fire from the gun. Blinded by the smoke, many soldiers fell into the wolf holes, mixed up with the Russians who were inside, and the line which had thrown itself to the ground at the moment of our regimental fire. Entering the redoubt, I defended myself with my sabre against the gunners; I sabred several of them and passed the redoubt. As we were not very strong, we were forced to retreat, to cross the redoubt, the Russian line which had risen and the wolf holes. This mêlée eventually destroyed the rest of the regiment, which rallied on the plateau where the division had been a moment earlier.

I have rarely found myself in such a mêlée, with soldiers as fearless and tenacious as the Russians. I was damaged: my shako was blown away by the grapeshot, along with the sides of my uniform; my stomach, flanks and thighs were bruised. A bullet that went through my left leg, combined with the one I had received the day before, left me shattered after a few minutes' rest and so weak from the loss of blood that I could neither move nor breathe. Having recovered a little from my weakness, some soldiers took me to the ambulance, where General Morand, who had been wounded in the chin, was being bandaged. The general touched my hand and, having bandaged it, signalled to the surgeon to do the same for me. The doctor came over to me, put his little finger in the bullet hole and with his scalpel made the customary crosses at each hole, put a probe through my leg between the two bones and said: 'happy wound', then he put the first appliance on me and told me to go to the army ambulance in Kologha, where there were thousands of wounded. The ambulance was in a convent. I went into a room where there were 27 officers from the regiment, including five amputees, lying on straw, lacking absolutely everything. This ambulance had more than 10,000 wounded. Eight to 10 days after this battle, three quarters of these unfortunate wounded had died for lack of help and food ...

---

bayoneted twenty times and taken prisoner by the Russians.

> In the evening, some of the regiment's soldiers, who had been slightly wounded, were walking through the wards; one of my companies said to me when he saw me: 'Ah, Captain, it was said that you were killed, and I'm so glad to see you again; so why did not you make do with the wound you received yesterday?' These soldiers were a great help to me and my comrades. He told me that my lieutenant had been killed and that my second lieutenant had had the underside of his left arm and part of his thigh blown off by a cannonball. My sergeant major, three sergeants, six corporals, 57 soldiers and a drummer had been killed; the company had only five men left, the regiment about 300 and 11 officers, out of the 4,100 it had in the morning. During the night, seven officers from the same barracks room as myself died.[133]

After the story of this battle as told by an infantryman, here is the account of a cavalryman:

> Before daybreak, we were ordered to move forward along the Moscow road and stop at Borodino. The division formed up in column by brigade in front of a ravine which crossed the whole battlefield, and at the bottom of which was a coloured stream. No sooner had the sun begun to shine on the horizon than one of General Grouchy's aides-de-camp brought and handed to the colonel, to be read in front of the regiment, this admirable proclamation by the Emperor ... The weather was magnificent and the whole battlefield was revealed to us. Our cavalry corps formed the extreme left of the battle line. We had to protect 25 artillery pieces placed between us and the Montbrun division, and to guard and light the road to Moscow and the village of Borodino. The battle began on the whole line almost at once. Opposite us, on the enemy's extreme right, we had a redoubt whose fire was engaged by the artillery on our right, but some of whose guns were reserved for us. All the cannonballs ricocheted through our ranks, and we waited for them, sabres at our shoulders. We remained in this terrible position for six hours. I was riding a charming grey horse from the King of Bavaria's stud farm, which I had bought when we were in Munich; this animal was extremely lively and, for the first few hours, couldn't help jumping sideways at every cannonball it saw coming, until finally, exhausted and sweating, it agreed to stand still. But it seemed that he had the courage to resign himself to his fate, for no sooner had he calmed down than a terrible shock made him reel and fall on top of me. He had been hit in the middle of the chest and the cannonball had come out of his right flank.

133. Charles-François François, op. cit., pp. 661–7.

I got up at once, dazed by the fall, but I felt a numbness in my right leg that prevented me from putting my foot on the ground. I thought I had lost my leg, knowing from numerous examples that, in the first moment, that's the only feeling you get. My comrade Guilleminier was quick to reassure me: 'Your foot is at the end of your leg, do not worry; but you can boast that you're getting off cheaply,' he said.

However, I felt that I was wounded and that I had some blood in my boot. I made my Chasseurs take my horse's harness, which he placed on his back, and went down into the ravine. After removing my shoes with a great deal of pain and suffering, I realised that the big toe of my right foot was broken, and the nail broken in the flesh ... I bandaged the injured part with my handkerchief, cut off my boot and headed for the other side of the ravine, towards the place where I was to find my servant and the only horse I had left. The battle was at its hottest and there was no sign of victory. I limped past the ambulances. There, near a van, lay a crowd of unfortunate wounded formed in a circle around a fire placed in the centre and used to cook bouillon tablets. The surgeons and their assistants, dressed in shirtsleeves and with their sleeves rolled up, held the fatal scalpel or the terrible saw in their hands. They cut off an arm or a leg, tore apart flesh and, covered in blood, were busily bandaging the wounds. Terrible curses, cries of despair and lamentable groans signalled the approach of these improvised ambulances, constantly renewed by the results of the battle ... However, I had been hoisted onto my bay mare, which was all I had left, with another more than mediocre horse, ridden by Bastien, and, crossing the battlefield for a second time to rejoin my regiment through a hail of cannonballs which criss-crossed the earth around me, I replaced myself at the head of my platoon, and as a reward for my zeal received the most flattering praise from my brave colonel.[134] The poor 8th Chasseurs were more than decimated; their ranks were sadly thinned, and a large number of corpses of men and horses littered the ground we had occupied since sunrise. It was about 11 o'clock; a frightful din of artillery was resounding across the plain; the earth was shaking under the sound of cavalry charges, when at last we saw an aide-de-camp of General Grouchy running at full speed, bringing us the order to charge by making a movement to our left to cross the road just above Borodino ... No man condemned to

134. Alexandre-Edmond de Talleyrand-Périgord (1787–1872). Second lieutenant in 1804, fought in the 1806–1807 campaign, aide-de-camp to Marshal Berthier. Appointed colonel of the 8th *chasseurs à cheval* in January 1812. Prisoner on 19 September 1813; released in 1814. After the fall of Napoleon, became lieutenant-general and inspector general of the cavalry. Danielle and Bernard Quintin, *Dictionnaire des colonels de Napoléon*, Paris, 1996, p. 816.

torture ever felt more joy at receiving his pardon than we did at carrying out this manoeuvre, which freed us from such disastrous inaction. The regiments formed into a squadron at a gallop and maintained this pace until, when they reached the enemy's right flank, they found themselves in the presence of the Russian cuirassiers. We formed forward in battle, and in column by regiment en masse. The 6th Hussars were in the lead; they charged vigorously and shook the Russian cuirassiers, so that the 8th Chasseurs, who came in second line, rushed forward like lightning and completed their defeat. They turned on their heels in the greatest disorder, and we sabre-rattled furiously, as if to compensate ourselves and make up for the time lost ... We were so relentless that many of us pursued them long after the trumpets had sounded the rally, and, to rejoin our division, we had to make our way through a cloud of Cossacks. The cuirassiers finally rallied and charged forward. They stopped 100 paces from our front. We stood firm in the stirrups, sabre in hand, ready to receive them. The Cossacks, as was their custom, had withdrawn on both sides to leave the field clear. The enemy, at the sight of our good composure, seemed to hesitate; he did not dare to start the charge and executed a half-turn by platoon, at a walk with as much regularity as in a manoeuvre on the field of Mars ... as I was suffering a great deal from my wounded foot, the colonel authorised me to squeeze in as well as possible with three of my comrades who were also wounded and the assistant surgeon-major named Gérard, whom we liked very much in the regiment.

The morning that followed this memorable day was very deadly for the 8th Chasseurs. It was our turn to take the head of the column. At dawn, the outposts were attacked, and we went forward to support them; but we had to fight, in addition to a very strong rearguard, an innumerable crowd of Cossacks and a battery of 30 cannon, which waited for us at close range and riddled us with grapeshot. More than 60 chasseurs were killed, and we had a large number of wounded, especially among the non-commissioned officers ... Finally, we managed to get out of the path of the enemy artillery and, the smoke having cleared, we found ourselves on the right flank of the position they occupied. Artillery captain Dufour, whom we had nicknamed 'Captain Grapeshot' because he always got close enough to the enemy to shoot him, had just taken up position in battery and was firing like hell to dismantle the Russian guns ... Relying on our help as on himself, he had advanced too rashly, when a large number of regular Cossacks and others, rushing from a nearby wood where they were in ambush, surrounded him on all sides in the hope of taking him and his pieces. But he defended himself like a lion until, seeing the danger he was in, with one accord, moved as

> if by the same thought, we rushed at full gallop on our horses to free him. Some cannons were already in the hands of the Cossacks; we immediately took them back and brought them to Captain Dufour, who received them with the joy and tenderness of a good father finding his children. We formed up in battle, between his artillery and the wood; in less than an hour the enemy pieces had been dismantled, and, after a few vigorous charges, we were in control of the position, where our fires were established in the bivouacs occupied the day before by the Russians.[135]

A letter from a captain of the 9th cuirassiers to his sister also described how the men waited under enemy fire, forced to stand still and suffer heavy losses throughout the battle, without ever going into action:

> The regiment did not make a charge, but also remained constantly under cannonball and grapeshot. We stayed nine lines from the squadron I was in. Everywhere we saw only the dead and dying. Twice during the battle, I went to look at the faces of the cuirassiers in my company to see who the brave ones were. I was quite pleased with them. I told them about it in the field. When I went to congratulate a young officer (M. de Grammont) on his good behaviour, I saw some terrible things. As he was telling me that he had nothing to complain about and that he would only like a glass of water, a cannonball came along when he had hardly spoken and split him in two. I turned round to another officer and told him that I was very sorry for poor Mr Gramont. Before he could reply, his horse received a cannon shot which killed him. Finally, a hundred other things; I gave my horse to hold for half a minute, the cuirassier who was holding it was knocked over dead. I was covered in earth that the shells had thrown at me, but I did not get the slightest scratch. That's what gave me the calm I needed. I said to myself: 'It's a lottery, if you come back, you still have to die; would you rather live in dishonour or die with honour?' The choice was easy.[136]

The battle of Borodino was one of the bloodiest of the Napoleonic era. Only the battle of Leipzig in 1813 claimed more victims. The 18th *Bulletin of the Grande Armée*, written at Mojaisk on 10 September, concluded the account with a toll disputed by contemporary historians:

135. Julien Combe, op. cit., pp. 82–92.

136. Aristide Martinien, op. cit. t. 1, p. 531, confirmed the death of Second Lieutenant Gramont on 7 September 1812.

> The enemy's loss was enormous: 12 to 13,000 men and 8 to 9,000 Russian horses were counted on the battlefield; 60 cannon and 5,000 prisoners remained in our power. We had 2,500 men killed and three times as many wounded. Our total loss can be estimated at 10,000 men; that of the enemy at 40 or 50,000. We have never seen such a battlefield. Out of six corpses, there was one French and five Russians. 40 Russian generals were killed, wounded or taken; General Bagration was wounded ...[137]

According to contemporary historians, the actual figures for losses on both sides during the battle are very different from those declared by Napoleon in the *Bulletin de la Grande Armée*, intended for French public opinion. At this battle, the French and their allies had 103,000 men and 587 cannons. They lost 6,600 killed and 21,400 wounded. In addition to the generals killed and wounded mentioned in the *Bulletin*, there were Major General Tharreau and Brigadier Generals Damas, Lanabère, Romeuf, von Breuning and von Lepel who died of their wounds, and several others. The Russians had pitted 103,800 regular soldiers, 640 cannon, 7,000 Cossacks and 10,000 militiamen against Napoleon. Their exact losses are unknown. They are estimated at around 43,000 killed and wounded and 1,000 prisoners; 20 cannon were taken by the French. General Prince Bagration died of his wounds, as did Generals Tuchkov and Kutaisov, Kanownitzin and many others.[138]

Although both armies claimed victory, the French remained in control of the battlefield, as they had at Eylau. The Russians were able to withdraw towards Moscow, taking their wounded and artillery with them. However, the outcome of the great battle of Borodino was not what Napoleon had anticipated. Despite suffering significant casualties, the Russian army had retained its capability to resist the French forces. The inconclusive outcome was blamed on Napoleon himself by the generals, who claimed that he refused the use of the Imperial Guard, which would have undoubtedly prevented the enemy from escaping:

> What is certain is that at the time, when the Russian losses were known to us, I heard Napoleon blamed for having left his Guard inactive during this great day. There seems to be no doubt that fresh troops, especially those of the Guard, had they fallen on the enemy, then overwhelmed with fatigue and exhausted by the fight, would have completed their crushing and would have made their retreat to the Mojaïsk defile very difficult.[139]

137. 18th *Bulletin de la Grande Armée*.
138. Digby Smith, op. cit., pp. 390–2.
139. Pierre de Berthezène, op. cit., p. 57.

While the army had already entered Moscow, news of the battle of Borodino spread among the troops who had stayed behind. Jean-Charles Lesure, serving in the 7th *Chasseurs à cheval*, wrote the following:

> Tilsit 18th September 1812
>
> My Dearest Father and Mother, I am writing you these lines to let you know that I have been in this town for six weeks, with two sick horses, both of which died three weeks ago, and I have been waiting for the new detachments which passed through this town on the 14th of this month, believing I could continue my journey with them, but the Captain did not want to because I had two crews in ... My Dearest Father and Mother, I have nothing new to write to you at present, except that the French won the strongest town in Russia on the 15th of August, and I hope that in a short while they will go to Turkey. From what the world says, the French are already 280 Leagues into Russia. It was my Captain who told me this at Tilsit. My very dear father and my very dear mother I have finished. With a thousand heartfelt kisses to you, my dear brothers and my dear sister.[140]

In Paris, the announcement of the 'victory' at La Moskova (the French name for the battle of Borodino) was well received by the public, who rushed to buy the 18th *Bulletin of the Grande Armée*: '55,500 copies of the Bulletin were sold last Sunday. This figure does not include copies of the Monitor or bulletins posted on street corners.' A Te Deum was sung at Notre-Dame cathedral for La Moskova and the other victories on Sunday, 4 October in the presence of the Empress.

Moscow! Moscow! The promised land

After the battle of Borodino, Napoleon, aware that the Russians still had a large army, thought that he would still have to fight to reach the capital of the empire.[141] This prediction was inaccurate. General Kutuzov did withdraw in the direction of Moscow, but he did not stop there and he did not defend the approach to the city. His rearguard, led by General Miloradovich, crossed the city on 14 September without stopping. Baron Larrey, surgeon-in-chief of the Grande Armée, described the march of the days following the battle of Borodino:

> No sooner had we moved a few miles from Mozaïsk than we were astonished to find ourselves, despite our proximity to one of the

140. AEL, FFP, 1042–1044, letter of Jean-Charles Lesure.
141. Napoléon Bonaparte, *Correspondance générale*, t. 12, p. 1091.

> world's greatest capitals, on a sandy, arid and completely deserted plain. The gloomy aspect of this solitude, which threw all our soldiers into despondency, seemed to foreshadow the complete desertion of Moscow and the misfortunes awaiting us in this city, whose wealth should have promised us a different fate. The army crossed this space with difficulty. The horses were exhausted, worn out by hunger and thirst. For water was as scarce as fodder. The men also suffered greatly. They were overwhelmed by fatigue and deprived of sustenance. The troops had not received any food for a long time, and the few resources that could be found in Mozaïsk were used only by the Young and Old Guards. Quite a few conscripts from this first corps fell victim to the abuse of schnapps (local brandy). You could see them take a few steps away from their companions, stagger, turn around, then fall on their knees or sit down involuntarily. They would remain motionless in this attitude, and would soon expire without uttering a single complaint.[142]

Napoleon, accompanied by the Imperial Guard, followed the Russians by a few hours. He arrived in sight of Moscow. For the army, it was the entry into the promised land. Sergeant Bourgogne recounts the arrival in his memoirs:

> On 14 September, at one o'clock in the afternoon, after crossing a large forest, we saw an elevation in the distance. Half an hour later, we reached it. The leaders, who were already on the highest point, signalled to those who were still behind, shouting 'Moscow! Moscow!' Indeed, it was the great city in sight: it was where we thought we would rest from our fatigues, for we, the Imperial Guard, had just travelled more than twelve hundred leagues without resting. It was a beautiful summer's day; the sun was reflecting off the domes, steeples and golden palaces. Many of the capitals I had seen, such as Paris, Berlin, Warsaw, Vienna and Madrid, had only produced ordinary feelings in me, but here it was different: for me, as for everyone else, there was something magical. At that moment, pain, danger, fatigue and deprivation were all forgotten, so that all I could think about was the pleasure of entering Moscow, taking up good winter quarters there, and making conquests of another kind, for such is the character of the French soldier: from combat to love, and from love to combat. While we were contemplating the city, the order came to dress in full uniform.[143]

142. Dominique-Jean Larrey, *Mémoires de chirurgie militaire et campagnes du baron D. J. Larrey*, t. 4, Paris, 1817, pp. 61–2.
143. Adrien Bourgogne, op. cit., pp. 11–12.

A cuirassier captain, in a long letter to his sister written six months later, also recounts this arrival in one of the two capitals of the empire:

> Finally, at noon on the 14th, we saw this capital of the world. We all felt a certain *je ne sais quoi* at the sight of it, something I've felt many times before and cannot define. It was so far from my country! At two o'clock in the afternoon we arrived at the gates of Moscow without any resistance. The Emperor was there, on foot, in his headquarters, waiting for the keys to be brought by the city's leaders. But not at all, the city was partly abandoned; there was only a bad rabble and perhaps twenty thousand Russians who were responsible for burning it. At a quarter to three we entered the town and it took us five hours to pass through it without stopping, which is proof enough of its size. In the evening we bivouacked three quarters of a league from the town and stayed there for two or three days. The next day I spent part of the day there; the fire was already in several quarters, but I did have some fun. I had fallen into a French house of origin where the kind ladies received me with welcome, or at least apparent welcome; I took advantage of this without trying to penetrate their hearts. However, I do not think I displeased them, because the city was being pillaged, and in such a case you must be happy to have an officer in your home.[144]

General Armand de Caulaincourt, who had previously served as an ambassador in St Petersburg and grand equerry to the French emperor, accompanied Napoleon during his campaign in Russia. Caulaincourt also documented the French army's entry into the Russian capital. On 14 September 1812, under the leadership of Napoleon, the French army entered Moscow, marking a significant departure from previous triumphs where Napoleon had marched through Vienna, Berlin and Madrid in front of their respective residents. Caulaincourt, who was at his side, has left us an account of incidents that depict Russian fanaticism against the invader:

> During the month which the Russian troops occupied in marching through Moscow, the city resounded with cries of 'Death to the French!' A serf, who had been emancipated in the reign of Paul I, and who at the time to which I am now alluding, was a blind old man of eighty, had thirteen sons or grandsons serving in the Russian army as volunteers. 'Go,' said he, on taking leave of them, 'and do not spare your blood in the defence of your country and your religion. You will return

144. Jean Bréaut des Marlots, *Lettre d'un capitaine de cuirassiers sur la Campagne de Russie*, Paris-Poitiers, 1885, pp. 24–5.

victorious. God is just. But if the heavenly wrath should light upon our city – if it be ordained that foreigners shall profane our capital, I swear that they shall march over my body before they enter it.'

The Russians lost the battle of the Moskowa, and the French troops advanced to the ancient capital of the empire. The inhabitants fled and the city was speedily deserted. Petrowisk the blind old man, resisted the tears and entreaties of his family, and refused to depart.

'This is the soil that gave me birth,' said he, striking the ground with his stick; 'here I have lived for eighty years, and here I am resolved to die.' This old man was inexorable. All the family emigrated, taking with them the little property they could rescue from the pillage of the soldiery. At the moment of departure, four generations on their knees implored the blessing of the revered head of their family. The old figure of Petrowisk, his white hair and flowing beard, his large dark eyes open and fixed, imparted a sort of poetic interest to the scene.

The blind man remained in his dwelling. All his family departed, with the exception of one of his grandsons, a youth of sixteen, who had resolved to share the fate of his grandfather. Next day, the French advanced guard defiled on the high road: the head of the column touched the gates of Moscow. At intervals several musket shots penetrated the ranks. They were evidently fired by a practised hand and not a single ball missed its aim. Many soldiers were killed and wounded. An officer struck in the head by one of the balls fell dead from his horse. All eyes were turned in the direction whence the shots had been fired. An old man, whose long white beard covered his breast, was seen sitting on the ground, and resting his back against a tree. Our soldiers rushed towards him with their drawn bayonets in their hands.

At this moment a young man descended from the tree and throwing himself before the old man fired two pistols which he had in his girdle and then drew a large poignard to defend himself. But he was speedily overpowered by numbers and fell bleeding and lifeless at the feet of Petrowisk. 'Now,' exclaimed he, 'kill me, accursed French! That brave youth is my grandson, and it was I, Petrowisk, who armed him.' About an hour afterwards, the Emperor, attended by his staff, passed the spot where this incident had occurred. 'Ah!', exclaimed he, turning his horse to the opposite side of the road, 'this is a cowardly murder! An old man!' All who beheld the appalling sight turned away from it with horror. The old man was still in a sitting position; his eyes were open and fixed, his white beard was clotted with blood, and his garments were pierced by the swords of his assailants. At the foot of the tree, the lifeless corpse of a young lad lay weltering in a pool of blood. The

Emperor was naturally superstitious, and this horrible spectacle made a profound impression on his mind.

As [Napoleon] passed through the streets of Moscow, on his way to the Kremlin, he was struck with the aspect of the city. All the houses were closely shut up, and not one of the inhabitants was to be seen. It would be difficult to form an idea of the melancholy effect of this silence and torpor in the midst of a great capital. On first descrying the city our soldiery raised the cry of 'Moscow! Moscow! the promised land!' But their joy was speedily succeeded by depression. 'This solitude is awful,' said the Emperor to me.

In the evening a man was discovered concealed under the staircase leading to the Emperor's apartments. The Emperor wished to see and question him, but the man could not speak a word of French, and an interpreter was sent for. The Emperor, who was agitated and impatient, paced rapidly up and down the room, and several times spoke to the prisoner, forgetting that he could neither understand nor answer him. At length the interpreter arrived. A long colloquy ensued, and it was curious to observe the air of pride and inspiration which sat upon the countenance of the man. He was about fifty years of age, of tall stature, and his features had a fierce expression. 'What does he say? what does he say?' inquired the Emperor every moment. We elicited from him that his name was Ivan, and that he was the son of Petrowisk, the blind man. He had solemnly sworn to his father that he would assassinate Napoleon; and to accomplish that purpose he had disguised and concealed himself. He had stripped one of our soldiers, who had been killed on the road, and, disguised in the French uniform, he experienced no difficulty in gaining access to the place where he had been found concealed.

'Why this furious hatred towards me? How have I injured this Petrowisk personally?' said Napoleon. 'I spare this man's life,' added he; 'let him be conducted out of the city, and I desire that he be not harmed. This matter must rest among ourselves,' he said, addressing himself to the persons present. 'I desire it may not be mentioned.'[145]

Soon after Moscow's capture, a fire broke out. There are many accounts of the incident but the best, in our opinion, but also one of the least known, was made by Abbé Surrugues, priest of the St-Louis parish in the Russian capital. Abbé Surrugues had been a French immigrant for many years. His account of the fire was written immediately after the event and was intended for his superior. He died in 1820:

---

145. Armand de Caulaincourt, *Recollections*, t. 1, London, 1838, pp. 65–9.

Moscow, 19 October 1812.

Abbé Surrugues, parish priest of the church of St-Louis, Moscow, to Father Bouvet, Jesuit.

During the six weeks that the French spent here, I did not even see the shadow of Napoleon, nor did I try to see him.

However, a project born of the enthusiasm of patriotism was already beginning to be carried out, that of sacrificing the city of Moscow to the salvation of the empire, and of preparing a pyre for the French army by setting fire to this immense city. For several weeks, a sort of arsenal had been prepared at Vironow, the country house of the Prince of Repnin, situated six versts from the city, where artificial fireworks, fuses and other instruments intended for the execution of the great project were being made. To dispel or prevent the people's worries or suspicions, a bulletin from the Governor General had announced in advance that a large aerostatic balloon was being prepared, with which it was certain to destroy the entire French army. A few days before the arrival of the French, these fireworks had been tested. There was nothing but talk of fire; some with an air of mystery, others more openly. The eagerness of the inhabitants to leave the city heralded some sinister plan. On the very day that Moscow was evacuated by the Russian army, a globe of fire had broken out in the Yauza district, which seemed to give the signal to the arsonists; one house had fallen prey to the flames; while on the other side, near the stone bridge, the large shop of brandy belonging to the Crown was on fire, and they were forced to sacrifice part of this depot to preserve the other. But that same day, around 11 o'clock in the evening, the fire broke out with the greatest violence in the shops near the Bourse. The shops, which were filled with oil, tallow and other combustible materials, became an unquenchable fire. People asked for the city's pumps, but they were nowhere to be found. The rumour spread that the police had had them removed, along with all the firefighting equipment. They tried to extinguish the fire on one side, but it erupted on the other with greater violence.

On Tuesday 3rd, when a north-easterly wind blew, the fire spread, and all the shops were on fire. Napoleon had come to live in the Kremlin palace. He had been struck by the sight of such a huge fire beneath him, and had given orders to extinguish it, when it was reported to him that the fire was breaking out in several places at once; that it was widely rumoured that a plan had been hatched to deliver the city to the flames, and to leave the French nothing but heaps of ashes for their conquests! Napoleon could not believe such an extreme plan; but the number of arsonists, caught in the act, their names, nicknames and status, and their carefully collected statements. Their uniform confessions, recorded in a document published for this purpose, left no doubt in this respect, and several of them were condemned to be shot: their bodies were exposed on various poles. It is said that most of them were police, Cossacks in disguise, soldiers who were supposedly wounded, and even people attached to the churches who declared that they considered this work meritorious before God.

However, the mob violently broke down doors and broke into the cellars of shops threatened by fire. Sugar, coffee and tea were soon looted, followed by leather, furs, fabrics and all luxury items. The soldiers, who at first had been quiet bystanders, soon became active participants. The flour shops were pillaged; wine and brandy flooded all the cellars; some soldiers were found drowned in the wine; in a word, the town fell prey to a scourge more terrible than fire: in fact, once the plan to set fire to the town had been established as a war measure employed by the Russian government, pillaging became an inevitable reprisal on the part of an enemy who saw himself frustrated by the hope with which he had been flattered. What compensation could be offered to troops exhausted by three months of fatigue and fighting, tested by hardships of every kind, and assured by solemn promises that Moscow would be the end of their suffering and the universal resource for all their needs?

The city fire continued its ravages, the Tverskaya was ablaze and had begun to engulf the Nikitki; part of the Pakvoska was also engulfed in flames, when a wind from the north-west accelerated the fire's progress prodigiously. Indeed, on the morning of Wednesday 4th, all that remained untouched by the flames were the houses of the booksellers and others adjacent to the Ouprava Blagot-Cheme; everything else was consumed. A rocket was even thrown at one of the buildings of the Kremlin, no doubt with the intention of setting fire to this enclosure; but the fire was immediately smothered by the activity of the Imperial Guard. Then Napoleon, who saw himself surrounded by fire on all sides, realised the arsonists' plan and thought he should prudently abandon the Kremlin and retreat to the Petrowski palace.

Towards four o'clock in the evening, the shifting wind blew from the south-west with all the violence of a hurricane. The fire, which had been set in a few houses beyond the Yauza and the Moscowka, being fed by the wind, developed with such activity that it was as if we were looking at an immense volcano whose crater was spewing out torrents of flames and smoke; it was a deluge of fire which consumed, in less than a few hours, all the districts beyond the two rivers and the whole Lubyanka, while on the other side the Moskavoua, the Pretchinska and the Artbate offered the same spectacle. You had to be there to see it. All you could see everywhere were unfortunate people, laden with the wretched debris they had plucked from the flames, uttering pitiful cries, and who seemed to have escaped the fire only to fall into the hands of brigands who robbed them mercilessly. Many of these unfortunate people went to Napoleon's camp at Petrowski to beg for his benevolence. He seemed moved by their plight and promised to look into ways of remedying it. More than 400 of them were taken in with as much zeal as generosity in Zapatoff's devastated house at the Red Gate, where they found not only a safe haven but also care and sustenance.

On Thursday 5th, the wind, which was blowing directly from the west, continued to blow with the same impetuosity as the day before, and carried clouds of fire from the Stretinska, over all the Meszinsky and the Trouba successively enveloped in the same whirlwind, part of the Meszinska, the Red Gate, the wood market, the old and new Bassemanne, and finally the whole of the German Slobode.

A sea of fire flooded all parts of the city. The ripples of flame stirred by the wind perfectly imitated those of the waves in a storm. It was as if the hand of the arsonists had been joined by that of divine vengeance, so supernatural did the cause of the fire seem. The unfortunate inhabitants of the Slobode, chased from place to place by the fire, were forced to take refuge in the cemeteries beyond the large military hospital, but even there they did not think they were safe.

In the meantime, the fire was engulfing the lower part of Patrowka and consuming all the shops adjacent to the bottom of the Marshal's Bridge. The flame, driven by the wind, threatened to cross the entire bridge and devour all the shops inside it as it rose towards the Lubyanka. Already the inhabitants of this district, each with a bundle on their back, seemed prepared for this final sacrifice. … Around three o'clock in the morning, the sky clouded over and the heavy rain that fell for the rest of the night calmed the wind, so the fire slowed down. All that escaped the storm were a few houses scattered here and there, Gozokora and Dimidova Street, which leads to the Summer Garden.

On Friday the 6th, the rain that continued to fall having knocked down the wind, the fire seemed to be coming to an end. Nevertheless, in the evening, the fire still broke out in a few places, but with less violence.

On Saturday 7th, Napoleon thought he could return to the Kremlin palace with greater confidence. Towards the evening, the fire consumed a few more shops at the Tverskoy gate: this street still contains the entire section between the Governor General's palace and the boulevard.

On his return to the Kremlin, Napoleon's first concern was for the unfortunates of all classes. He ordered that administrators be appointed

> to identify all those who found themselves without shelter or sustenance; he had refuge warehouses opened to receive them, and promised to distribute rations to them. He went to the *Maison des Enfants-Trouvés*, which had escaped the fire, summoned the director, General Toutolmin, asked him to give an account of the house, asked him to make his report to Her Majesty the Empress Mother, and undertook to send it by courier. (This report remained unanswered.) Napoleon then took care of the hospitals, a large part of which had been spared from the fire. But what was his astonishment when he was told that these houses were in the greatest destitution of necessary help; without doctors, without remedy, without surveillance; that a prodigious quantity of dead had been found there; that, of more than 10,000 wounded who had recently arrived from the army, half had perished for lack of help; that the rest were struggling between need and death.
>
> On Sunday 8th, people thought they could breathe a sigh of relief, thinking that calm would finally replace the storm, but what calm! During the first week, no one had dared to leave their house without being exposed to public robbery. … All the streets were strewn with human corpses, lying jumbled with those of horses and other animals that had perished, either from want or in the flames ... Such was the destiny of the former capital of Russia, the largest city in Europe. … Last July, there were some 9,300 mansions and more than 800 noble mansions in which art competed with rich ornamentation. Today, by calculating the number of houses that escaped the flames, we can estimate this number at about one fifth of the city.[146]

A few days later, on 8 November, Father Surrugues, in another letter to the same addressee, returned to points already dealt with in the previous letter and provided some interesting details about what the Muscovites thought of Napoleon's intentions:

> It was noted that the Moscow populace had played the greatest role in the looting: it was they who started looting the shops: it was they who discovered the most secret cellars of the French soldiers, in order to share the booty: it was they who introduced Cossacks into private homes when the French left, and the peasants from around Moscow, who came to take part in the brigandage, took home and buried everything they

146. Abbé Surrugues, *Lettres sur l'incendie de Moscou écrites de cette ville, au R.P. Bouvet de la Compagnie de Jésus, par l'abbé Surrugues, témoin oculaire et curé de l'église de Saint Louis à Moscou*, Paris, 1823, pp. 9–40.

could. In general, the householders betrayed their masters and enriched themselves with their spoils.

The French, thanks to the safeguards we had been given on our arrival, respected our enclosure, and it remained intact until the entry of the Cossacks, who replaced them without there being any authority to restrain them. I am very happy, on my own account, to have been compensated for a few pieces of silver cutlery, bottles of wine and provisions of sugar, fish, etc. Fortunately, everything went off without a hitch, which was what we had most to fear. Abbé Perin was so horrified by the banditry of the French army that he did not dare follow it, even though he had received orders to leave. He preferred to run the risks than to leave the empire with the country's enemies ... Since the old order was re-established, many of those who had remained in Moscow have been cruelly disturbed. I was viewed very favourably by everyone, because they knew that I had only stayed out of duty, and that I had no kind of relationship with the leaders of the French government that could compromise me ... On leaving, the head of the French army swore to reduce St Petersburg to ashes next spring, as well as Riga, and to fill my ports. To judge his plans by his hasty retreat, one would be tempted to believe that he was deluding himself; but, in the meantime, 200,000 conscripts had been ordered to set out, 100,000 Poles had been organised by the Duke of Bassano; 80,000 men were in the vicinity of Danzig under Marshal Augereau; 40,000 under Marshal Victor; and the contingents of the Confederation of the Rhine were to be complete, counting the Austrian troops, and perhaps other enemies that he would try to arouse in Russia, to take revenge; because he wants to take revenge and he has terrible means. The safest thing is not to fall asleep. I repeat, if your fathers have precautions to take, let them not neglect them. The way this man handles the minds of his soldiers and masters his army gives him monstrous power. None of his generals, not even the most intimate, know his thoughts; none dare contradict him, and he says that the word impossible was not made for him.[147]

While some present-day historians challenge the theory that the Russians intentionally set fire to Moscow, the multitude of witnesses eliminates any uncertainty. According to contemporaries, beginning with Napoleon himself, released convicts and police personnel in Moscow were responsible. The existence of convicts appears to have been verified, but to what extent? Were all of the men who were shot arsonists? The purported confessions are dubious,

147. Abbé Surrugues, op. cit., pp. 41–8.

and there are no reliable documents to make a definitive statement. Sergeant Bourgogne recalled the event:

> We took our prisoners with us, thirty-two in number, and, as I had been in charge of the police guard during the night, I was also in charge of the rear guard and the escort of the prisoners, with orders to bayonet those who wanted to escape or who did not want to follow. At least two thirds of these unfortunate men were convicts, with sinister faces; the others were middle-class bourgeois and Russian police, easy to recognise from their uniforms.[148]

Were all these prisoners taken to their deaths guilty? It is doubtful, especially as a few days later the military commission responsible for repression was much less severe. The *Journal de l'Empire* of 30 October 1812 published the judgments handed down on 24 September 1812 against twenty-six people accused of arson by the military commission set up to judge the perpetrators of the fire on 14 September and subsequent days. On trial were nine police soldiers, two blacksmiths, three painters, three servants, a beadle, a merchant, a labourer, an officer, a soldier, an upholsterer, a tailor, and two men whose occupation was unknown. Of the twenty-six defendants, only ten were sentenced to death: the officer, a police soldier, a merchant, two painters, a blacksmith, a servant, a tailor and the two whose occupation was unknown. As for the other defendants, 'the military commission, considering that they are not sufficiently convinced, condemns them to be held in Moscow prisons, to prevent any harm they might do'.[149] It should be noted that these late defendants do not seem to fall into the category of convicts (except perhaps for the two with unknown occupations), and that the soldiers of the Moscow police (often accused of having taken part in the fire), who are overwhelmingly present in this group, fared rather well, since only one was sentenced to death. The merchant sentenced to death had a French name (Jean-Christophe Thomas).

Far from having been reduced to misery by the fire, the French army was enjoying itself in what remained of the Russian capital. Eugène Labaume, captain and executive officer to Eugène de Beauharnais, viceroy of Italy, noted what he saw in Moscow in the light of the fires. He entered the city on 15 September. The first flames devoured a few buildings, and the looting began:

> The further I went, the more the avenues of the stock exchange were clogged with soldiers and beggars, carrying with them effects of all

148. Adrien Bourgogne, op. cit., pp. 34–5.
149. *Journal de l'Empire*, 30 October 1812.

> kinds; disdaining the least precious, they threw them on the ground. Thus, in a few moments, the streets were littered with quantities of goods. At last I entered the interior of the building, but alas! It was no longer the building so renowned for its magnificence, but rather a vast furnace from which flaming beams fell on all sides; it was no longer possible to walk under the porticoes, where there were still numerous shops, and it was there that the soldiers, breaking open the crates, shared out a booty beyond all their expectations. No cries, no uproar could be heard in this horrible scene, so much so that everyone found enough to satisfy their greed; nothing could be heard, apart from the fizzing of the flames and the sound of the doors being broken down.[150]

The chaos extended beyond the plundering of personal possessions: the tombs of the czars were opened, and whatever precious objects they might contain were taken by the soldiers. Additionally, the women who remained within the capital were also subjected to the aggression of the triumphant army:

> Cruel licence, but unavoidable in a monstrous war, where sixteen nations, different in morals and language, thought they could do anything, in the belief that their disorders would never be attributed to any one of them. The abundance enjoyed by the army made them forget their fatigue; they consoled themselves for having the rain on their backs and their feet in the mud, by the good food and the profit that everyone made trading in the goods brought from Moscow. For, although it was forbidden to go to this city, the soldiers, attracted by the lure of gain, violated the orders and continually returned laden with food and merchandise. Under the pretext of going on a marauding expedition, they would return to the Kremlin and rummage through the ruins and ashes, uncovering untouched shops from which they profusely extracted objects of all kinds. Thus our camp no longer resembled an army, but a great fair where each soldier, transformed into a merchant, sold the most precious things at a low price; and although camped in the fields, exposed to the insults of the weather, by a singular contrast, they ate from porcelain plates, drank from silver vases, and possessed everything that luxury had imagined richer and more elegant for the comforts of life.[151]

150. Eugène Labaume, *Relation circonstanciée de la campagne de Russie*, Paris, 1814, pp. 200–1.
151. Eugène Labaume, op. cit., p. 214.

Labaume also looked at the remaining population within the city:

> Although the population of Moscow had entirely disappeared, there nevertheless remained many of those unfortunate people whose misery forces them to regard all events with indifference. They ran through the streets with the soldiers, acting as their servants, feeling very happy to be rewarded with the things that the soldiers despised. There were also many public girls, and this class was the only one to reap any benefit from the sack of Moscow; for everyone, eager to have a wife, welcomed these creatures who, having entered our homes, immediately became mistresses and squandered all that the flames had spared. There were others who really deserved respect because of their upbringing, and above all because of their misfortune: hunger and misery often forced their mothers to come and introduce them to us. This immorality in such circumstances fell on those who did not have enough virtue to triumph over a brutal passion, and who were corrupt enough to seek pleasure from a mouth that was discoloured by hunger. For this empire that mothers gave us over their daughters was the effect of a public calamity.[152]

Sergeant Bourgogne tells us how, with another non-commissioned officer, he hired the services of two young women whose duties were probably not limited to ironing uniforms:

> I opened the door to the second bedroom and, as I entered, I saw the two sweethearts sitting on a sofa. When they saw me they did not seem surprised; they both spoke to me at once, but I could never understand a word they said. I wanted to know if they had anything to eat; they understood me perfectly, for they immediately served me cucumbers, onions and a large piece of salted fish with a little beer, but no bread. A moment later, the youngest brought me a bottle which she called 'Kosalki'; when I tasted it, I recognised it as Danzig gin, and in less than half an hour we had emptied the bottle, for I realised that my two Muscovites drank better than I did. I stayed with the two sisters for a while longer, as they had made it clear to me that they were; then I went back to my room.
>
> On entering, I found a non-commissioned officer from the company who had come to see me, and who had been waiting for me for a long time. He asked me where I had come from; when I had told him my story, he was no longer surprised at my absence, but seemed delighted, because, he told me, we could find no one to launder the laundry; since chance had provided us with two Muscovite ladies, they would certainly

152. Eugène Labaume, op. cit., pp. 228–32.

> find it a great honour to launder and mend that of the French soldiers. At ten o'clock, when everyone had gone to bed, as we did not want anyone to know that we had women, the non-commissioned officer returned with the sergeant-major to fetch our two beauties. At first they made a few difficulties, not knowing where they were being taken; but, having made it clear that they wanted me to accompany them, I went as far as the accommodation, where they followed us willingly, laughing. As a study was available, we put them in it, after having furnished it suitably with what we found in their room; much better, with all the beautiful and elegant things we could find that the noble Muscovite ladies had not been able to take with them, so that, from the large servants they appeared to be, they were immediately transformed into baronesses, but laundering and mending our linen.[153]

Napoleon was convinced that the capture of Moscow would force Czar Alexander to negotiate. This was probably because he saw nothing coming from the court in St Petersburg, but also because it was difficult for him to admit that the burning of the capital had been carried out with Alexander's agreement. A few days after the fire, Lieutenant Combe was sent to hold a position a few leagues from the capital. He arrived at the village of Voronowo, where Count Rostopchin's castle was located:

> This governor of Moscow, making ample use of the carte blanche given to him by the Emperor of Russia, ordered the evacuation of the city and took all necessary measures to ensure the execution of his fire, a barbaric and patriotic work. What's more, he set the example himself, for I read on a stone, in the remains of his burnt castle, these words written in French with charcoal: 'I set fire to my castle to prevent the French dogs from taking control of it. Signed: ROSTOPSCHIN.' We had done well to take precautions with provisions carried by our horses, as the castle and its vast outbuildings offered us no resources. Everything that could not be taken away was soiled and devastated. Barrels of beer, wine and brandy were smashed and strewn about; heaps of black ash, surrounded by the debris of the walls, were the only sign of the straw and hay barns.[154]

Was the fire in Moscow a decisive factor in the campaign of 1812 or even the ultimate reason for the French disaster? This remains uncertain. Sergeant Bourgogne reflected on this matter when he penned the following:

153. Adrien Bourgogne, op. cit., pp. 65–6.
154. Julien Combe, op. cit., pp. 114–15.

> Many people who did not take part in this campaign say that the burning of Moscow was the army's undoing: as for me and many others, we thought the opposite, for the Russians could very well not have set fire to the city, but could have taken away or thrown into the Moskova the supplies and ravaged the country for ten leagues around, which was not very difficult, for part of the country is deserted, and at the end of a fortnight we would necessarily have had to leave. After the fire, there were still enough dwellings to house the whole army, and, supposing they were all burnt down, the cellars were there.[155]

In support of Sergeant Bourgogne's claims, many accounts of life in Moscow in the days following the great fire, as well as those describing the early stages of the retreat, state that there was no shortage of accommodation and food. It should be borne in mind, however, that Sergeant Bourgogne was a member of the Imperial Guard, a corps that enjoyed many privileges, and his view of the situation was perhaps somewhat optimistic. This was not the case with Captain Labaume, who was part of Prince Eugène's immediate entourage and viewed things from a higher perspective:

> While negotiations were being discussed, everything was being prepared to start the war again, but nothing was being done to prevent the rigours of winter. However, the future was frightening: the longer we stayed in Moscow, the more difficult it became. As we exhausted the neighbouring villages, we had to go to places that were further and further away. The distances involved made our journeys as perilous as they were tiring: having set off at dawn, our foragers rarely returned before nightfall.[156]

The main effect of Count Rostopchin's spectacular gesture was probably psychological. In fact, once he was convinced that the fire had been set with the czar's agreement, Napoleon had to realise the weakness of his position. Alexander did not even deign to respond to his proposals. Empty of inhabitants and economic activity, Moscow had become nothing more than a field of ruins and was no longer of interest. The city was far from the French rear bases and exposed to encirclement by the Russian army, which could reinforce itself without limit.

The news of the capture of Moscow reached Paris on 30 September. The *Journal de l'Empire* reported the event briefly on 1 October:

155. Adrien Bourgogne, op. cit., p. 41.
156. Eugène Labaume, op. cit., p. 240.

> The French army entered Moscow on 14 September. The capture of this great city was the result of the memorable victory at Moskowa. The troops found immense resources there. Moscow has always been regarded by the Russians as their real capital, because it is situated in the centre of the empire and surrounded by the most fertile and populous provinces. Petersburg, on the other hand, is surrounded by sand, marshes and barren lands. Thus, the French armies, in reaching Moscow through a series of increasingly astonishing successes, struck at the heart of the enemy they had defeated.[157]

It was not until 4 October that the French learned all the details of the capture and burning of Moscow from the 19th *Bulletin de la Grande Armée*. There was great consternation. This was not the victorious entry into an enemy capital to which they were accustomed. Following the 19th *Bulletin*, the *Journal de l'Empire* published a violent diatribe, which we suspect was written by the Minister of Police, against the Russian authorities who had seen fit to destroy their capital:

> If anyone could ever have doubted the awful barbarity of the Russians, the way they behave in their own country would make it better known than anything that has been printed about the customs of these ferocious peoples. Defeated by our weapons, they take revenge for their defeat by burning the towns they were unable to guard; women, children, the elderly, even their own wounded are the victims of their senseless rage and brutal pride. We only seem to pursue them to save them from their own fury. And those for whom the intoxication of victory could make them forgive a few disorders, only ever arrive to save a people from the excesses of the army charged with defending it. What would become of civilised Europe if this cloud of incendiaries could penetrate it? The ruins of Rome and Italy provide the answer. The barbarians of today are still the barbarians of yesterday; if ever there was a national war, it is undoubtedly the war undertaken to bring down this bloodthirsty colossus which, for a century, has been advancing on Europe with the noise of the chains with which they threaten its freedom, in the light of the torches with which it wants to illuminate its ruin ... It was necessary for a powerful genius to unite and transport all the forces of civilisation to the very centre of barbarism, in order to strike it to the heart. Such is the great picture that is unfolding today before the eyes of the astonished world, and of which the capture of Moscow forms one of the main aspects ...[158]

157. *Journal de l'Empire*, 1 October 1812.
158. *Journal de l'Empire*, 4 October 1812.

In the Parisian press, news of the Russian campaign was not extensive and was often limited to mocking Russian claims to victory, whereas hardly a day went by without news of the war in the Iberian Peninsula being discussed. Although no new military actions were announced, texts describing a comfortable situation for the army appeared regularly in the newspapers. Most of these were certainly invented. For example, on 4 November 1812 the *Journal de l'Empire* reported:

> Moscow, 14 October. Extract from a letter written by a staff officer. Reinforcements are arriving every day; our army looks formidable. Moreover, we have been joined by a large number of wounded; the healthiness of the air we breathe has singularly accelerated their recovery, and the fine weather, which has lasted for a long time, has made communications as quick as they are easy. Fortune has favoured us in every way; winter usually starts very early here, and we have had a fine French autumn; it was only two days ago that we saw the first snow fall. There is no country in the world where people know how to protect themselves better from the cold: the industry of the French will add to everything that is being done; It would be difficult to imagine the ease with which our soldiers acclimatise to all regions and become familiar with the new habits they are obliged to adopt. We lack absolutely nothing; we are well clothed, well fed and well heated. As for pleasures, we must admit that they are not common. However, we have the show, and we find it perfect. You do not have the right to be fussy 960 leagues from Paris. From time to time we see Russian deserters arriving: most of them are Poles who have come to line up under the flags of their homeland; they all agree that the Russian army is in the worst condition. Only the front rank is made up of soldiers; the rest are peasants from new levies, who are poorly armed and poorly dressed ...[159]

To fully appreciate this text, it should be remembered that the retreat of the French army had begun sixteen days before it was published.

Financial circles were also impressed by the entry into Moscow, which appeared to be a great victory for the French army. The Amsterdam stock exchange, the main European financial centre where governments borrowed money, reacted strongly to the news:

> Amsterdam, 24 October. For as long as anyone can remember our stock exchange has not seen such a rapid fall in funds as that of the Russian funds; the bonds of the loan negotiated with the bankers Hopa and

159. *Journal de l'Empire*, 4 November 1812.

> company were quoted at 64 the month before the beginning of the war; they fell little by little to 33, towards the beginning of September; the Grand Army entered the city of Moscow on 14 September, and the Russian funds are quoted today at 27%. Our newspapers said, according to the London gazettes, that the English government had sent some money to Petersburg; but what is a few hundred thousand pounds sterling to a power which has already lost so many provinces, as well as all its credit in Amsterdam, Frankfurt and Leipzig?[160]

In Moscow, once the fire had died down, optimism returned to the French ranks for a time. Administrator Denniée recounted in his memoirs:

> The storm has been replaced by calm: we breathe, we wait, we live in a sort of quietude. Our outposts are in the direction of Kolomna; they communicate familiarly with the Russian outposts. The regular Cossacks complained about the fatigue of war; the officers chatted with our Cossacks; there were exchanges; there were differences, to the point of giving up ground, even a village with more fodder, to the Russians, to the point of sometimes giving us useful information. General Sébastiani informs the Emperor of the enemy's peaceful disposition and of the impatience shown by the Russians to see the war come to an end; his confidence increases as a result of his hopes, and perhaps he shares them with the Emperor. He flattered himself that overtures would be all the more forthcoming, as the Russian army, it was said, had no infantry left, its cavalry was exhausted, and its officers and soldiers longed for nothing but rest. But this enemy, so discouraged, so little feared, found himself on 22 September, unbeknownst to us, at the height of Galitzin Castle, on the road to Moscow; he took two convoys from us, several estafettes and, a few days later, a squadron of dragoons of the Guard and a battalion of marchers.
>
> It was then that the Emperor dictated this order: 'General ... You have allowed yourself to be grossly deceived; I forbid, on pain of death, any communication with the outposts; it is only with rifle and cannon that one communicates with such a disloyal enemy.'
>
> Since we had taken up our position on the Pakra, this river had, so to speak, formed a line of tacit neutrality; talks had begun between the chiefs, and they had become serious enough for the Emperor to send General Lauriston to Kutuzof's headquarters on 4 October. On his return he announced that Kutuzov was going to send an officer to St Petersburg to urge the Emperor of Russia to adhere to the peace

160. *Journal de l'Empire*, 31 October 1812.

> proposals, and he added that the Russians' intentions seemed entirely satisfactory. ... On the 15th, in his impatience, he sent the Duke of Vicenza to Kutuzov; the Duke returned on the 16th without any news. During these delays, our cavalry and infantry were melting away day by day. In blind confidence, our outposts ventured into difficult positions; this pernicious security still reigned on the 17th, when, on the 18th, the most unexpected event came to open our eyes; in fact the cavalry reserve corps, commanded by General Sébastiani, was attacked from all sides. Overwhelmed by the numbers, it was forced to abandon part of its artillery and could only save itself by impetuously marching across the fields towards the main road to Kaluga, from which it was cut off and which it could only reach by overthrowing several Russian infantry battalions that tried in vain to oppose its passage. At the same time, the King of Naples was attacked along his entire line and was powerless to rescue Sébastiani. At noon on the same day, the Emperor learned of the attack and the defeat, and at the same time, no doubt, knew that the day before Kutuzov had received 10,000 regular Cossacks from the army of Wallachia. On this sad occasion, the departure order was given at the same time, for the 19th, at eight o'clock in the morning.[161]

Army morale was beginning to sink. Letters from conscripts, rarely literary works, showed the slow deterioration since the start of the campaign. Joseph Sainte, a French soldier from Liège, wrote to his wife:

> From Stettin this 6 October 1812
>
> I will tell you that I left Berlin on 2 September to go to Sweden, as safe as ever. On our arrival, we received orders to leave for Russia, where I am going to suffer cold and hunger. I long to know the end of my fate in a way that will either bring me happiness or ruin me. It is God's will. I cannot tell you the value of the Russian war; common sense prevents me from saying so. However, I am happy to go to war. In the last affair, one hundred thousand men were found out of action, after having risen to the attack twelve times. I will tell you all about it when I am out of there.[162]

The French soldiers thought they had seen the worst. Yet now they were preparing to face the cold of the Russian winter.

---

161. Pierre-Paul Denniée, op. cit., pp. 101–7. Pierre-Paul Denniée (1781–1848) was an inspector-general of reviews under the Empire, and therefore an important figure in the administration. He was in constant contact with Napoleon.
162. AEL, FFP, 1042–1044, letter of Joseph Sainte.

Chapter 6

Retreat!

Leaving Moscow

The first indication that Napoleon was thinking of evacuating Moscow can be found in a letter written on 9 October 1812 to Maret, the Minister of Foreign Relations.[163] The decision for the French army to leave Moscow was taken several days before it was implemented. This is suggested by letters intercepted by the Russians. It was on 16 October, in a letter, that the Emperor announced his firm decision to abandon his conquest. Father Surrugues' letter, mentioned in the previous chapter, described the departure of the French troops:

> Finally, on Sunday 6 October, at four o'clock in the evening, the roll-call was sounded and the troops were ordered to prepare for departure. An hour later, some of the regiments set off, and Napoleon left the Kremlin, after having had the Cross removed from the Ivan-Veliqui tower, which he had sent to France as a monument to his victory. The next day, Marshal Mortier moved his residence and his chancellery to the Kremlin; all the remaining troops, numbering around 5,000 men, were concentrated there. The last convoys of sick were hastily dispatched. On Tuesday 8th, a party of Cossacks entered through the Tverskoï, identifying themselves as parliamentarians, and tried to break through to the Kremlin: the French gathered round and forced them to give in. A few days earlier, the Petrovsky palace, thought to be a retreat for the Cossacks, had been given over to the flames, and soon afterwards the house of the Count Rostopchin, on the Kalinka, suffered the same fate. Finally, on Thursday 10 October, the general's departure was announced to two Russian officers who had advanced as far as Tverskoï, identifying themselves as parliamentarians; the officer commanding the post in this street arrested them and took them with an escort to Governor General Mortier, who told them that as they had not been announced either by a trumpeter or by a junior officer, in accordance with the laws of war, they were prisoners by right, and that he

163. Napoléon Bonaparte, *Correspondance générale*, t. 12, p. 1176.

> was going to have them taken to the Emperor Napoleon's headquarters. They were Wintzingerode, Lieutenant General of the Cossacks, and Leon Alexandrovitch Narichzin, squadron leader of the hussars. In the evening the troops began to march around seven o'clock, and by 11 o'clock the Kremlin and the town had been completely evacuated by the French. Some sinister event was expected that same night. Around two o'clock in the morning, a terrible explosion was heard, followed by a general commotion. It was the arsenal, which had just been buried under its ruins by a mine. At the same time, the Czars' palace was on fire and fell prey to the flames. This first explosion caused such a tremor that all the windows in the city were shattered. Of the two women retreating to the house of refuge, one was suffocated and the other, pregnant, was surprised by the pains of childbirth. Three other explosions, less considerable than the first, destroyed the Kremlin gate opposite the Nikolski, part of the Senate and the outer towers of the Kremlin. It is added that when the Cossacks arrived, they managed to cut the fuse that was supposed to ignite 48 barrels of gunpowder, intended to blow up the cathedrals and Ivan Veliki's tower. In the great commotion, the bell of Ivan Veliki was detached and fell. When the French evacuated Moscow, they left more than 2,000 wounded Frenchmen to the generosity of their enemies, who found them in the Galitzin hospital and the hospital of the Lost Children. About forty of these unfortunate men, on learning that they had become prisoners of war, tried to withdraw, but they were massacred by the peasants as they left the town, and the next day the road was found covered with their corpses.[164]

Captain Labaume explained how his stay in Moscow came to an end:

> We were anxiously awaiting the return of the courier sent to Petersburg, when General Lauriston left again to go to Kutuzov, but in such a hurry that he was forced to use the Emperor's relays. In the belief that all these conferences would have a favourable outcome, our army guarded itself badly and believed itself to be in perfect security. The enemy took advantage of this error to attack (October 18) at Winkowo, near Tarutino, the cavalry of the king of Naples, and to take away a park of 26 pieces. The King of Naples ... mounted his horse and rode with his staff into the middle of the action, which he led fearlessly as our cavalry formed up ... The Cossacks, obliged to flee, abandoned the 26 cannons; the Russian infantry advanced to support them, then the combat became general, and, on both sides, they fought fiercely. The riflemen and some

164. Abbé Surrugues, op. cit., pp. 34–8.

> Polish regiments, less tired than the rest of the cavalry, helped to avenge the honour of our arms ... on our side, more than 2,000 men were the object of our regrets ...[165] The Emperor was in the Kremlin, reviewing his troops, when he received this unexpected news; he immediately became furious and, in the heat of his anger, exclaimed that this was treason and infamy; that the King of Naples had been attacked in defiance of all the laws of war, and that only barbarians could violate conventions in this way. On the spot, the parade was disbanded, hopes of peace dashed, and the order to leave was given for that very evening. All the corps were to leave Moscow and take the main road to Kaluga. It was hoped that they would go to the Ukraine to find, under milder skies, regions that were less ravaged and much more fertile. But those who seemed best informed assured us that our movement on Kaluga was only a false manoeuvre, made with the intention of masking from the enemy our plan to retreat to Smolensk and Vitebsk.[166]

While Napoleon in Moscow was still hoping for peace with Russia, the first cracks appeared in his alliance with Austria. The Russian army, liberated by the peace with the Ottoman empire, was manoeuvring to encircle the capital. Until then, the 30,000 men of the Austrian expeditionary corps, commanded by Marshal Schwarzenberg, had behaved like a faithful ally. Napoleon had rewarded the Austrian marshal by giving him command of the second corps, responsible for protecting the army's right. Marbot remarked:

> Around 12 October, the Second Corps, which had been living in abundance and tranquillity in Polotsk and the surrounding area since 18 August, had to prepare to take the chance of fighting again. We learned that Admiral Tchichagov, commander-in-chief of the Russian army in Wallachia, having made peace with the Turks through the intermediary of the English, was heading for Mogilev, in order to follow in the footsteps of the Emperor Napoleon, who, not having yet left Moscow, was still lulled by the hope of concluding a treaty with Alexander. People were astonished that Prince Schwarzenberg, who was in charge of guarding the Russian corps in Wallachia with 30,000 Austrians, our allies, had allowed Tchichagov to pass; but the fact was no less real. Not only had the Austrians not blocked the way of the Russians; but,

165. This was the battle of Winkowo on 18 October 1812. Murat's 18,000 men were attacked by Kutuzov and Miloradowitch's 36,000. The French lost General Déry, 2,000 killed and wounded and 1,500 prisoners. They lost 36 cannon. The Russians had 800 killed and wounded and 700 prisoners. The Russian general Baggovut was killed. This battle, fought by surprise, showed that the Russian army had overcome the consequences of the battle of Borodino (see Digby Smith, op. cit., pp. 395–6).
166. Eugène Labaume, op. cit., pp. 244–6.

> instead of following them at the rear, he had remained very quiet in the Volhynia cantonment. Napoleon had relied too much on the good faith of the ministers and generals of his father-in-law, the Emperor of Austria, in entrusting them with the task of covering the right wing of the great army ... There was flagrant treason on their part, and history will tarnish their conduct![167]

On 21 October, having just left Moscow, Boniface de Castellane witnessed one of the first atrocious scenes of this retreat:

> In the evening, 1,200 Russian prisoners arrived escorted by a Portuguese battalion; the major commanding them found three small dead horses on the road; he gave them to the prisoners to eat. These unfortunate men had previously been fighting over pieces of the cadavers. The Portuguese claim to have orders to shoot any Russians who do not march. So they put the ends of their rifles to their heads and blew the brains out of all those exhausted men who could no longer walk. They do this cruelly and clumsily; if they shot them on the side of the road, you would think that these corpses were those of people who had tried to escape; they carry out their beautiful executions in the middle of the road. This barbaric behaviour will, I fear, cause us terrible reprisals.[168]

Three days later, on 24 October, he wrote in his diary:

> On the road we saw around forty Russian prisoners killed by the Portuguese. One of them owed his life to the laziness of a soldier in their rearguard; this Russian, having fallen, could go no further; the Portuguese shot him at point-blank range. His rifle missed twice; the third time, he shouted 'I'll be good! My rifle needs cleaning. It's better to leave it there.' The unfortunate prisoner crawled off the road on all fours, fearing the troops that were following.[169]

This treatment of prisoners was confirmed by Heinrich Roos, who wrote about it on 30 October 1812. On 21 October Roos, whose regiment had been fighting the Russians on the outskirts of Moscow throughout the occupation of the city by French troops, joined the main army corps, which had left the capital on the 19th:

---

167. Marcellin Marbot, op. cit., p. 296.
168. Boniface de Castellane, *Journal du maréchal de Castellane*, t. 1, p. 175.
169. Boniface de Castellane, op. cit., p. 177.

> During this march, I noticed how much the battalions of our troops had been reduced, but also how the small number of those who had stayed in Moscow were rebuilt, well clothed and abundantly supplied with food. I also noticed that, despite their small numbers, they still took all their cannons with them. That same day, we came into contact with Napoleon's Old and Young Guards, who had returned from Moscow. Their appearance was superb and magnificent; fresh and cheerful, their columns flowed with order; the men were well dressed and heavily laden with food. Each man had three or four loaves of white bread strapped to his pack and a flask of brandy hanging from the straps of his sabre or cartridge belt. Behind the columns followed a crowd of baggage, the like of which had never been seen in any war. All the generals and senior officers had new carriages; the junior officers had local light carriages, all full of valuables and provisions. The married soldiers also had vans, loaded with everything that could be useful to them sooner or later; they had entrusted them to their wives. The food wagons were filled with wine, brandy, sugar, coffee, tea and everything else needed to keep them going for a long time; in short, this indescribable column was carrying riches as varied as they were unimaginable, and the fine weather did its bit to make the spectacle extraordinary and astonishing.[170]

Three days later all these loads were forced to stop in the vicinity of the town of Borowsk. Roos continued:

> A large number of carts, most of them loaded with beautiful things, riches and food from Moscow, were there; all of this appeared to be waiting for what was going to happen up ahead, on the army side. The drivers were unpacking their loads, partly to examine and review them, but mainly to trade them, sell them and finally lighten their load. With this in mind, many objects were set aside and thrown away forever. I saw magnificent blankets and carpets, the like of which I had never admired before, tapestries and curtains of great size and graceful form, fabrics of great price, enriched with embroidery, borders and fringes of gold and silver. I saw a host of silk pieces of every colour and beauty, embroidered and sparkling garments of both sexes, such as can only be seen in princely courts. People said that this one was rich in precious stones; that one had a jewel representing a small cat made of brilliants; that one had rolls of ducats and that one had ingots of silver. I heard all this in amazement. I was certainly more sad than envious at the sight

170. Heinrich Roos, op. cit., pp. 140–1.

Paul I, Czar of Russia. (*Wellcome Trust*)

The battle of Zurich. (*François Bouchot, 1835*)

The battle of Castricum. (*Frederik Bierweiler, between 1799 and 1805*)

Czar Alexander.
(*Stepan Shchukin, 1808*)

Jean Gheerbrant after the Napoleonic Wars. (*Private collection*)

On the eve of the battle of Austerlitz. (*Baron Lejeune, Palace of Versailles*)

Above left: Talleyrand, Napoleon's minister of foreign relations. (*François Gérard, 1808*)

Above right: Marcellin Marbot. (*Private collection*)

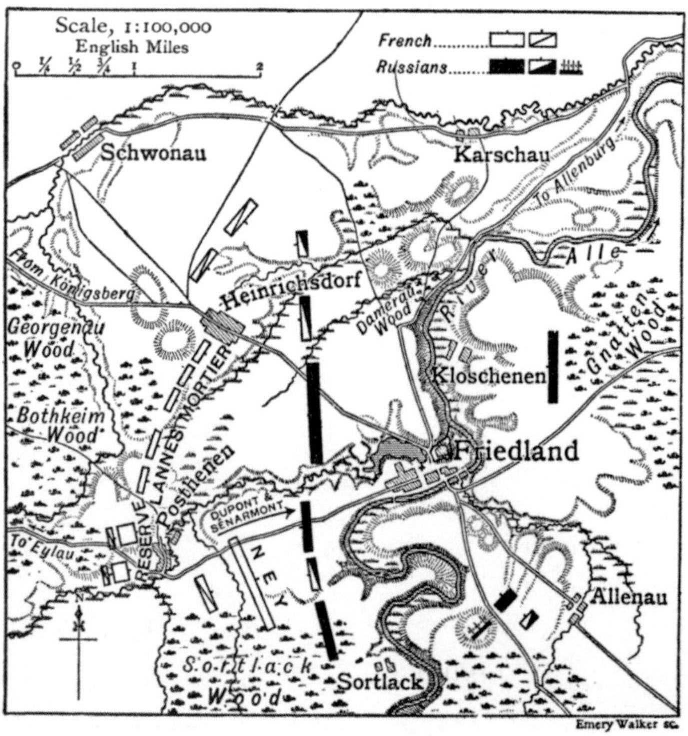

Map of the battle of Friedland. (*Encyclopaedia Britannica, 1911*)

Above left: Armand de Caulaincourt. (*Private collection*)

Above right: General Kutuzov. (*Volkov, between 1812 and 1830*)

The battle of Borodino. (*Baron Lejeune, Palace of Versailles*)

The burning of Moscow. (*Albrecht Adam, 1841*)

The crossing of the Berezina river. (*Musée de l'armée*)

Victory declaration after the battle of Leipzig. (*Deutsches Historisches Museum*)

Louis XVIII wearing his coronation robes. (*Robert Lefèvre, 1822*)

The capture of Paris. (*Private collection*)

Napoleon signs his abdication at Fontainebleau. (*François Bouchot and Gaetano Ferri*)

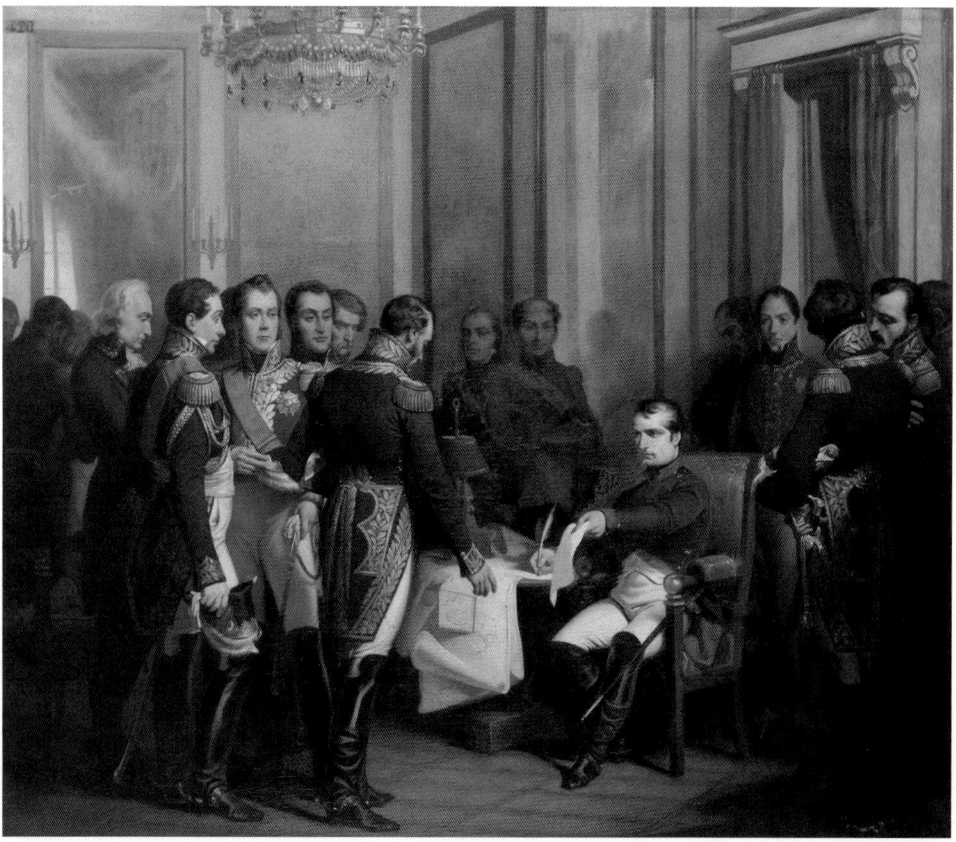

> of all this splendour, for I was convinced that these people did not have long to be happy. On the morning of the 25th the cannonade began again, the clouds of smoke closed in on us and we soon noticed the clear signs of a retreat. We returned to Borowsk. The general rumour was that Napoleon had fought a battle, that he had had to give up his attempt to penetrate the fertile southern provinces, that the army was turning back and that it was already arriving. All these rumours were soon confirmed. Amid an appalling roar of bangs, surrounded by fire and smoke, the army arrived at Borowsk. Orders had been given to burn or consign to the flames everything left behind. The villages between Maloyaroslavets and us had already been set on fire; the ammunition caissons that had not been taken along, or could not keep up, were flying through the air with thunderous explosions. If the Russians had been a great nuisance to us during our invasion, burning villages, destroying the harvest in the fields and the hay in the meadows, ours carried out the recent order to ravage everything in an even crueller and more appalling manner. The romantic and beautifully situated town of Borowsk was delivered to the flames by the furious arrivals.[171]

On 25 October, while on reconnaissance with horsemen of the Guard and Poles, Napoleon was attacked by a group of Cossacks who almost seized him. Several accounts mentioned this event. Boniface de Castellane, who was part of the 'Sacred Squadron', the soldiers responsible for personally protecting the Emperor, wrote in his diary:

> Leaving Maloyaroslavets at daybreak, a squadron of Cossacks almost caught the Emperor. They came within 15 paces of His Majesty without him being recognised. The Emperor fled at full gallop. The horse guard charged. The aide-de-camp to the Prince of Neuchâtel, Lecoultoux, a brave officer returning from a charge against the Cossacks, spear in hand, having lost his hat, was taken as an enemy; a mounted grenadier wounded him with a sabre through the body.[172]

The army's numbers were drastically reduced by the increasingly bitter cold, guerrilla warfare by the Cossacks and desertion. Boniface de Castellane wrote in his diary:

> 6 November. Snow sets in for the first time. The 5th Polish Corps, with 28,000 men entering the field, has detached the Dombrowski Division,

171. Heinrich Roos, op. cit., pp. 143–6.
172. Boniface de Castellane, op. cit., p. 177.

> with 9,000 men. Of the remaining 19,000, 700 are now under arms. All this is not lost; a large number are travelling as amateurs, this corps numbered 4,000 men when it passed through Moscow ...
>
> 7th November ... General Marchand arrives with his Württemberg division, which was 13,000 men strong at the start of the campaign and is now down to 450. General Fouché, in command of the artillery of the Third Corps, is in despair, his horses are falling and cannot get up again. He is forced to abandon many of his cannons ... the soldiers who live only on horseback are attacked by a singular illness: they look drunk, make hasty movements, fall to the ground saying: 'I have no more strength' and die (9 remained on the road that day, at the bivouac left this morning).[173]

In Paris, public opinion was shaken by two almost simultaneous events: General Malet's conspiracy[174] and the arrival of the 25th *Bulletin of the Grande Armée* announcing the withdrawal from Moscow. Back in Russia, the sick and wounded were sometimes left to fend for themselves. One of them, Joachim Delmarche, who was wounded in the knee at the Moskova and hospitalised at Mosaïsk for six weeks, described his flight, as well as an encounter with a group of partisans who attacked the isolated or small groups:

> News of the French army's retreat! Convoys were already passing through from Moscow! I set off with a comrade, each with a pair of crutches, with no food and no hope of finding any. It was more than 40 leagues from there without being able to find a single hamlet. We had been told that a marching battalion was to be formed, including many soldiers from the regiment to which we belonged. We travelled about three leagues a day, which was not a small distance for men with only one leg and nothing in their bodies. Our ordinary food was horse. We could not do without it, but it was not of excellent quality, as the horses died of fatigue and need. We always walked with great fear, because the path was covered with French corpses that the Russian partisans had killed. One day, we were resting in a pine forest. A carriage came to meet us; they were dragoons from the Guard. We begged them to let us get in, and they agreed to our request. We had hardly gone a quarter

173. Boniface de Castellane, op. cit., pp. 181–3.

174. General Claude-François de Malet, who had already been interned for conspiracy, claimed that Napoleon had died in Russia and fabricated a decree setting up a provisional government. On 23 October 1812 he and his republican and royalist accomplices attempted to rally the Paris garrison. The plot almost succeeded. Most of those involved were executed.

> of a league when we were attacked by a crowd of peasants coming out of the wood, shouting and screaming at the top of their voices. They threw themselves headlong at the little convoy, and I was thrown off the carriage over the wheel, my nose in the mud, in despair, and shouting at the top of my voice. Their weapons were scythes, pitchforks and other farming implements. The unfortunate wounded, thrown into the mire, begged for their lives. They replied: 'niema pardonn', meaning 'no forgiveness'; they chopped as much as they could: the first blow of the scythe, so to speak, cut a dragoon in two! They unhitched the horses, searched and looted the carriage and the men, kicked us in the legs, in the stomach, etc. Luckily, I only received the latter, but so many that I was left for dead! Finally, when the brigands returned to the woods, those of us who were still there dragged ourselves along as best we could. At the end of the day, we reached the exit of the wood. From a distance we saw an open van filled only with reform crews, whose drivers had just been murdered by the partisans. When we got close to them, we realised they were still warm.[175]

The army arrived in Smolensk in November, where Napoleon had thought to establish his winter quarters and where, in principle, important supplies were waiting. The disillusionment was great: 'All kinds of provisions for the army had been stored in the town. The Guards got the lion's share. There was little left for the fighters.'[176] Disappointment was widespread:

> At last we were in Smolensk, the promised land that we had always been led to believe would be the end of our efforts, the end of all our suffering and hardship. It was here that the prediction was to be fulfilled: we were to find abundance in richly stocked shops, heated dwellings were to welcome us; it was here that, in well-secured winter quarters, we were to find rest after the most horrible suffering. Until then, this hope alone had sustained our courage; it alone had still weakly held together the almost broken bonds of discipline. But the prediction turned out to be a lie in every respect. It was only then that an immense abyss of misery opened up before us; and this Smolensk, where we were to meet the end of all our troubles, still marked only the beginning and foretold the dreadful but certain destruction of the entire army. In 18° cold, a bivouac set up in the middle of deep snow, on the rubble and in the courtyard of a burnt-out house, a few meagre items of food, for

175. Joachim Delmarche, *Les Soirées du grenadier ou Mémoires de Joachim Delmarche, de Philippeville, Cerfontaine*, 1980, pp. 26–7.
176. Heinrich Roos, op. cit., p. 161.

> the possession of which we still had to grapple at the gates of the shops with thousands of spectres who were enraged by hunger, and with that, a single day's rest: that was all we found in Smolensk, in its much-vaunted winter quarters. We had to continue our journey, and with the cold and misery increasing day by day, we still had 30 days to walk to reach the Russian frontiers. We again uncoupled a few cannons, in order to obtain the carriage, we needed to continue our march for four six-pieces, the only ones left of all our artillery: and we tried to place our sick and dying in the houses in the new square, which had been converted into hospitals. These hospices, which were far from being able to cope with the immense influence of all the sufferers, presented a heartbreaking picture of desolation. We could see these unfortunate people piled up in a jumble under the arches of these houses or in the wagons which had been used to transport them, abandoned by everyone, deprived of any help, they would infallibly become victims of the cold of the first night. It was also in this bivouac to the hum of the cannon, which, getting closer and closer, announced to us the approach of Kutuzov and his army. For the glorious days of Smolensk and Valutino-Gora, we were given the marks of honour that had been sent to us from our homeland and which were waiting for us here.[177]

Eugène Labaume, aide-de-camp to Prince Eugène, was rather severe with the Emperor:

> A premature winter caused Napoleon's plan to fail, since, if he had been able to hold out between Smolensk and Vitebsk, he could easily repair the losses he had made at that time. The main and only cause of his ruin was that he wanted to go to Moscow, without thinking of what he was leaving behind, and to do at the cost of our blood what the most imprudent of monarchs had not thought prudent to do. The desire to sack this capital, the pride of giving it laws, made him sacrifice everything; and, forgetting the winter and its rigours, he went to burn the Kremlin without remembering that Wittgenstein had never abandoned the Dvina, and that Tchikagov, back from Moldavia, would attack him on the return from his mad expedition.[178]

The cold continued to wreak havoc on the ranks of the French army. From 14 to 16 November the thermometer registered 16 to 18 degrees below freezing. The horses of the French army died by the thousands. More than 30,000

177. Christian-Guillaume Faber du Faur, *En Russie avec Napoléon*, pp. 253–4.
178. Eugène Labaume, op. cit., pp. 300–2.

perished in a few days; the cavalry found themselves on foot; the artillery and the transports were without carriages; some of the guns and the munitions of war had to be destroyed. Marshal Ney, with the 3,000 men of the Third Corps, was charged with blowing up the walls of Smolensk after the army had left and with slowing down the advance of the Russian armies pursuing the French. The situation of the army after leaving Smolensk became even worse. Some authors even mention cases of cannibalism or autophagy:

> The road was covered with soldiers who no longer had human form, and whom the enemy disdained to take prisoner. Every day these wretches made us witnesses of some painful scenes to tell. Some had lost their hearing, others their speech; and many, through excessive cold or hunger, were reduced to a state of frenzied stupidity that made them roast corpses to devour them, or that drove them to the point of gnawing their hands and arms. Some were so weak that, unable to carry wood or roll a stone, they sat down on the dead bodies of their brothers, and, their faces all decomposed, stared at some burning coals; soon the coals were extinguished, and these livid spectres, unable to get up, fell down beside those on whom they had sat. Some of them, with convulsive laughter, threw themselves through the flames and perished, uttering horrible cries and making horrible contortions, while others, with equal insanity, followed them and died the same death.[179]

The Russians cautiously pursued the remnants of the Grande Armée, still led by Napoleon. The Emperor was defeated at Krasnoi by General Milodarovich but managed to escape despite heavy losses. For the first time since the start of the Russian campaign, the French emperor sent into battle the Imperial Guard, the best-preserved corps in the French army:

> While we were in and around Krasnoi, the Russian army, said to be 90,000 strong, surrounded us, because in front of us, to the right, to the left and behind us, it was all Russians who probably thought they could make good use of us. But the Emperor wanted to make them feel that things were not as easy as they thought, because although we were unhappy, dying of hunger and cold, we still had something to sustain us: honour and courage. So the Emperor, tired of being followed by this swarm of barbarians and savages, resolved to get rid of them. On the evening of our arrival, General Roguet received the order to attack during the night, with part of the Guard, the fusiliers-chasseurs, grenadiers, voltigeurs and tirailleurs regiments ... At eleven o'clock in

179. Eugène Labaume, op. cit., pp. 400–1.

the evening, a few detachments were sent to reconnoitre and ascertain the position of the enemy, who were occupying two villages in front of which they had set up camp, and whose direction was known from the position of their fires; it is probable that they feared something, for when we attacked them, some of them were already in a position to receive us. …

It was two o'clock when the movement began; we marched in three columns: the fusiliers-grenadiers, of which I was a member, and the fusiliers-chasseurs formed the centre column; the tirailleurs and voltigeurs formed the right and left columns. It was as cold as the previous days; we marched with difficulty through the middle of the land, knee-deep in snow. After half an hour's march, we found ourselves in the midst of the Russians, some of whom had taken up arms, for a large line of infantry was on our right, less than eighty paces away, firing murderously at us; their heavy cavalry, composed of cuirassiers dressed in white and wearing black armour, was on our left, at a similar distance, howling like wolves to excite each other, but not daring to approach us, and their artillery, in the centre, firing grapeshot. This did not stop our march, because, despite their fire and the number of men who fell among us, we approached them at full speed and entered their camp, where we made a terrible carnage with bayonets. Those who were further away had time to take up arms and come to the aid of the first. Then a different kind of battle began, as they set fire to their camp and the two villages. We were able to fight by the light of the fire. The right and left columns had overtaken us and entered the enemy camp from the extremities, while our column entered from the centre.

I forgot to say that as we were charging forward and the head of our column was driving the Russians back, routing their camp, we came across several hundred Russians lying on the snow, who were thought to be dead or dangerously wounded. We overtook them, but as soon as we were above them, they jumped up with their weapons; they fired, so that we were obliged to turn back to defend ourselves. Unfortunately for them, a rear-guard battalion that they had not been able to see arrived. They were caught in the crossfire; in less than five minutes, there was no longer any battalion: this is a ruse of war that the Russians often use, but in this case it did not work ...

When we had crossed the Russian camp and entered the village, after forcing them to throw some of their artillery into a lake, a large number of their infantry had retreated into the houses, some of which were in flames. That is where we fought fiercely, hand to hand. The carnage was terrible; we were divided; each man fought for himself. I was close to our colonel, the oldest colonel in France, who had fought in the Egyptian campaigns.[180] We were at the entrance to a kind of farm where many Russians had retreated and were blocked by men from our regiment; all they had to retreat to was an exit into the large courtyard, but it was closed by a fence that they had to climb over.

During this isolated battle, I noticed, in the courtyard, a Russian officer mounted on a white horse, beating his soldiers with the flat of his sabre, who were in a hurry to flee, wanting to jump the barrier, and leaving him no means of escape. Eventually, however, he gained control of the passage, but just as he was about to jump to the other side, his horse was hit by a bullet and fell under him, making the passage difficult. The Russian soldiers were then forced to defend themselves. From then on, the battle became fiercer. In the glow of the flames, it was a slaughter. Russians and French were on top of each other in the snow, killing each other at point-blank range. I wanted to run after the Russian officer who had freed himself from under his horse, and who was trying, with the help of two soldiers, to save himself by passing the barrier; but a Russian soldier stopped me two paces away at the end of the barrel of his rifle, and fired; Feeling that I was not wounded, I withdrew a few paces from my adversary who, thinking that I was dangerously wounded, quietly reloaded his weapon. Adjutant Major Roustan, who was near the colonel and had seen me in danger, ran to me and, taking me in his arms, said: 'My poor Bourgogne, are you not wounded?' – 'No,' I replied. – 'Then don't miss him!' This was indeed my thought. Supposing my rifle was missing (something that often happened, because of the snow), I would have run at him with my bayonet. I did not give him time to finish reloading, as a bullet had already gone through him. Although mortally wounded, he did not fall immediately; he staggered back, looking at me menacingly, without dropping his weapon, and fell on the officer's horse which was against the barrier. The adjutant-major, passing by him, struck him in the side with his sabre, accelerating his fall; at the same moment, I returned to the colonel, whom I found exhausted and no longer able to command; he had only his sapper with him. …

It was not five minutes after the sapper had huddled, that the Russians who were in the farmhouse and whom we held tightly blocked, seeing themselves on the point of being burnt, wanted to surrender: a wounded non-commissioned officer came in the midst of a hail of bullets to make the proposal. The adjutant-major then sent me to order a halt to the firing: 'Cease firing!' replied a soldier from our regiment, who was

180. Pierre Bodelin (1764–1828) had indeed fought in Egypt and later became a general. He retired in April 1813.

wounded; 'cease firing whoever wants to, but since I am wounded and will probably die, I will not stop firing until I have no more cartridges!' In fact, wounded as he was from a bullet that had broken his thigh, and sitting on the snow, which he was reddening with blood, he did not stop firing and even asked the others for cartridges. The adjutant-major, seeing that his orders were not being carried out, came himself, he said, on behalf of the colonel. But our soldiers, who were fighting desperately, did not hear him and carried on. The Russians, seeing that they no longer had any hope of salvation, and probably having no more ammunition to defend themselves, tried to leave en masse from the building to which they had retreated and where they were beginning to roast, but our men forced them to return. A moment later, unable to hold out any longer, they made another attempt, but as soon as a few men were in the courtyard, the building collapsed on the rest, where perhaps more than forty perished in the flames; those who had got out were no happier. After this scene, we collected our wounded and gathered around the colonel with our weapons loaded, waiting for daylight. Meanwhile, all around us was the noise of rifle shots from those still fighting on other points, mingled with the cries of the wounded and the complaints of the dying. There is nothing as sad as a night battle, where fatal mistakes are often made.

We waited for daylight in this position. When it appeared, we were able to recognise each other and judge the result of the battle: the whole space we had covered was littered with dead and wounded. I recognised the man who had tried to kill me: he was not dead; the bullet had gone through his side, regardless of the sabre blow the adjutant-major had given him. I had him put in a better position than the one he was in, because the white horse of the Russian officer, near which he had fallen, and which was struggling, could have hurt him. The interiors of the houses in the village where we were, I do not know whether it was Kircova or Malierva, as well as the Russian camp and the surrounding area, were covered with corpses, some of which were half-burnt. Our battalion commander, Mr Gilet, had his thigh broken by a bullet and died a few days later. The riflemen and voltigeurs lost more people than we did; in the morning, I met Captain Debonnez, who was from the same place as me, and who commanded a company of voltigeurs of the Guard; he had come to find out if anything had happened to me; he told me that he had lost a third of his company, plus his second lieutenant, who was a Vélite, and his sergeant-major, who were killed first. As a result of this deadly battle, the Russians withdrew from their positions, without however moving away, and we remained on the battlefield throughout the day and night of the 16th and 17th, during which we were always on the move. At every moment, to keep us on our toes, we were called to arms; we were always on the alert, without being able to rest or even get warm ...

On the morning of the 17th, as soon as it was light, we took up arms and, after forming up in close columns by division, we set off to take up positions on the side of the road opposite the battlefield we had just left. When we arrived, we saw part of the Russian army in front of us, on an eminence, and leaning against a wood. We immediately deployed in line to face them. We had our left up against a ravine which crossed the road and to which our backs were turned; this road, which was hollow and dominated from the sides, could shelter and protect those who were on it from enemy fire. On our right were the fusiliers-chasseurs, with the head of their regiment within rifle range of the town. In front of us, 250 paces away, was a regiment of the Young Guard, the first voltigeur, in close column by division, commanded by Colonel Luron. Further forward, and on our right, were the old grenadiers and chasseurs, in the same order, that is to say, as well as the rest of the Imperial Guard, cavalry and artillery, which had not taken part in the battle on the night of the 15th to the 16th. All this was commanded by the Emperor himself, who was on foot. Advancing with a firm step, as on the day of a grand parade, he took up a position in the middle of the battlefield, facing the enemy batteries. Just as we were taking up a position on the side of the road to form up in battle and face the enemy, I was marching with two of my friends, Grangier and Leboude, behind Adjutant-Major Delaitre, and just as the Russians were beginning to see us, their artillery, which was not far off at half a range, let loose its first volley on us. The first to fall was Adjutant-Major Delaitre: a cannonball cut both his legs just above the knees and his tall riding boots; he fell without uttering a cry or even a complaint. At that moment, he was holding his horse by the bridle, which he had passed through his right arm, and was walking on foot. No sooner had he fallen than we stopped, because the way he had fallen was blocking the little path we were walking on. To continue walking, we had to step over him, and as I was walking after him, I was obliged to do this. As I passed, I examined him: his eyes were open and his teeth were chattering convulsively against each other. He recognised me and called my name. I went over to listen to him. Then he said to me in a rather loud voice, and to the others who were watching him: 'My friends, I beg you, take my pistols from the pommels of my horse's saddle and burn my brains!' But no one dared to do him this favour, because in such a position it was one. Without answering him, we passed on our way, and very fortunately, because we had not taken six steps, a second shot, probably from the same battery, killed three other men among those who were following us and who were immediately taken away, as well as the adjutant-major.

From the crack of dawn, we could see the Russian army on three sides, in front of us, to our right and behind us, with its artillery, pretending to want to surround us. At that moment, a moment after the adjutant-major had just been killed, the Emperor arrived; we had just completed our movement: then the battle began. With his artillery, the enemy sent us terrible broadsides which, each time, brought death to our ranks. On our side, all we had to retaliate with were a few guns, which also made deep breaches in their ranks with each shot, but some of ours were soon dismantled. Meanwhile, our soldiers were dying without moving; we were in this sad position until two o'clock in the afternoon. During the battle, the Russians had sent part of their army to take up positions on the road beyond Krasnoi and cut off our retreat, but the Emperor stopped them by sending a battalion of the Old Guard.

While we were exposed to enemy fire and our strength diminished by the number of men who were being killed, we saw, behind us and a little to our left, the remnants of Marshal Davoust's corps, in the midst of a cloud of Cossacks, who did not dare approach them, and whom they quietly dissipated, marching on our side. I noticed in their midst, when they were behind us and on the road, the canteen-keeper's carriage where his wife and children were. At the same moment we heard cries of despair from the wife and children, but we could not tell if anyone had been killed or wounded. At the same time as Marshal Davoust's debris was passing, the Dutch grenadiers of the Guard had just abandoned an important position which the Russians had immediately covered with artillery, which was directed against us. From that moment on, our position was no longer tenable. Another regiment, the first of the voltigeurs, which was in front of us, made a move in its turn and reached the foot of the batteries, but immediately a mass of cuirassiers, the same ones with whom we had had dealings on the night of the 15th, and who had not dared to charge us, came to stop them. Then they withdrew a little to the left of the batteries and almost in front of our regiment and formed themselves into a square; no sooner had they formed than the cavalry tried to push them in, but they were received at point-blank range by a discharge from the voltigeurs, which caused a large number of them to fall. The rest turned around and retreated. A second charge took place; it had the same fate, so that the sides of the square where the cuirassiers had presented themselves were covered with men and horses; but they succeeded a third time with two cannons loaded with grapeshot, which crushed the regiment. Then they entered the square and finished off the rest with sabre blows:

these unfortunate men, almost all young soldiers, some of whose feet and hands were frozen and who could no longer use their weapons to defend themselves, were almost all massacred. This happened in front of us and we could not do anything. Eleven men returned; the rest were killed, wounded or taken prisoner, and led with sabres into a small wood opposite us. The colonel himself, covered in wounds, as well as several officers, were taken prisoner. I forgot to mention that when we were going into battle, the colonel had ordered: 'Flags, general guides on the line!' and I became the general guide on the right of our regiment; but they forgot to send us back and, as it was my principle to remain at my post, such as it was, I remained in this position, rifle butt in the air, for nearly an hour, and despite the cannonballs to which I could serve as a target, I did not move.

During this time, and at a moment when the Russian artillery was wreaking the most havoc in our ranks, the colonel had a pressing need (a natural need); the position and the place were not very suitable for such a task, but, as the matter was urgent, he took his decision and, withdrawing about sixty paces from the regiment, and with his rear facing the enemy, he quietly completed his business. If anything bothered him, it was the cold, but for the Russians for whom he served as a focal point, it did not worry him, although he could see them well, and it was as he rose from this position that he commanded, 'Flags and general guides to your places!' It could have been two o'clock, and we had already lost a third of our men, but the fusiliers-chasseurs had been treated worse than us: being closer to the town, they were exposed to more deadly fire. For half an hour, the Emperor had withdrawn with the first regiments of the Guard and following the main road; there was only us left on the battlefield, and a few platoons from different corps, facing more than fifty thousand enemy men. At that moment, Marshal Mortier ordered a retreat, and we immediately began our movement, withdrawing at a walk, as if on parade, and followed by the Russian artillery, which crushed us with its grapeshot. As we withdrew, we took with us those of our comrades who were least wounded. The moment when we left the battlefield was terrible and sad, because when our poor wounded saw that we were abandoning them in the middle of a field of death, surrounded by enemies, especially those of the 1st voltigeur, some of whose legs had been shattered by grapeshot, we saw several of them crawling on their knees, reddening the snow with their blood; they raised their hands to the sky, crying out in heart-rending cries for our help; but what could we do? The same fate awaited us at every moment, for as we withdrew, we were obliged to leave behind those we had lost. As we passed the position occupied by the fusiliers-chasseurs on our right, who were marching ahead of us, and as our second battalion, the one I was part of, was at that moment forming the rearguard and the extreme left of the retreat, I saw several of my friends lying dead on the snow and horribly mutilated by the grapeshot ...

After passing the fusiliers-chasseurs emplacement, and as we were at the entrance to the town, we saw, on our left, ten paces from the road and against the first house, cannons which, to protect us, were firing on the advancing Russians. They were supported and followed by about forty men, both cannoneers and voltigeurs; they were the rest of a brigade commanded by General Longchamp; he had just come out of the Imperial Guard; he was there with all that he had left, to save them or die with them. As soon as he saw our colonel, he came to him with open arms; they embraced like two men who had not seen each other for a long time and who were perhaps seeing each other for the last time. The general, his eyes full of tears, said to our colonel, showing him the two cannons and the few men he had left: 'Here, look! This is what I have left!' They had fought the Egyptian campaigns together.

This battle prompted Kutuzov, general-in-chief of the Russian army, to say that the French, far from allowing themselves to be brought down by the cruel situation in which they found themselves, were all the more enraged to run after the cannon that were crushing them. The English general Wilson, who was present at this battle, called it the battle of the heroes; this was certainly not because he was there, as this word is only applicable to us who, with a few thousand men, were fighting against the entire Russian army, which was 90,000 strong. General Longchamp, with the rest of his men, had to abandon his cannon, almost all of whose horses had been killed, and follow our retreat, taking advantage of accidents on the ground and in the houses to withdraw while defending himself. No sooner had we begun to enter Krasnoi than the Russians, with their guns mounted on sledges, came to position themselves at the first houses and let loose several cannon shots loaded with grapeshot. Three men from our company were hit. A Biscayan that touched my rifle and damaged the wood by shaving my shoulder, hit a young drummer walking in front of me in the head and killed him without him making the slightest movement.

Krasnoi is divided by a ravine that we had to cross. When we reached it, at the bottom we saw a herd of oxen dead from hunger and cold; they were so hardened by the frost that our sappers could not chop them up with their axes. Only their heads were visible, and their eyes were open as if they were still alive; their bodies were covered in snow. These oxen belonged to the army and had been unable to join us; the extreme cold and lack of food had caused them to perish. All the houses in this

> wretched town, as well as a large convent there, were full of wounded, who, on realising that we were abandoning them to the Russians, cried out in agony. We were obliged to abandon them to the brutality of a savage and merciless enemy, who stripped these unfortunate wounded without regard for their position or their wounds. The Russians were still following us, but sluggishly; a few pieces were still firing on the left of the road, but they could not do us much harm; the road on which we were marching was dug in; the cannonballs passed over it and could not reach us, and the presence of the little cavalry we had left, which was also marching on our left, prevented them from approaching us more closely. When we were a quarter of a league on the other side of the town, we were a little calmer; we walked sadly and silently, thinking of our position and of our unfortunate comrades whom we had been forced to abandon; I seemed to see them still begging us to rescue them. Looking back, we saw some of the least wounded, almost naked, whom the Russians had already stripped, and whom they had then abandoned; we were lucky enough to save them, at least for the moment; we hastened to give them what we could to cover them.[181]

Crossing the Berezina

The French army crossed the Borysthenes at Orza, but found before it the Berezina, a river that was difficult to cross at this time of year and bordered by marshes. The Russians occupied all the crossings. On 23 November the Russian army was determined to stop the French at Borissov along the Berezina. Napoleon decided to cross the river at Studianka, where the river was only 20m wide and 2m deep. Two bridges were built by the sappers, one for pedestrians and the other for wagons. The tragic crossing of this river remains in the French imagination the most striking symbol of the Russian retreat. Second Lieutenant von Kausler of the Württemberg army was at the Berezina crossing. He recounts this dramatic page of the campaign:

> On 26 November, long before dawn, we left the bivouac at Nimanitschi to head for Borissov with the remnants of the Grande Armée, which was returning from Moscow. Borissov had been taken on 23 November by Chichagov and recaptured on 24 November by the Duke of Reggio. It was still dark when we passed this town, as well as a stretch of two leagues of road up the river; the glow of the Russian fires on the right bank guided us on our march. When day broke, this movement was masked by a forest that stretched as far as Studianka, four places above Borissov. The cannonade and fusillade, which had been heard faintly all

181. Adrien Bourgogne, op. cit., pp. 87–9.

morning on the right bank, became more animated after dinner. It was Oudinot who, with the 2nd corps, had crossed the trestle bridges built near Studianka and was pushing Chichagov back towards Borissov. It was only slowly and after several long halts that we finally reached Studianka towards evening, situated on the left bank, on the slope of a hill, the crest of which was manned with cannon to defend the trestle bridges. These bridges had been started on the morning of 26 November and completed in the afternoon by General Éblé, at a distance of 100 toises from each other, immediately below Studianka; the one on the right, situated above, was for infantry and cavalry; the one on the left, which was lower down, was for artillery and vehicles of all kinds. At this point, the Berezina is 54 toises wide; its dried-up banks are marshy; the water was about six feet deep at the time. The bridges were reached by ramps, the approaches to which were flooded as the river overflowed in places. The houses had provided the wood needed to build the bridges and barracks, and as it was also used to fuel the fires, the village was disappearing more and more; the slopes on which it was built were covered with the remnants of the Moscow army, who were bivouacked there awaiting the passage scheduled for the following day. It was so overcrowded with men, horses and carriages that we were happy to find shelter for the night behind the outer wall of a hut in the French gendarmerie quarters, sheltered from the icy wind. On 27 November at two o'clock in the morning, the guards, the third corps and, with it, the 25th division (from six infantry regiments, four cavalry regiments and 1,000 artillery men, it now had only 150 men without cannon in its ranks), left the bivouac and crossed the bridges to the right bank. The supernumerary officers followed this movement at seven in the morning. This departure was a signal for several thousand stragglers of the Grande Armée who were scattered far and wide in the surrounding bivouacs to also rush to the bridges. At the crack of dawn, a thick and confused mass of men, horses and carriages made their way towards the narrow passages of the bridges and, as it were, stormed them. Although the enemy was not yet close by, the crowd was no less frightening, and what made it even more so was that the gendarmerie and the pontoniers, in accordance with the orders they had received, would only allow detachments of troops in line, or armed officers and soldiers, to cross the bridge, and would repel all others from the entrance, even using force of arms. In the press, hundreds of men were crushed against the bridges or underfoot or thrown into the water. Those who were allowed to cross the bridges were in less danger only when, by a fortunate chance, they were able to stand in the middle of the crowd on the extension of the ramps and were carried over the railings by this moving mass. But as soon as you missed them, you were in danger of either being crushed underfoot or falling into the ice of the Berezina.

In the midst of this terrible turmoil, the Emperor, serenity on his forehead, stopped on the shore between the bridges and made every effort to bring order to the confusion and calm to the tumult, to unravel the chaos. He led the way until evening, then went with his retinue to the right bank and set up his headquarters in the hamlet of Zaniwski, half a league from the Berezina ... Driven back from our fire, where we had established ourselves as comfortably as possible, we withdrew to the hamlet of Zaniwski, situated halfway up the Berezina, on the slope of a hill; we arrived at dusk in the midst of heavy snow. All the imperial headquarters, the remnants of the guards and, successively, all the troops who had crossed the Berezina that day had already gathered there, and who, without maintaining order or rank, had been able to drag themselves through the snow, attracted by the fires of the bivouacs, whose glow extended into the distance. All the houses were occupied; everywhere we were forbidden to approach. It was only with difficulty and after a long search that we found a place in front of a house with our headquarters and most of our officers and soldiers. We had to conquer a few beams at sword point to light a fire, around which we spent the night, camped in three or four lines in deep snow and deprived of all food. But most of those who had taken the houses did not enjoy them for long, for bloody battles ensued everywhere, not to find space in the houses, but to get the houses themselves. The soldiers, who had become furious due to the extreme cold, and the guards in particular, began by uncovering the roofs to obtain fire and ended by demolishing them completely, despite the desperate but useless resistance of the inhabitants. The next day, Zaniwski had disappeared, consumed in the fires of the bivouacs.

However, as night fell, calm had also returned to the left bank among the innumerable crowds who, during the day of 27 November, had not yet crossed the bridges. They had stopped moving to this side, and everything was resting peacefully under the debris of Studianka, on the slopes of these heights, and in the middle of the immense mass of carriages of all kinds placed in a jumble, and forming, over a depth of several hundred paces, a vast circle around the entrance to the bridges; the lights of the bivouacs illuminated the whole region. No doubt most of these unfortunates, dulled by suffering, had become insensitive to danger; perhaps they were also counting on the protection of Victor's corps, which, occupying the heights of Studianka with its left wing and leaning against the Berezina with its right, covered the approaches to the bridges on the left bank. In addition, there were thousands of sick, wounded and crippled people who, abandoned by their guides and held back by their helplessness in their wagons or sleds, were relegated to this inhospitable land. This was how the night of 27–28 November passed. But at the crack of dawn on the 28th, the cannon thundered on both banks of the river, announcing that on the left, Wittgenstein with 40,000 Russians was crossing the Borissov road, and on the right, Chichagov with 27,000 men, was marching against the entrances to the bridges, and that the last day had undoubtedly come for most of these unfortunate men. Then, but too late for a large number of them, they tried to cross, and again rushed towards the bridges, of which the one on the left, intended for carriages, ended up breaking for the third time under the weight of the mass, and could no longer be restored in the midst of the tumult and the press. From then on, a single idea, a single goal occupied all their minds, that of reaching the only bridge still standing; and to reach it, knocking down everything around them, everything that stood in their way, leaders, comrades, women and children, they trampled them underfoot, or pushed them into the waters of the Berezina or into the flames of the house that was burning between the two bridges. Victor, with his corps reduced to about 6,000 men, made incredible efforts to stop Wittgenstein; and Oudinot, Ney and Dombrowski and their 9,000 men drove Chichagov back to Stachowa; but Wittgenstein, whose forces were too superior, advanced further and further towards the bridges; so that in the end he was able to direct the murderous fire of his far superior artillery not only on Victor's force, but also on this thick group of defenceless men, on this heap of carriages and horses, and even on the bridge. Then the misfortune and despair of this hurried crowd were at their height. The cries of these unfortunate people drowned out the thunder of the cannon and the whistle of the bullets, and they rushed towards the bridges with renewed fury. Around the bridges, like hills, rose heaps of men and horses trampled underfoot or killed by enemy fire; to reach the bridges, it was necessary to pass over their bodies while fighting; the waves and ice carried by the river swept them away from time to time, but it was only to make way for others. At last night came, the enemy's blows became more uncertain and finally ceased altogether; at around nine o'clock in the evening Victor managed with his corps to fight his way through this scene of horror and desolation; he went to the right bank, leaving a rearguard at Studianka. Many neglected to take advantage of this night, although they could have, to reach the opposite bank; and it was only when, on the morning of the 29th, the Russians again advanced against the bridges, and there was no longer time, that they made a desperate but

> useless attempt, for at 8.30 a.m. the bridge was set on fire, and all means of salvation lost forever.
>
> The same fate awaited the remnants of the Grande Armée on the right bank, if, on the only line of retreat they still had, Chichagov had destroyed the bridges which, between Zaniwski and Zembin, led across the marshes, and which he had occupied immediately before crossing the Berezina. Fortunately, he had not recognised the importance of this pass; the army arrived at Zembin, destroyed the bridges, and thus put the marshes between itself and the pursuing enemy.[182]

French losses were very heavy: 25,000 combatants and more than 20,000 non-combatants. In the nineteenth century the battle of the Berezina was considered a Russian victory. Today, French historians believe that because the remnants of Napoleon's army managed to escape the enemy's numerically superior forces, it should be considered a victory for the Emperor.

Napoleon was alarmed by the news of General Malet's conspiracy, which had almost succeeded. The precise date on which he was informed is unknown. His correspondence mentioned the event for the first time on 7 November, but the situation of the army did not allow him to reach Paris immediately. On 5 December 1812 the Emperor summoned Murat, Prince Eugène, Marshal Berthier, Marshal Ney, the Dukes of Danzig, Treviso and Istria, and the Prince of Eckmuhl to his headquarters in Smorgony', where he announced that he had to return to France to get the army back on its feet and that he was entrusting command of the Grande Armée to his brother-in-law Murat, King of Naples. He then left the army in a hurry, by sledge, accompanied only by Caulaincourt. The greatest secrecy had been kept regarding the imminence of this departure. Squadron Leader Dupuy reported his reaction and that of his fellow officers when they were informed of the Emperor's departure by General Sébastiani:

> We were invited to dismount and go up to the rooms of the general, who announced the Emperor's departure for France, urged us not to become disunited and informed us that, in a few moments, we would be marching back to Kaunas ... This departure of the Emperor, which had been foreseen for three or four days and which was spoken of, albeit vaguely, caused some officers whose spirits were embittered by misfortune and suffering to murmur; but those for whom it was still possible to reflect, and this was the greatest number, immediately understood that Napoleon would be in a better position in France than at the head of the debris of his army, to organise the means of repairing

182. Faber du Faur, op. cit., pp. 269–81.

> the disasters of the Russian campaign ... Moreover, if he had stayed with them, the march on Prussian territory, from the Niemen to the Elbe, would not have been so peaceful, the hostile dispositions of Prussia already showing in some of its generals.[183]

Two leagues from Wilna, Major Noël, dismayed, encountered the retreating remnants of the Grande Armée for the first time:

> On 8 December ... I encountered the first remnants of our army. At first, I could not believe that this was the Grande Armée. But soon there could be no doubt. These were the wretched remnants of the magnificent army of 400,000 men which, six months earlier, had crossed the Niemen, and which, in all encounters, had constantly beaten the Russians. The sight of this disorderly crowd was pitiful. It is impossible to imagine such a sad picture, and it is impossible for me to give an account of what I saw and to express the grief and despair I felt. It was a crowd, a mass of haggard, scruffy, dishevelled men, walking in front of them or jostling each other, seeming to see nothing, hear nothing, understand nothing. All ranks mixed together, officers and soldiers, horsemen and infantrymen, French, Italians, Germans, unarmed, covered in rags, pelisses, old sacks, freshly flayed animal skins, with shoes on their feet made of old clothes and old hats.[184]

From then on, Noël took part in the rout of the Grande Armée. He noted:

> The retreat to Kowno. From the 8th to the 10th, at the summit of Ponary, I had lost 20 men, all Dutch, who had frozen to death; others were also mistreated. The cold was so intense that I could not stay on horseback for long. When I tried to put the traces of a carriage back on, the tips of my fingers froze and my skin remained attached to the iron of the buckles. In addition to my waistcoat and woollen knitwear, I was wearing my uniform capote, a jacket with sheepskin sleeves, with the hair inside, and over my greatcoat, and despite all this gear, the cold penetrated me. The loss of soldiers in the train forced me to entrust the driving of the guns and carriages to gunners, and it was with this beginning of disorganisation that I set off again on the 10th, marching all day and part of the nights, without regular lodgings. The cannoneers, the temporary drivers, were not very happy with this kind of service, which was in any case very arduous, so they neglected the horses and

183. Victor Dupuy, op. cit., pp. 207–8.
184. Jean-Nicolas Noël, *Souvenirs militaires d'un officier du Premier Empire*, Genève, 1971, p. 428.

> deliberately abandoned or overturned the carriages. Without the help of the discouraged officers, I was unable to save a single carriage; the gunners were lost in the crowd. But the main cause of my losses was a disastrous measure taken by General Bessières to save one of the army's treasuries. Treasury vans were abandoned on the road. The marshal had my convoy stopped and, despite my observations, because pressed as we were by the Russians, we needed cannons more than money, he ordered me to load my crews with barrels from the treasury. What I had foreseen happened. The bait was tempting, so cars with loads of barrels soon disappeared. The mess was so great, and it was so easy to evade detection, that no one knew who was responsible for these losses.[185]

The army approached Vilnius, where, in principle, large quantities of supplies were waiting and where it could take some rest. The prevailing indiscipline upset the established plans:

> On the 9th of December, we arrived at Wilna, where there were some stores; but as the Duc de Bassano and General Hogendorp had left for the Nieman, there was no one to give orders, so that there, as at Smolensk, the officials demanded proper receipts for the issue of food and clothing, which was virtually impossible because of the disorganisation of almost all the regiments. We lost some precious time in this way. General Maison broke into several stores and his men took some supplies, but the remainder was taken the next day by the Russians. Soldiers from other corps wandered round the town in the hope of being taken in by the inhabitants, but the people who six months previously had welcomed the French with open arms, closed their doors to us when they saw us in distress. Only the Jews would accommodate those who could pay for temporary shelter.
>
> Admitted neither to the stores nor to private houses, the majority of famished men headed for the hospitals where, although there was not enough food for all of them, they were at least sheltered from the piercing cold. This respite was enough to decide 20,000 sick and wounded, among whom were two hundred officers and eight generals, to go no further. They had reached the end of their physical and mental resources.
>
> Lieutenant Hernoux, one of the most vigorous and brave officers in my regiment, was so overcome by what he had been through that he lay down on the snow, refusing to move, until he died. Several soldiers, of all ranks, blew their brains out, to escape from their suffering.

185. Jean-Nicolas Noël, op. cit., p. 429.

> During the night 9th–10th December, in thirty degrees of frost, some Cossacks came and began shooting at the gates of Wilna. Many people thought this was the entire army of Kutuzov, and in a panic they fled from the town. I regret to say that King Murat was among them. He left without giving any orders, but Marshal Ney stayed and organised the retreat as best he could. We quitted Wilna on the morning of the 10th, leaving behind not only a great number of men, but also an artillery park and a part of the army's funds.[186]

Captain François was also at the Ponary crossing and told about his arrival in the Prussian town of Thorn, where there was a French garrison and invaluable supplies. He displayed the typical anti-Semitism of the time:

> 10 December. Our passage through Vilnius, after the Berezina affair, was one of the most disastrous episodes of the retreat. We entered the town, pushed by the Cossacks. We had endeavoured to get there in the hope of some relief after having endured all the rigours of the weather. For many, the change was a cause of death. Soldiers, officers and generals crammed into the houses and suffocated, like my two comrades. Those who stayed outside, sleeping along the walls, froze to death. Many of these unfortunate people were murdered, especially, we were told, those staying with Jews. I only left Wilna at six in the morning and by a roundabout route, and I saw thousands of corpses, completely naked, many with stab marks. It was certainly not the Poles who committed these crimes; they showed us great affection and often exposed themselves to the blows of the murderers to defend us. Just as I was leaving Vilnius, the Russian vanguard entered ... That day, heavy snow obscured the air. The road was barely visible, and the army had great difficulty in reaching the foot of the mountain about a league from Vilnius. At this position the army was surrounded by Cossacks and, as many of their officers spoke French, they said to us: 'You need crampons to climb this mountain. Just wait, Chichagov and Platov will bring you some.' In truth, the icy, steep path made us despair of following it. The horses we had left were badly shod, slipped, fell and had no strength to get up again. We had to abandon the rest of the equipment, the baggage and the Emperor's treasure, which was said to contain 15 million, as well as his gold and silver crockery; the soldiers pushed the dishes and vases with their feet or threw them into the snow. When I got to the top of the mountain, I saw the grenadiers of the guard defending the last caissons against the Cossacks, but they ended up taking them. The army

186. Marcellin Marbot, op. cit., p. 334.

> had a hard time climbing the mountain. Me, with my stick and my arm in a sling, I do not know how I managed to get to the top. I fell more than 100 times and dragged myself across the ice ... During the night, some soldiers came to join us. Like me, they had left Vilnius very late. The Cossacks on the plateau, they told us, had murdered the wounded and sick that the inhabitants, terrified by these brigands, had chased from their homes.[187]

After some tough marches, the remnants of the great army finally reached Prussian territory. Commander Coudreux summarised in a letter his disastrous campaign:

> I arrived at my regiment on the evening of the sixth, after having travelled 72 leagues in six days, and I was with it on the business of the seventh and eighth, where we were reduced to 540. I crossed Moscow on the 14th with the vanguard; the next day, we pursued the enemy and exchanged a few hundred cannonballs with them every day until we reached the outskirts of Kaluga, where we had another very heated affair on the 4th of October which earned me the rank of battalion commander. The fatal retreat finally began on the 18th; I was in the rearguard. We fought often, and on 3 November I had a horse killed under me by a cannon shot ... I was captured at Krasnoi on 18 November, after being bayoneted in the chest and sabred in the head during an attack on a battery. How can I tell you what I had to suffer during a four-month march across the whole of Russia? Wounded, penniless, covered in rags, devoured by vermin, exposed to being massacred at any moment by an exasperated and furious population, I saw most of my unfortunate comrades die around me of misery and hunger. Courage never deserted me, however, and I arrived at Saratov, where we had the good fortune to find a generous and humane man as our governor, whose noble and sensitive conduct completely avenged the infamous way in which we had been treated all along the road.[188]

Like all the others, Marbot, who was serving in the rearguard, explained why the Russian campaign had failed:

> We may now cast a glance at the causes which led to the failure of the Russian campaign. Of these the chief was undoubtedly the mistake into which Napoleon fell when he thought he could go to war in the north of

187. Charles-François François, op. cit., pp. 699–701.
188. Gustave Schlumberger, op. cit., pp. 221–2.

Europe before making an end of that which he had long been waging in Spain, in which country his armies had just undergone heavy reverses when he made arrangements to attack the Russians at home. As the genuine French troops, when thus divided between the north and the south, were in both parts insufficient, Napoleon thought to make up by uniting battalions of his allies with them. It was like diluting generous wine with dirty water.

The French divisions deteriorated; the allied troops remained as moderate as ever, and they it was who during the retreat threw the Grande Armée into disorder.

A cause, not less fatal, of our reverses was the bad organisation, or rather total want of organisation, in the conquered countries. Instead of doing as we had done in the campaigns of Austerlitz, Jena and Friedland, namely, establishing in the country left behind by the way small corps which could form from post to post regular communications, and so secure that our rear should be undisturbed, and that ammunition, solitary men and trains of wounded should move in safety, all our available forces were imprudently pushed on to Moscow, until between that place and the Niemen there was, with the exception of Vilnius and Smolensk, not a garrison, not a store, not a hospital. Two hundred leagues of country were thus given over to wandering bands of Cossacks; and the result was that the sick when cured could not rejoin, and that, for want of convoys to evacuate them, all those wounded at the Moskwa had to be left for two months in the convent of Polotsk. They were still there when the retreat began; nearly all were captured, and those who reckoned that they had strength to follow the army died of fatigue and cold on the high road. Lastly, the retreating troops had no assured supply of food in districts which produce corn in abundance.

To the lack of small garrisons in our rear was also due the fact that out of more than 100,000 prisoners taken by the French in the course of the campaign, literally not one ever left Russia, the reason being that no organisation existed for passing them to the rear. Accordingly, they all escaped with ease and returned to the Russian army; thus repairing in some degree its losses, while ours increased daily.[189]

While Napoleon, who had returned to France, set about rebuilding his army, the remnants of what had been the Grande Armée headed for Prussia and the Grand Duchy of Warsaw. What was left of the troops that had entered the Czarist empire in June 1812? There is no definite figure for the number of casualties in the 1812 campaign. Estimates of Napoleon's army's losses range

189. Marcellin Marbot, op. cit., pp. 337–40.

from 380,000 to over 500,000. French historian Thierry Lentz has reviewed the progress of research in this area. Between 550,000 and 560,000 men entered Russia. Between 25,000 and 30,000 men crossed the Niemen again. Kutuzov estimated the number of prisoners at 150,000. According to the Russian historian Vladène Sirotkine, between 50,000 and 60,000 deserters found refuge among the population. The number of dead and missing should therefore be around 200,000, a high figure, but much lower than those traditionally accepted since the Napoleonic era.[190] Let us conclude this chapter with some remarks by Antoine de Jomini, one of the great figures of military thought in the nineteenth century:

> If Napoleon's admirers were not fair to his rivals, neither were his personal enemies in all countries. He was not, in this campaign, below his high reputation. He did not throw himself madly, like an adventurer, into inhospitable lands; he had taken measures to provide for everything. The enormity of the distances, the masses, even the preparations, all worked against him. He attempted it boldly, but after having prepared everything within the reach of human foresight: unfortunately, he had dreamt the impossible.[191]

190. Thierry Lentz, *Nouvelle histoire du Premier empire, II, L'effondrement du système napoléonien 1810–1814*, Paris, 2004, pp. 319–21.
191. Antoine de Jomini, op. cit., pp. 215–16.

Chapter 7

Decline and fall of the French empire

Shifting the balance of power

In Paris, while the French expeditionary corps saw its numbers dwindle rapidly, the press, which was strictly controlled by the censors, endeavoured to give a positive image of the expedition to Russia, despite the retreat from Moscow, which was now public knowledge. The newspapers of 24 November announced to readers that 'the latest news of the Grande Armée is from 7 November; the movement it had begun continues to be carried out in the most perfect order. The Emperor, who was still in the best of health, was expected in Smolensk on the 8th.'[192] In addition, the newspapers of the same week emphasised the eagerness of the conscripts who had recently been called up to join the army. The *Journal de l'Empire* of 26 November published an article, which it claimed was taken from an English opposition newspaper, describing Russia in a particularly black light:

> From the sovereign down to the last slave, Russians, be they princes, nobles, priests or peasants, are covered in vermin; there is not one exception in a thousand ... If a foreigner has the misfortune to look at the soup being served, he will discover a few victims alive and in distress; a Russian will swallow without being moved ... Prince Potemkin took the vermin on his head and killed it on his silver crockery. There are beautiful princesses in Moscow who have no qualms about imitating his example. A true Russian eats breakfast with black bread and a glass of brandy. He dines on very fatty meats, the ascorbutic effects of which he corrects with salted cucumbers, sour cabbage and the juice of various berries ... A foreigner waits in vain for his fork and knife to be changed; if they are sent back, they are returned to him without having been cleaned. At the home of Count Alexis Orloff, one of the greatest lords of the empire, the servants drop their saliva in the most precious dishes,

192. *Journal de l'Empire*, 24 November 1812.

> and wipe them with dirty towels ... There is not a single bed in the entire Russian empire in which an Englishman would want to lie down after examining its condition ... If you ask what the Russians did with Crimea after conquering it by dint of perfidy and atrocities, the answer will be short; They devastated the whole country ...[193]

The 29th *Bulletin of the Grande Armée* arrived in Paris on 16 December. Its publication in the semi-official newspaper *Le Moniteur universel* on 17 December caused consternation in France. Since the announcement of the retreat from Moscow, the inhabitants of the French empire had known that the campaign against Russia would be difficult. However, the French had confidence in the Emperor's military skills, as he had already faced pugnacious opponents and had always turned the situation in his favour. This time, however, there was no longer any reason to doubt that the imperial army had been defeated. This *Bulletin* attributed responsibility for the disaster to premature bad weather, which had hit an army that was always victorious in battle. The 29th *Bulletin*, while admitting that the situation was difficult, did not give the full picture of the disaster and concealed the real losses suffered by the Grande Armée. It is true that when Napoleon had left the army, the worst moments of the French troops in Russia had not yet struck the imperial legions. Here is the beginning of the announcement that so dismayed contemporaries:

> Molodetchna, 3 December 1812
>
> Until 6 November, the weather was perfect, and the movement of the army was carried out with the greatest success. The cold began on the 7th; from then on, every night we lost several hundred horses, which died in the bivouac. By the time we reached Smolensk, we had already lost many cavalry and artillery horses. The Russian army of Volhynia was opposed to our right. Our right left the Minsk line of operations and took the Warsaw line as the pivot of its operations. On the 9th, the Emperor learned in Smolensk of this change in the line of operations, and assumed what the enemy would do. However hard it seemed to him to set off in such a cruel season, the new state of affairs made it necessary. He hoped to arrive in Minsk, or at least on the Berezina, before the enemy; he left Smolensk on the 13th; on the 16th he slept in Krasnoy. The cold which had begun on the 7th suddenly increased and from the 14th to the 15th and 16th the thermometer registered 16 and 18 degrees below freezing. The roads were covered in ice; cavalry, artillery and train horses perished every night, not by the hundreds but

193. *Journal de l'Empire*, 24 November 1812.

> by the thousands, especially French and German horses. More than thirty thousand horses perished in a few days; our cavalry was all on foot; our artillery and transport were without teams. We had to abandon and destroy many of our guns and munitions. This army, so beautiful on the 6th, was very different on the 14th, with no cavalry, no artillery and no transport. Without cavalry, we could not light up a quarter of a league away; however, without artillery, we could not risk a battle and wait on firm footing; we had to march in order not to be forced into a battle, which the lack of ammunition prevented us from wanting; we had to occupy a certain space in order not to be turned around, and this without cavalry to light up and link the columns. This difficulty, combined with the sudden excessive cold, made our situation unfortunate. Men whom nature had not tempered strongly enough to be above all the odds of fate and fortune seemed shaken, lost their cheerfulness and their good humour, and dreamt only of misfortune and disaster; those whom nature had created superior to all retained their cheerfulness and their ordinary manners, and saw a new glory in the different difficulties to be overcome ...[194]

Napoleon returned to Paris on 18 December. His arrival came as a surprise and was only briefly announced in the *Journal de l'Empire* of Sunday, 20 December: 'The Emperor arrived last night in his capital, in very good health. His Majesty was accompanied by the Duke of Vicenza ...'[195] Napoleon immediately set to work. On 21 December he solemnly received the Senate in his Tuileries palace. In his speech President Lacépède referred to the campaign that was drawing to a close:

> Your Majesty has flown the French eagles over the towers of Moscow. The enemy has only been able to halt his successes and thwart his plans by resorting to the dreadful resources of despotic governments, by creating deserts on all his borders, by setting fire to his provinces, by burning down his capital, the centre of his wealth and the products of so many centuries ...

In his reply, Napoleon justified his defeat: 'My army suffered losses, but it was due to the premature severity of the season.'[196] His first task now was to investigate General Malet's conspiracy. The prefect of the Seine department, Frochot, was dismissed. There was also the question of strengthening the

194. *Le Moniteur universel*, 17 December 1812.
195. *Journal de l'Empire*, 20 December 1812.
196. *Journal de l'Empire*, 22 December 1812.

morale of the population with regard to the military situation in central Europe and reconstituting the army, which had been severely tested by the Russian campaign. On 25 December Napoleon received the homage of the constituted bodies at the Tuileries palace. The speeches given on this occasion made extensive reference to the Malet conspiracy, but also to the military situation. From then on, the official language would constantly contrast the wisdom of Napoleon, a conscientious administrator and unconquerable general, with the Russians, barbarians who respected nothing and had to be stopped. Napoleon was also ardently concerned with resolving two problems of capital importance: firstly, reassuring the allied sovereigns, in particular the princes of the Confederation of the Rhine, whom he might have suspected of having been shaken in their loyalty by the disastrous campaign of 1812, which had shown that Napoleon himself could be defeated, as well as the loss of the expeditionary corps attached to the great army, and secondly reconstituting his military power.

Austria, led by the father-in-law of the French emperor, Francis I, whom Napoleon had defeated in 1805 and 1809, was an unreliable ally. The Austrian military corps led by Prince Schwarzenberg fought well, but sometimes behaved equivocally, bordering on treason. Was this because of instructions from the government in Vienna? On 7 January 1813 Napoleon wrote a long letter to Emperor Francis I, which began by explaining and justifying the reasons for the retreat and ended with mentions of potential peace negotiations with Russia:

> The consequence of all this must be that I will not make any representations for peace, because the latest circumstances having turned to Russia's advantage, it is up to this cabinet to make representations if it judges the situation of affairs correctly ... I will not refuse a peace that is honourable for all the belligerent parties. But it is quite clear that it is not in my power to go back on any of the provisions enshrined yesterday in our constitutional laws; none of the countries united by senatus-consults can be a subject for negotiation, either with Russia or with England. I will yield on the Treaty of Tilsit, insofar as it may compromise the complete independence of Russia, but I will not abandon a single village in the Duchy of Warsaw, and I will not allow Russia to receive any increase from Austria, Prussia, Turkey or Sweden ...[197]

As we can see from this extract, Napoleon refused to acknowledge his military defeat and, sure of his resources and his superiority, he set conditions for the signing of peace with Russia that the latter could not accept. What is more,

197. Napoléon Bonaparte, *Correspondance générale*, t. 13, pp. 56–9.

Napoleon did not seem to show the slightest concern. General de Caulaincourt, in his memoirs, recounted that as soon as he arrived in Paris, that:

> the disposition of minds in France would reassure him about the consequences that all the events could have. He complacently enumerated all the means he would have at his disposal three months later, calculating that he could gather 800,000 men under arms. Once this number was found, with the certainty of arming and equipping it, the rest depending on his genius, he truly believed he had regained the empire of the world and could count on his fortune and the future.[198]

Napoleon did not seem to distrust the King of Prussia, who bent to his will when it came to supplying troops for the Russian expedition. On 5 January 1813 he wrote to his ally Frederick VI, King of Denmark and Norway, 'I am assured of Austria's good feelings, I have only to praise the King of Prussia ...'[199] A few days later the French learned that General Yorck, head of the Prussian corps of the Grande Armée, had concluded an armistice with the enemy at Tauroggen on 30 December, in which he proclaimed his neutrality towards Russia. Under this agreement, the part of East Prussia where the Prussian troops were located was deemed neutral, while General Yorck and 4,000 of his men were integrated into the Czar's army. The government in Berlin was panicked by Yorck's premature action, while the kingdom of Prussia was still occupied by a series of French garrisons that could seize the king. A court martial, convened urgently by Frederick William III, sentenced the disobedient (or too impatient) general to death in absentia. Napoleon was convinced of Frederick William's sincerity, a fact highlighted in a letter to his brother Jerome, King of Westphalia, on 18 January.[200]

Napoleon was completely mistaken. At the same time as this Council was being held, a Prussian ambassador was meeting Czar Alexander to conclude an alliance. On 3 February 1813 the *Journal de l'Empire* published an entry drowned out by other news: 'It is written from Berlin that His Majesty the King of Prussia left his residence at Potsdam on the 22nd to go to Silesia. The purpose of His Majesty's journey is to preside over the preparations for the next campaign and to raise the 20 new battalions that he has ordered to be formed.'[201] Frederick William III's departure for Silesia, which went almost unnoticed, was in fact intended to put the king and his family beyond the reach of French forces. As for the troops that were to be raised, they were to be used

198. Armand de Caulaincourt, op. cit., p. 398.
199. Napoléon Bonaparte, *Correspondance générale*, t. 13, p. 44.
200. Napoléon Bonaparte, *Correspondance générale*, t. 13, p. 120.
201. *Journal de l'Empire*, 3 February 1813.

to wage war against France. Austria, for its part, was preparing to make a declaration of neutrality, while keeping Marshal Schwarzenberg's corps away from the Grande Armée. Moreover, Russia had no intention of signing a peace treaty with France.

At the start of the Russian expedition, Napoleon had been able to count on the support of the Ottoman empire, which was at war with Russia. The signing of a peace agreement between these two powers had freed up large Russian forces to intervene against the retreating French army. Napoleon tried without success to persuade the Turkish sultan Mahmoud to resume the struggle. In the letter to his brother Jérôme, quoted above, Napoleon estimated that the Grande Armée, thanks to the garrisons left throughout Germany, still numbered 200,000 men. To this must be added the 120,000 men of the class of 1813, mobilised by the senatus-consult of 1 September 1812, armed and trained but not yet used, as well as the 88 cohorts of the National Guard which had been raised in 1812 to protect the territory of the empire during the Russian expedition. There was one obstacle to using the National Guard: by law, it was exclusively dedicated to defending the national territory. The leaders of the its cohorts were encouraged to ask for their units to be attached to the army. In December and January the pages of the newspapers frequently carried letters from officers, non-commissioned officers and soldiers to the Emperor, asking for the honour of fighting for the country. These so-called wishes were fulfilled by a senatus-consult of 11 January 1813. The combined cohorts provided the Grande Armée with 22 regiments. At the same time, the same text called up in advance 150,000 men of the class of 1814. Meanwhile, all of France's institutions were showing their patriotism by offering to equip cavalrymen. For example, the city of Paris supported 500 cavalrymen from the Grande Armée. Everyone wanted to show their zeal. Similarly, a large number of private individuals imitated the official authorities. One of the Emperor's first concerns was to reconstitute the Imperial Guard. On examining the first personnel reports, he found that it had been severely affected by the end of the campaign and that it required significant recruitment to bring it up to strength.

A glance at Napoleon's correspondence on this subject reveals a certain mistrust of soldiers from regions where public opinion seemed to be turning against the empire: 'The 400 men needed for the four companies on foot will be drawn from the cohorts, taking care not to take any Belgians, Dutch or [men] from the new departments of Italy.'[202]

The number of conscripts raised exceeded anything seen before. Before Napoleon left for the army, a series of decrees and senatus-consults were published:

202. Napoléon Bonaparte, *Correspondance générale*, t. 13, p. 28.

- 11 January 1813: National Guard, 100,000 men; classes 1809 to 1812, 150,000 men; early call-up of class 1814, 150,000 men;
- 11 February 1813: supplement of 10,000 men of the class 1814; and
- 3 April 1813: 10,000 honour guards, 80,000 National Guards and a further 90,000 men from class 1814.[203]

The aforementioned raising of the 10,000 honour guards shows that Napoleon was wary not only of the populations that had recently become French, but also of the higher social classes from which these men would be recruited and who would serve as hostages to the loyalty of their families. The establishment of the new army was going well. Napoleon organised, stimulated his collaborators and gave instructions from all sides. No fewer than 1,748 letters written by him between his return to Paris in December and his departure for the army on 15 April 1813 were preserved. The majority of these letters contained detailed instructions that show the Emperor's astonishing breadth of knowledge.

On 16 March 1813 Frederick William III of Prussia declared war on France. Russia was no longer alone in its war against Napoleon. Armand de Caulaincourt, one of the men closest to Napoleon, wrote:

> [Napoleon] therefore believed that he could tempt the fate of arms and have a good chance of success, by presenting himself early on the battlefield. He also felt that he needed a success to wash away our setbacks and to be able to speak the language that suited the power of France. Our new corps were being formed, some cohorts had already crossed the Rhine; the remnants of the Russian army, rallied and reorganised, were nevertheless obliged to withdraw in the face of superior forces that were growing daily. Ours were also increasing. Since the month of March, the Emperor's departure had been announced because the enemy, master of Dresden, was already on the Saale when all the means prepared and put into action so quickly were brought together and gave the Emperor the means to enter the campaign. Only the Guard had a few squadrons; the rest of our cavalry was in the rear, with the exception of a few small detachments, made up of conscripts, placed on horseback en route and which were then emerging from Mainz. As for the infantry, with the exception of the cohorts made up of men who had remained in France and had been in the army for a year, the rest had left their villages. The most highly trained had had rifles for a month, and most of them since their passage to Mainz, in other words for 24 hours. Many did not even receive one until Erfurt and on the road, on the eve of the battle of Lützen.[204]

203. Alain Pigeard, op. cit., p. 347.
204. Armand de Caulincourt, *Mémoires du général de Caulaincourt*, t. 2, p. 404.

On 23 March 1813 Bernadotte, Crown Prince of Sweden, although of French origin and Marshal of the Empire, signed an alliance with Russia, but did not yet declare war on France. Constant, the valet de chambre and sometime secretary of the French emperor, wrote in his memoirs:

> Since the Emperor had left the army and, as we have seen, left the command to the King of Naples, His Sicilian Majesty had himself abandoned the command entrusted to him, and had handed it over, on leaving for his states, to Prince Eugène. The Emperor was very eager for the news he received from Posen, where the main headquarters was located towards the end of February and the beginning of March; but the Prince Viceroy had under his command little more than the remnants of various corps, some of which were no longer represented by more than a very small number of men. Moreover, each time the Russians appeared in force, there was no other option but to withdraw; and each day, during the month of March, the news became more and more worrying. So at the end of March, the Emperor decided to leave very soon for the army ... No one was surprised when, before leaving, he entrusted the regency to the Empress Marie-Louise ... The Emperor left Saint-Cloud on 15 April at four in the morning. The following day at midnight, he entered Mainz. On arriving, His Majesty learned that Erfurt and the whole of Westphalia were in the grip of the most vivid alarms. Nothing could express the speed with which this news made him set off. In eight hours, he was in Erfurt ... On 1 May, he was in Lützen.[205]

The Russian army, taking advantage of the poor condition and inadequacy of the troops that made up the Grande Armée at the time, advanced without encountering any major obstacles in East Prussia and along the Baltic Sea. Welcomed favourably by the Prussian population, the Russians entered Königsberg on 5 January 1813. They surrounded Danzig, where there was a French garrison. Eugène de Beauharnais, commander of the remnants of the Grande Armée, was forced to evacuate the Grand Duchy of Warsaw. His rearguard and the Saxon allies were defeated on 13 February at Kalisz. The Russian army then resumed its march on Berlin, leaving troops along the way to block the French garrisons in a series of Prussian and Polish strongholds. Wittgenstein entered Berlin on 11 March, followed on 17 March by the Prussian corps, formerly part of the Grande Armée, led by General Yorck. At the same time the two duchies of Mecklenburg abandoned the French alliance. On 18 March the port city of Hamburg opened its doors to the Cossacks and created a volunteer corps, the Hanseatic Legion, to ensure the independence

205. Constant, *Mémoires intimes de Napoléon Ier*, t. 2, Paris, 1967, pp. 298–301.

of the German ports. On 26 March Frederick Augustus, King of Saxony and Grand Duke of Warsaw, who had remained loyal to Napoleon, was forced to flee before the Prussian army that occupied his capital, Dresden. At the beginning of April the duchies of Saxony-Anhalt joined the alliance of Russia and Prussia. On 21 April Frederick William of Prussia decreed the raising of the Landsturm, which included all Prussians between the ages of 15 and 60 who had not been drafted into the army. Prussia now had an active army of 280,000 men. Faced with this worrying situation, the French counter-attacked. General St-Cyr beat a British corps that had just landed but was himself beaten on the Elbe on 21 March. The Russians abandoned Hamburg, which was entrusted to Marshal Davout. He powerfully fortified the Hanseatic port and expelled 25,000 of its inhabitants. Napoleon, considered by all to be the only man who could turn the situation around, arrived with a new army, joining the one commanded by his adopted son Eugène de Beauharnais. As soon as he arrived, he confronted the Russo-Prussian army at Lützen.

Captain Pierre Robinaux, of the 130th line infantry regiment, described the Emperor's arrival at the army on 29 April:

> The Emperor soon passed through with part of his Guard; he was arriving at the army; we had not yet seen him since crossing the Rhine; so the cannon soon began to be heard; we saw the smoke a moment after we had passed the town. Then we said: 'Napoleon has arrived, everything will be fine.'[206]

Désiré Chlapowski, squadron leader of the Polish lancers of the Imperial Guard, described the battle of Lützen, the first victory of this campaign:

> On 2 May, the march continued towards Leipzig ... Around 10 a.m. we heard a very heavy cannonade and musketry fire behind the village of Kaja. Behind the Guard followed the corps of Marshal Marmont, and finally the corps of General Bertrand, aide-de-camp to the Emperor. The entire Prussian and Russian army suddenly attacked Marshal Ney's corps, which consisted only of young soldiers from the first bench. They were unable to withstand this vigorous attack by the enemy infantry, supported by a large artillery force, and abandoned Kaja. Ney's entire corps was routed, and the young soldiers threw down their weapons, which littered the ground on which we had just arrived. The moment was critical. The Emperor was on horseback at the head of the Guards on the march; he ordered Prince Eugène to deploy on the right; in this way he drew closer to the Emperor. The latter, turning his horse, ordered

206. Pierre Robinaux, *Journal de route du capitaine Robinaux, 1803–1832*, Paris, 1908, p. 127.

us to follow him at a trot, and ordered the Guards infantry which was behind (it was the Young Guards) and the Guards artillery to follow us. After half an hour we stopped between the road and the village of Kaja, and deployed in a line opposite this village, on the fields where the remnants of Ney's young soldiers were still fleeing. The entire French army, with its 120,000 men, marched in columns towards Leipzig, where the Emperor hoped to find the enemy; he had therefore prepared to deploy it in front, and it was even easier for him to manoeuvre to deploy it on the right. All the French corps, by a flanking movement, moved to the right, while the Guard alone moved backwards for half an hour to reach the threatened point, opposite the village of Kaja, already occupied by the enemy.

When we arrived in front of Kaja, we were met by artillery salvos and a fusillade from the gardens. The Emperor gave the order not to let Ney's fugitives pass between our squadrons: they were obliged to withdraw behind our left wing, that is to say between us and the Young Guard which was advancing. As a result, instead of scattering across the plain, they were forced to mass to escape the enemy's cannonballs. Most of them were officers and non-commissioned officers, all old soldiers: it was therefore fairly easy to reform them behind us, as they had not thrown down their weapons like the younger soldiers, but they were few in number. The artillery finally arrived. The Emperor immediately had two batteries put into position, and had the Young Guard form up behind us in columns.

The enemy did not emerge from the village, all the houses of which he had put in a state of defence, and the thick column of his cavalry took up position on the left of Kaja, so close to us that we could recognise in the front line a regiment of cuirassiers and a regiment of black hussars alongside. We could clearly hear their commands during the very short intervals when the cannon fire ceased. We could also see various movements in the columns to the rear of these regiments.

We were sure that the enemy was going to pounce on us and attack us with cavalry large enough to surround our right. We were well prepared to receive them, but they had wasted too much time in preparatory movements, and the decisive moment for them passed very quickly. In war, an army commander must be quick to decide, because a move that is advantageous at one moment becomes unworkable five minutes later. Decision and presence of mind are the sine qua non qualities of a leader.

The French batteries followed one another at every moment on the battle line. The Emperor ordered all artillery to direct fire on the village, and also had my two squadrons advance by platoon to the right. The other two squadrons commanded by Jerzmanowski did the same

> on the left, leaving an interval between us. The Emperor drew his sword, placed himself between the two columns of the Young Guard, threw himself with them towards the village and entered it without a shot being fired; the shooting in the gardens had ceased. The enemy cavalry did not move. The situation had changed: we had gone from the defensive to the offensive. Marshal Marmont's corps could be seen in the distance on our right wing. It is probable that at the sight of Marmont's corps on the march, the enemy cavalry, so numerous, stopped to prepare some manoeuvre; the enemy's attack to envelop the French right wing would have had a better chance of success if he had used this cavalry usefully instead of defending with all his forces the villages of Kaja, Bahna and Görschen, which became his tomb … a few moments later, the Emperor sent us the order to follow him, and we crossed the village filled with dead and wounded: In several places these unfortunate people, both French and enemy, were lying pell-mell on top of each other. In particular, we saw a gigantic soldier of the Prussian Guard and a small, very young French soldier standing there as if they were embracing: they looked like father and son, as General Lefebvre-Desnouettes, who was at the head of my squadron, remarked when he saw them ...
>
> After crossing Kaja, we formed up behind the Young Guard, which was pursuing the retreating enemy from all sides. Prince Eugène had more difficulty on our left wing. He had in front of him a Russian corps commanded by Wittgenstein, which only began to withdraw when it saw the Young Guard in hot pursuit of the Prussian corps, and when the artillery attacked from the flank. The entire enemy line was then in retreat in front of us; the enemy cavalry on our right wing was also withdrawing, pursued by Marmont's marines, and further to the right by General Bertrand's corps. At daybreak, Napoleon ordered all the corps to halt, but to remain under arms. Before it was completely dark, we saw the enemy cavalry stop, while the infantry continued its retreat.[207]

In his account of the battle of Lützen, Chlapowski made a remark that highlighted the main weakness of the new Grande Armée, which was to limit the impact of Napoleon's victories: the lack of cavalry, which prevented him from pursuing defeated enemies: 'We only had 2,400 cavalry left, and the Emperor did not want to use them, so as not to reduce the number.'[208] Squadron Leader Mathieu Hubert commanded an artillery company. He was present at the battle of Lützen and confirmed Chlapowski's remark: 'Seeing that we did

207. Désiré Chlapowski, *Mémoires sur les guerres de Napoléon, 1806–1813*, Paris, 1908, pp. 306–13.
208. Chlapowski, op. cit., p. 312.

not move, they stopped, and an hour later we saw their rearguard withdraw. We set off in pursuit, but we did not have enough cavalry to take advantage of our situation.'[209]

As was often the case during the great victories of the past, for this new campaign Napoleon had a proclamation read out to the troops, which was immediately echoed throughout the empire:

> Soldiers! I'm so pleased with you! You have fulfilled my expectations! You have made up for everything with your good will and your bravery. On the famous day of 2 May, you defeated and routed the Russian and Prussian armies commanded by Emperor Alexander and the King of Prussia. … We will send these Tartars back to their dreadful climates which they must not cross. Let them remain in their icy deserts, dwellings of slavery, barbarism and corruption, where man is reduced to the equal of brute. You have well deserved civilised Europe. Soldiers! Italy, France and Germany give you thanks! From our imperial camp at Lützen, 3 May 1813.[210]

It should be noted that this proclamation was mainly directed against the Russians, with the Prussians barely mentioned. In Paris, on hearing the news of this victory, the authorities decided to celebrate it with a simple mass of thanksgiving, to be held on Sunday, 23 May in the presence of the Empress Marie-Louise.[211] On the other side, the official Bulletin of the Russo-Prussian army presented the battle as won by Wittgenstein and Blücher and confirmed the lack of cavalry on the French side.[212] As is often the case, the assessments of the battle presented by the adversaries proved to be inaccurate. The allies lost 12,000 men dead, wounded or missing, and Lieutenant Generals von Scharnhorst and Kanownitzin died of their wounds. The French suffered 2,757 killed and 16,898 wounded, two generals were killed and five cannon fell into enemy hands.[213]

After the defeat of their armies, Frederick William and Alexander retreated towards Dresden, the capital of Saxony, Napoleon's ally. Napoleon pursued his enemies and marched on the city, which the allied sovereigns were forced to abandon. After a short stay in Dresden, Napoleon resumed the pursuit of the enemy army. The Russians and Prussians had halted their march and dug in at the village of Bautzen.

---

209. Mathieu Hubert, *Souvenirs du chef d'escadron Mathieu Hubert*, Paris, 1910, pp. 29–30.
210. *Journal de l'Empire*, 19 May 1813, p. 3.
211. *Journal de l'Empire*, 19 May 1813, p. 3.
212. *Bulletins officiels de la Grande Armée, recueillis et publiés par Alexandre Goujon, Campagnes de Russie et de Saxe*, Paris, 1821, p. 209.
213. Digby Smith, op. cit., pp. 416–19.

Bautzen and Wurschen

The war was not over and May 1813 was to prove bloody. The newspaper *Le Moniteur universel* of Sunday, 30 May 1813 reproduced the account of the days leading up to the battle of Bautzen, as sent by Napoleon to Empress Marie-Louise:

> The Emperor left Dresden on the 18th; he slept in Harta, and on the 19th, at 10 o'clock in the morning, he arrived in front of Bautzen. He spent the whole day reconnoitring the enemy positions. On the 20th, at eight o'clock in the morning, the Emperor moved to the high ground behind Bautzen. He ordered the Duke of Reggio to cross the Spree and attack the mountains supporting the enemy's left, the Duke of Taranto to build a trestle bridge over the Spree between Bautzen and the mountains, and the Duke of Bragg to build another trestle bridge over the Spree, in the depression formed by this river, on the left, half a league from Bautzen; to the Duke of Dalmatia, to whom His Majesty had given the higher command of the centre, to cross the Sprée to threaten the enemy's right; finally to the prince of the Moscowa, under whose orders was the third corps, Count Lauriston and General Régnier, to close on Klix, to cross the Spree, to turn the enemy's right, and to move on his headquarters of Wurschen and from there on Weissenberg.[214]

Désiré Chlapowski, who was at Napoleon's side during this battle, reported the following anecdote at the time:

> We formed the centre and put in communication the left wing and the right wing, because the Emperor carried from the centre to the left the corps of Marshal Marmont and the cavalry of General La Tour-Maubourg; Marshal Ney had in fact warned that he had encountered bad roads and could not arrive in line until around midday. On receiving this news, the Emperor ordered the infantry attack to be suspended, but the cannonade did not cease, and on our right wing, in the mountains and in the middle of the scrub, the fire of the skirmishers continued uninterrupted on both sides. It was to the sound of this artillery and musketry that the Emperor lay down on a cloak unfolded on the ground and gave orders that he should not be woken up for two hours; he fell asleep as peacefully as possible in front of us. During these two hours, on our right wing, in the mountains, the whistling of the skirmishers' bullets and the cannonballs of a dozen cannons that the French had

214. *Bulletins de la Grande Armée*, 1813, pp. 69–70.

brought up there could be heard continuously. The enemy had more guns on this point than we did, as they had had plenty of time to prepare to receive us. In the centre, only the guns in front of us were firing, and we could hear a fairly weak fire from the skirmishers in the ravines. From time to time we received enemy cannonballs; about fifteen of them ricocheted off us, but rolled towards us without hurrying and without doing us any harm. One fell near the Emperor. ... Napoleon was still sleeping peacefully when the orderly Béranger arrived from Marshal Ney, bringing the news that the Marshal's corps, after having travelled along sandy roads, was emerging on the right wing of the enemy, who was placed on a height which he had fortified with entrenchments, as could be seen. Marshal Duroc, who was walking beside the Emperor, did not want to wake him before two hours had passed, so accustomed was everyone to carrying out his orders meticulously. He looked at his watch and said, 'Twenty minutes to go.' These twenty minutes had not yet passed when loud detonations of artillery were heard on the Russian positions on our left wing; one could see not only the smoke, but even the flashes of the salvos. This cannonade began so suddenly that the Emperor woke up shouting: 'It's Ney who's attacking!' He mounted his horse, sent his officers to all the marshals with orders to attack, and added: 'In an hour's time, victory will be ours.'

But he was wrong in his prediction of the time, for an hour had passed and the enemy's right wing was still holding its ground, the fire did not cease and seemed, on the contrary, to increase; salvos could be heard from the companies. The Emperor sent his officers off one after the other almost every 10 minutes; none of them came back ... He called me and said: 'Quick, go near Ney, and tell him to hurry up and attack with all his forces! Marmont is already approaching his right wing to support him.' I found Marshal Ney at the height of the fire, in the middle of the infantry columns that had been pushed back and were forming up again. The first columns I encountered were Württemberg, retreating in great disorder, then French columns also in retreat, but with more order. I repeated the Emperor's words to the marshal; Marshal Ney swore in reply: 'Tell the Emperor that I have Russians in front of me. If I had had Prussians, I would have taken the position a long time ago. Now I only want to use the French; I'm going to send the allied troops back, they are no match for the Russians.' ... Ney knocked the enemy off their feet at the village of Klix, crossed the Spree, and pushed what was in front of him as far as the village of Preilitz. The Duke of Dalmatia began to push forward at one o'clock in the afternoon. The enemy, who had realised the danger he was threatened with by the direction the battle had taken, felt that the only way to sustain the fight against the Prince of Moskowa with any advantage was to prevent us from emerging, and wanted to oppose the Duke of Dalmatia's attack. The moment to decide the battle was now. In 20 minutes, the Emperor moved to the left, with the guard, the four La Tour-Maubourg divisions and a large quantity of artillery, on the right flank of the enemy's position, which had become the centre of the Russian army. The Morand division and the Württemberg division took the hillock that the enemy had used as a stronghold ... General Devaux set up a battery and directed its fire on the masses trying to retake the position ... The Duke of Treviso headed for the Klein-Baschwitz inn, cutting the road from Wurschen at Bautzen. The enemy was forced to clear his right to counter this new attack. Ney took advantage of this and marched forward. He captured the village of Preissig and, having outflanked the enemy army, advanced on Wurschen. It was three o'clock in the afternoon and when the army was in the greatest uncertainty of success, and a frightful fire was heard, the Emperor announced that the battle was won. The enemy, seeing his right turned, retreated, and soon his retreat became a flight ...

At four in the morning on the 22nd, the French army set off. Throughout the night, the enemy had searched every road and every direction. His first positions were only found beyond Weissenberg, and he only put up resistance on the heights behind Reichenbach; the enemy had not yet seen our cavalry. General Lefebvre-Desnouettes, at the head of 1,500 horses of the Polish lancers and the red lancers of the guard, charged the enemy cavalry on the plain of Reichenbach and knocked them out.

The enemy, believing that they were alone, brought forward a cavalry division and several divisions engaged in succession. General La Tour-Maubourg with his 14,000 horses and the French and Saxon cuirassiers came to their aid and several cavalry charges took place. The enemy, surprised to find 15,000 to 16,000 cavalry men in front of them, when they thought we had none, withdrew in disorder ... In the battles of the 20th and 21st, the Württemberg general Franquemont and General Lorencez were wounded. Our losses during these days can be estimated at 11 or 12,000 men killed or wounded. On the evening of the 22nd at seven o'clock, the Grand Marshal, Duke of Frioul, lay on a small eminence talking with the Duke of Treviso and General Kirgener, all three standing on the ground and quite far from the fire, ... one of the enemy's last cannonballs grazed the Duke of Treviso closely, ripping open the Grand Marshal's lower abdomen and throwing General Kirgener to his death. The Duke of Frioul was immediately stricken to death and died 12 hours later.[215]

215. Désiré Chlapowski, op. cit., pp. 325–8.

The death of Marshal Duroc, Duke of Frioul, who was a close collaborator and one of the Emperor's few friends, was a heavy blow for Napoleon.

On 23 May a parliamentarian sent by the Russian and Prussian sovereigns arrived at the Emperor's residence bearing several letters. The rumour immediately spread that the enemies were asking to negotiate an armistice. From 30 May to 2 June armistice negotiations were held between General de Caulaincourt for France, Count Schuvalov for Russia and General Kleist for Prussia. Instructions had been given for a cessation of hostilities between the two armies. The armistice was signed on 4 June and was to endure until 20 July, to allow the belligerents to discuss the terms of a possible peace. The allies, frightened by Napoleon's initial successes, wanted a break in the fighting, in which Napoleon had a clear superiority, to allow Austria, which they knew was ready to join the anti-French coalition, to complete its mobilisation. Aware of his strength, Napoleon had almost refused this truce, but his situation was not easy. The losses on the battlefields of Lützen and Bautzen had been heavy, the army, largely composed of young soldiers, was exhausted, there was a shortage of cavalry (although reinforcements were expected) and, moreover, the generals were showing signs of weariness. His entire entourage had put pressure on the Emperor to accept the truce. In addition, the news from France was not good: despite the Te Deum celebrating the victories in Saxony, the public mood was increasingly worried and the desire for peace was growing.[216]

Nicolas-Joseph Petitjean, a rifleman in the 147th line infantry regiment, wrote to his parents from Breslau, announcing the provisional cessation of hostilities:

> Since we left Munster, we have been on the march without knowing our destination. We are fighting with the Russians every day and pursuing them. The first day, we had a lot to do. The enemy attacked us at dusk and after an hour and a half we drove them off. The next morning we entered Breslau armed. On 2 June we were told that there had been a suspension of arms and that there was hope of peace. We were billeted to await the outcome.
>
> We have not been fighting since 2 June! We are waiting for peace or else war, stronger than ever.[217]

The armistice between the belligerents was signed on 4 June 1813 at Pläswitz, under the patronage of Austria, a neutral power, but a power whose entry into the war Napoleon was beginning to fear.[218]

216. Thierry Lentz, op. cit., pp. 412–13.
217. AEL, FFP 1042–1045, Letter of Nicolas-Joseph Petitjean.
218. Napoléon Bonaparte, *Correspondance générale*, t. 13, p. 1069.

The planned congress in Prague was slow to open. However, the coalised nations agreed on a minimum number of conditions for the signing of an eventual peace. The projects accepted at the time essentially provided for the end of French hegemony over the Confederation of the Rhine, the end of the Grand Duchy of Warsaw and the return of Illyria to Austria. On 14 June Prussia and the United Kingdom signed a treaty of alliance at Reichenbach, in which Prussia agreed not to negotiate with Napoleon without the consent of Britain, which for its part wanted France to evacuate Holland and Spain; Prussia was granted a subsidy of one million pounds. On 15 June Russia also signed an agreement with England in which the Czar accepted the clauses of the Treaty of Reichenbach and received £600,000.

The congress intended to conclude the peace opened on 9 July in Prague. Emperor Francis I of Austria, assisted by Count Metternich, was the mediator. France was represented by Caulaincourt and the Count of Narbonne. Metternich presented the demands of the Austrian empire: abandonment of the Grand Duchy of Warsaw, independence of the Hanseatic cities, withdrawal of the French from Spain and Holland, cession of the Illyrian provinces, and Napoleon's relinquishment of the titles of Protector of the Confederation of the Rhine and Mediator of the Helvetic Confederation. Napoleon, informed of the Austrian proposals, agreed to give up Illyria and Spain and to cede the Grand Duchy of Warsaw to Russia, but without accepting the other demands. As the discussions failed to produce any concrete results, the armistice was extended until 10 August. At midnight on 10 August Count Metternich declared the congress over. On 12 August Austria declared war on France. In the meantime France had signed a treaty of alliance with Denmark on 10 July. Denmark claimed possession of Norway. As a result, France declared war on Sweden, and Denmark on Russia, Sweden and Prussia. Sweden's entry into the war, although it was not a major military power, would have important consequences for the rest of the campaign since its army was led by Prince Charles-Jean – none other than Bernadotte, Napoleon's former marshal, whose advice would be invaluable for the rest of the offensive: it was he who advised the allies to refuse to fight when Napoleon was in command in person and to attack when they were dealing with one of his marshals. This tactic proved effective. The coalition announced the resumption of hostilities on 17 August. Much to the indignation of his opponents, however, Blücher attacked the French on the 14th.

When the decision was taken to break the armistice, Brigadier General Antoine de Jomini abandoned Marshal Ney's staff and joined the Russian army; he was received by Emperor Alexander, who took him on as aide-de-camp. This desertion was not without consequences, as Jomini was in possession of all the documents for the forthcoming campaign and it was too late to change the plans.[219] A former French general, Moreau, who had been exiled to America since the Consulate because of his involvement in a conspiracy against Bonaparte, joined the allied camp and was given the title 'Feldmarschall' by Emperor Alexander.

Artilleryman Joseph Gougnard of the 1st marine artillery regiment, in a naive letter on the eve of the resumption of hostilities, gave his family news of the war:

> Grandemberg, 12 August 1813
>
> The armistice is always extended and postponed until 15 August. Today we received orders to leave on the first whistle. I am therefore taking the opportunity of writing to you to let you know that I am in good health. The war will start again on the 17th of this month. We must resume our line of battle where we had the present armistice. The strength of the Russian army is along the river Oder, as well as the Prussian army, where we expect to have a great battle.
>
> You will also be aware that the Russians and Prussians, retreating into Saxony, burnt down villages and even towns. The inhabitants had fled. In my first letter I gave you an account of three major battles. The first great battle was on the second of May last, a battle which was so honourable in the eyes of the French. The enemy outnumbered us by one hundred and fifty thousand men. This battle began on the ninth at ten o'clock in the morning and ended at 11½ o'clock in the evening. There was fire in various villages and in the Russian camp, which lit us up at dusk. The enemy cavalry charged our regiment three times in succession, believing they were more successful than during the day, but always poorly received. Victory remained undecided for a very long time. This battle is known as the battle of Luxenne.[220] We crossed the river Lippe on 8 May, which is about as strong as the Rhine. Here is where the forces of the Russian, Prussian, French and allied armies were combined, namely at the battle of Bautzen, which is the battle of the 20th and 21st, where we were, on both sides, 1,100,000 men combined. The fire lasted for two days without ceasing. Around twenty villages were burnt on the battlefield. The cannon fire was like a two-row fire. The shells burst in the air. You could no longer tell whether it was French or Russian as long as there were shells. At the battle on the twentieth, I enlisted as a skirmisher. I played dead on the battlefield. If

219. *Bulletin de la Grande Armée*, 6 September, pp. 133–4.
220. Lützen.

I had not taken that precaution, I would have been killed. We used the principle necessary for many. They showed no mercy to anyone. They slashed at the wounded they saw moving around. They wanted to enter the town of Bautzen. They were poorly received. When they got close to the town, the horses refused to move, they just stood up in the air. As you know, you cannot make an omelette without breaking eggs. If I had to tell you about my adventures, I would not need a letter but a book. I can tell you frankly that in the three great battles, I was in the front line. My moustache was curled many times by cannonballs, grapeshot, and bullets. The shako on my head also saved my life. A bullet cut the grenade from my plate. It did me no great harm. I can also tell you that countries that suffer the scourge of war are to be pitied. If I spoke to you in person, I would make you open your ears. ...[221]

The road to Leipzig

The second part of the Saxon campaign began on 14 August with an offensive by Blücher with 200,000 men towards the centre of the French position, while Marshal Schwarzenberg at the head of the Bohemian army headed towards Leipzig. Napoleon repulsed Blücher and decided to confront Schwarzenberg, who, on the advice of Moreau, was threatening Dresden, the capital of his Saxon ally; Napoleon entrusted the centre of the army to Marshal Macdonald. Meanwhile, Oudinot was charged with taking Berlin, where he would be joined by Davout from Hamburg. On 22 August Marshal Gouvion St-Cyr was beaten at Pirna by the Russians commanded by Wittgenstein. On 23 August Oudinot was defeated at Grossbeeren by Bernadotte, at the head of a corps of Russian, Prussian and Swedish troops, which prevented the French from advancing towards the Prussian capital. After various manoeuvres Napoleon, under the walls of Dresden with 155,000 men, found himself facing the army of the coalition, some 200,000 strong, commanded by Feldmarschal von Schwarzenberg.

Lieutenant de Bourgoing of the Young Guard was at the battle of Dresden:

The Russian and Austrian armies were already on the point of leading an attack that could be decisive: large masses were concentrated for this purpose, and the weak garrison prepared for a vigorous defence. The inhabitants of Dresden were deeply alarmed at the fate that threatened their city. A capture by force would have been a great misfortune for the capital. The Emperor arrived in person on the morning of 26 August, and his presence raised hopes that the enemy would be repulsed. Our columns followed him closely. From the heights that crown the horizon of this valley of the Elbe, a magnificent spectacle presented itself to our

221. AEL, FFP 1042–1045, Letter of Joseph Gougnard.

eyes. The two coalition armies covered the plain and spread out their long lines of infantry, we could make out the march of the battalions we were going to have to fight; but we too were running with numerous soldiers. The grenadiers of the Imperial Guard marched with us down the escarpments on the right bank of the Elbe; we were going to approach the enemy with enthusiasm and confidence. When our columns arrived at the bottom of this hill, in the first houses of the suburb of Dresden, we were told to halt, to wait for those who were following us and to make all the arrangements for a vigorous attack on the other bank of the river. Besides, our infantry, having covered more than 30 places in three days, needed a little rest. We were also given a few moments to dress for the battle that was about to begin. Our regiment had been placed in the gardens and courtyards of Link's baths, a place of pleasure much loved by the inhabitants of Dresden, to get ready for battle. One of my most esteemed comrades, whose name was Dolmery, then made a joke which has since taken on the character of a presentiment in our memories. He was the most handsome officer in the regiment; that day, after having shaved and dressed as well as he could, he said to me, laughing: 'At least, if I am picked up on the battlefield this evening, people will say: "he was a very handsome man!"' Two hours later he was blown away by a Russian cannonball. We had been directed towards one of the three bridges over the river, which we were about to cross under fire from the Russian batteries. The head of our column, having arrived at a narrow part of this suburb, was stopped for a moment by a congestion of carriages and wagons ... When we were on the other side of the bridge, an order from the Emperor led us into a street where we were to wait for the right moment to attack the enemy. The projectiles were aimed at this part of the city, shattering the tiles of the houses that sheltered us. This street was called Ziegelstrasse. I was on horseback to the right of the regiment and so found myself at the height of a low first floor where a whole peaceful Saxon family was groaning, very frightened at the moment by the tumult that was rumbling in the distance and the noise, closer up, produced by the enemy artillery fire ... The Young Guard's task was to emerge through the gates of Dresden closest to the Elbe and to attack the enemy threatening the city. These impetuous sorties by our regiments followed one another rapidly. Only the night stopped our momentum. We had pushed the enemy, who had been so threatening, away from Dresden. They had stopped a short distance away, and when night fell, the two armies were separated by only a few hundred paces. Our 9th regiment halted on the edge of the wood where the Russian infantry had withdrawn. At that moment, we received an order from an officer of the Emperor's command not to light any fires

> and to camp in square battalions, so as not to be surprised by a night attack. While our tired soldiers did their best to sleep in this position, I placed the chain of sentries. ... The next day, at daybreak, the battle began again. I was sent to the right of the wood on the road to Pirna. A skirmish, the usual prelude to a battle, had already begun between several of our regiments and the Russian infantry. I found one of my cousins, Richard de Soultrait, among the combatants. The day before, when the Young Guard was leaving, we had shaken hands and wished each other good luck ... At that moment I found him in line, safe and sound. I left him, and five minutes later he was wounded. At about eight in the morning, my regiment was ordered to cross the wood where the Russians had withdrawn. It had been completely evacuated during the night, but when our battalions emerged onto the plain, they were met by Austrian fire. The corps of the Duke of Treviso contributed mightily in these two days to the success of this victory, one of the most glorious that Napoleon had won.[222]

It is difficult to put a figure on the losses at this battle, as the various authors who wrote about it differ widely in their estimates. However, it is certain that the French lost at least 10,000 men. The allies suffered approximately 10,000 dead and wounded and 13,000 Austrian soldiers were taken prisoner. The French took 40 cannon and 15 flags from their enemies. During the battle of Dresden, the allies suffered one notable loss in the person of General Moreau, who, standing next to Czar Alexander, had both his legs blown off by a cannonball. He died on 1 September.

In the days that followed, various small encounters took place between the adversaries: the French won a victory on 27 and 28 August at Pirna under the command of General Vandamme, while they were defeated on 28 August at Retschow and on 29 August by the Russians at Plagwitz. In the latter battle the French suffered heavy losses: General Puthod, 100 officers and 3,000 soldiers were taken prisoner. Several regiments were completely wiped out. The French lost 16 cannon and three eagles. On 29 and 30 August General Vandamme's 37,000 men were beaten at Kulm by an army made up of Austrian, Prussian and Russian soldiers. The French suffered 5,000 killed and wounded and 10,000 taken prisoner, including Generals Van Damme, Haxo, Guyot and Heimbrot, while 21 cannon, 200 ammunition wagons, all the baggage, 2 eagles and 3 flags were lost. The 70,000 allied soldiers, commanded by the Russian general Barclay de Tolly, lost 11,319 killed or wounded. On 6 September Marshal Ney was defeated at Dennewitz by Prussian troops commanded by General von Bülow. The French suffered 6,500 killed and wounded and 13,500

222. Pierre de Bourgoing, *Souvenirs militaires du Baron de Bourgoing, 1791 -1815*, Paris, 1897, pp. 250-8.

captured. They lost 50 cannon, 300 ammunition wagons and 4 flags, while Prussian losses were slight. On 17 September Bavaria, Napoleon's oldest German ally and one of the most important, signed an armistice with the allies.

On the same day as the battle of Dresden, 26 August, the battle of Katzbach was fought between an army commanded by Marshal Macdonald and a Russo-Prussian corps commanded by Marshal Blücher. The battle was a disaster for the French and their allies. The French suffered 12,000 killed or wounded and 18,000 taken prisoner. They lost 105 cannon, 300 ammunition wagons and 2 eagles, while the Prussians lost 1,000 killed or wounded and the Russians 3,000.[223] The defeats of Napoleon's marshals rendered the Emperor's victory at Dresden useless.

In his memoirs, Marcellin Marbot explained the situation in which the French army found itself in October 1813:

> The iron circle within which the allies were preparing to enclose the French army, had not yet completely surrounded Leipzig, when the King of Württemberg, a man of violence but honourable, thought it his duty to warn Napoleon that the whole of Germany, incited by the English, was about to rise against him, and that he had barely sufficient time to retire with the French troops behind the Main, before all of the German Confederation abandoned him to join his enemies. He added that he himself, King of Württemberg, could not avoid doing likewise, as he was forced to accede to the demands of his subjects, who clamoured for him to go with the torrent of German public opinion and, breaking with Napoleon, range himself with the enemies of France. The Emperor, shaken by this advice from the most able and most faithful of his allies, is said to have considered retiring towards the mountains of Thuringia and Hesse, to get behind the river Saale and there wait for the allies to attack him, where they would be at a disadvantage on the difficult terrain, heavily wooded and full of narrow passes. This plan could have saved Napoleon; but it had to be executed quickly, before the enemy armies were completely united and near enough to attack us during the retreat. However, when it came to deciding to abandon a part of his conquests, the Emperor could not make up his mind; he was most unwilling to have it thought that he considered himself defeated because he sought refuge behind these inaccessible mountains. The over-boldness of this great captain was our undoing; he did not stop to consider that his army, weakened by numerous losses, contained in its ranks many foreigners who were waiting only for a favourable

223. Digby Smith, op. cit., pp. 442–3.

> opportunity to betray him, and that it was liable to be overwhelmed by superior forces in the great open plains of Leipzig.[224]

Captain Robinaux was at the battle of Leipzig in the 3rd corps commanded by Marshal Ney:

> On the 15 [October], nothing was done on either side, reviews and manoeuvres were the work of the day. Napoleon came to review our army corps: 3rd, 5th and 11th, commanded by the Duke of Taranto, Marshal Macdonald ... On 16, from seven o'clock in the morning, the enemy columns could be seen advancing at great speed; the army was staggered; everything presented the appearance of a great battle; immediately the cannon was heard on all sides; the most lively cannonade began on all points; At the end of an hour of fighting, our right had already made great progress; a considerable knoll situated to the north of the plain was taken by our columns of infantry who immediately went to crown this beautiful position; while our left wing faced the enemy, the right of our army put all its efforts into pushing back the left of the enemy army. Towards two o'clock in the afternoon, we had beaten the enemy on all points and gained more than a league of ground; the army fort had withdrawn to the support of a large wood situated to the south of the plain; immediately our corps moved forward and in close columns on a large village, Gossa; it was flanked by 80 cannon; this village was situated in an area where there were 10,000 Russians and Prussians who put up firm resistance. The village was taken and retaken several times; we took 200 prisoners. If all our soldiers had followed the attack with as much impetuosity as the brave General Bachelet had directed it, we would have taken 80,000 prisoners; the soldiers, mounted in the upper rooms and attics, fired through the windows; when they saw us enter the village, confusion became so great in their ranks and they found themselves so tightly packed in the streets that they could no longer use their weapons; More than 50 men had laid down their weapons, which they took up again when they saw us in such small numbers; we were pushed out of the village, which we recaptured a moment later; at the same time as we took control of the village for the second time, the brave General Bachelet-Damville fell dead at our side. At eight o'clock in the evening, we were forced to leave the village, which was taken back from us; then the fire ceased at all points, and everyone took up their positions; there were considerable losses on both sides; the night

224. Marcellin Marbot, op. cit., t. 2, pp. 490–1.

was very cold; each soldier lay on his pack, rifle between his arms, fearing to be surprised.

On 17, there was nothing on either side; we reorganised and held talks which had no beneficial effect; the day of the 17 passed thus; on the evening of the 17 we concentrated to gather all the forces ready to give battle on the 18 in the morning, which did not fail; at around eight o'clock, the attack began on all points. We put up firm resistance; until 11 o'clock we had not lost an inch of ground when suddenly the infamous treachery of the Saxons, who were part of our army and occupied part of the right wing, occurred; they turned 40 guns on us; what a fatal blow for France! What a sudden change! How could we repair such a disaster, such a foiled battle plan? We had to think about retreat; how could we sustain it with a breach, a break in the army? Finally, Napoleon the Great, undaunted and always prompt in his military dispositions, marched with a division of his guard and confronted the troops who had just turned their weapons on us. The enemy made every effort to shake our army, which resisted this terrible and disastrous shock on every point. It remained unshaken. Finally, the retreat was ordered and carried out at the same time. Our corps (3rd) and two regiments of the Young Guard had to support the most important point, the village of Reudnitz, situated to the east of Leipzig, which was the centre of the army (the troops of the Prince of Moskowa, that is to say the 3rd and 6th corps of the Durutte division, distinguished themselves above all by their heroic obstinacy). Less than 40,000 men had fought all day against 150,000 enemies without being supported, except in the evening by some cavalry and a division of the Imperial Guard. This position had to be held or the army would be driven in: the village was taken and retaken six times in succession; by the sixth charge we were in control; this unfortunate village became frightening to look at. By eight o'clock in the evening, it was ablaze with flames; not a single house was not damaged. The shooting continued until midnight; the last shots were very fatal for one of my great friends, a highly educated captain. We left the village at 11 a.m. to set up outposts and form a line of skirmishers under cover in a large ditch to support the retreat at daybreak. A bullet hit the captain in the lower abdomen; immediately I saw him fall to the ground saying to me: 'My dear Robineau, I'm dead!' I had him taken to the ambulance where the surgeons looked after him carefully. All the care was useless; two hours later he had passed away; throughout the night, the retrograde movement was carried out in the greatest order; all the Guard and cavalry had passed Leipzig.

On 18, 95,000 cannon shots were fired; in the five days of fighting, more than 250,000 were fired. On the morning of 19, the town was still very crowded; caissons were blown up to prevent them from remaining in enemy hands. All the army corps on the eastern heights of the town moved and took up positions on the glacis to support the retreat. The walls were all crenellated and the glacis bristling with cannon; finally, all measures were taken to evacuate our artillery and the army's baggage, which was numerous. The enemy army received a Saxon parliamentarian, who addressed the Emperor of Russia, to ask him to spare the city and its inhabitants; this request was rejected by the Emperor of Russia; a parliamentarian sent for the same purpose by the Duke of Taranto was no happier. Thus Leipzig, attacked by all the forces of the coalition armies, was destined to suffer the fate of a city taken by assault. Before starting the action, Blücher gave the French army the ridiculous summons to lay down their arms; he did not have the honour of a reply. Immediately the charge was heard on all points of the enemy army; we saw on the heights columns which followed one another and seemed to descend from the clouds; a redoubling of the cannonade was heard; the enemies immediately fell on the town; to make matters worse, the bridge which was to serve us for the retreat was mined; by clumsiness or treachery the fire was put there, and it blew up at the same moment; four corps of armies still occupied the town. The explosion of the bridge was heard; the noise spread through the ranks, terror seized the soldiers, confusion and the most terrible disorder multiplied throughout the army; the soldiers of the train cut the lines, and the gunners abandoned their guns; everything was immediately mixed up, artillery, cavalry, soldiers of the train and infantry. The Saxons fired through the cross-arms; the army rushed into the river; the surface of the water was soon covered with nothing but the dead and dying. Pitiful cries were heard from all sides! Prince Poniatowski rushed with his horse into the river, his horse fell under him, he was carried away by the current and disappeared. His body was found a few days later, in the place where he had lost his life ... During this unfortunate disaster, I noticed an infinite number of senior and junior officers who, fearing that they would not be able to cross the river, sat down on the naval pieces lying here and there along the river, saying: 'The enemy will do what he likes with me, I'm not crossing the river, I'd rather die on the spot!' There was still a small stone bridge over the river, closed by an iron gate surrounded by wire netting, which was also broken down and opened; this gate was three feet wide and eight feet high; in the space of two minutes it was surrounded by a crowd of more than 10,000 men. The more they tried to pass through it, the less the number of those who did pass; the crowd was so great that when I went to pass it, there were more than three feet of dead and dying men crushed by their own

> comrades. I wanted to get involved in this mess, so I almost fell victim to it; when I had penetrated a certain distance from this misguided mass, I felt my strength weakening and I was infallibly going to fall under the feet of this crowd which had lost all feeling of humanity and was thinking, each one, only of his personal safety; selfishness was at its height, men had lost all use of reason: They could no longer get along, leaders were no longer listened to, in short, misfortune was at its worst. I withdrew as best I could; I immediately went along the river to find the place least crowded with men, so as to pass more easily and not be caught by my clothes; that was all I had to fear; there were an infinite number who, although they knew how to swim, drowned in this way. I took my sword and my watch between my teeth, and I swam out; fortunately I made it through without any obstacles. … It was with difficulty that I climbed onto the bank, so heavy were my clothes, but at last I made it. The inhumanity with which the ladies of Leipzig saw the bloody spectacle will always remain engraved in my memory. When I was in the river, I turned round several times and saw quite a large number of ladies on the balconies of a palace and several neighbouring houses, laughing at the most distressing scene and applauding with handkerchiefs waving from their windows. What barbarity! Less civilised peoples would have recoiled in horror and dread, whereas a civilised nation laughs at misfortune![225]

Until 30 October, in Paris and throughout France, the population received news only of Napoleon's victories from the front. On Sunday, 31 October the Parisian newspapers published the *Situations de l'armée* sent to the empress, dated 4, 15, 16 and 24 October. It was not until reading the last of these that the defeat at Leipzig was revealed. It was attributed exclusively to the treachery of the Saxon army and, above all, to the destruction of the bridge over which several units of the army had to retreat. There was great consternation, for the blow was unexpected. A few days before the battle of Leipzig, a senatus-consult had ordered a new levy calling to arms all available conscripts from the year XI to 1814, and the early call-up of the class of 1815. This levy was supposed to provide the Emperor with 280,000 new soldiers. To arrive at the prescribed figures, the prefects were obliged to no longer take into account the reasons for legal exemption from conscription. As a result, the number of draft dodgers rose sharply in some départements, and operations to reconstitute the army were accelerated. On the other hand, the call-up of the 1815 class arrived unexpectedly and the municipal and departmental lists were not ready. The arrival of these young conscripts was therefore slower.

225. Pierre Robinaux, op. cit., pp. 160–8.

In Saxony, according to the news sent from Leipzig on 6 November and published in the *Journal de l'Empire*, the civilian population was suffering from the large numbers of Russian soldiers passing through. The King of Saxony, who remained Napoleon's ally to the end, was taken as a prisoner to Berlin, while the Russian prince Repnin was appointed Governor of Saxony on 1 November.

The last battles

After the battle of Leipzig, the French army retreated towards the territory of the empire. The Bavarians, who had just entered the war against France, tried to prevent the retreating army from passing through. In a letter to his father, sent from Mainz on 16 November 1813, Lieutenant Franconin of the Imperial Guard gave a brief account of this episode:

> We had enough trouble in our retreat from Leipzig. On the 16th and 18th, we were quite exposed and were lucky to lose only a few men per company. A more or less similar loss awaited us at Hanau, on October 30, for the unfortunate Bavarians, traitors to their interests and their oath, planned to stop the French army 16 leagues from its borders. There they learned what they had witnessed many times before, that French courage and intrepidity are equally formidable in reverses of fortune as in the most brilliant successes.[226]

On 1 November 1813 Napoleon arrived in Frankfurt and left the army for Mainz, where he arrived the next day with part of his guard and artillery, as well as the 6,000 Bavarian prisoners taken at Hanau. Jérôme Bonaparte, threatened by the allied troops, abandoned his capital and took refuge in Cologne. At the same time the French rearguard evacuated Frankfurt, pursued by the allied troops. By 7 November the entire imperial army had crossed the Rhine again. The Duke of Taranto organised the defence of the empire on the left bank of the river. Napoleon, hoping for an offensive comeback, nevertheless left behind the strongholds occupied by his army. In Erfurt, Dresden, Hamburg, Danzig and several smaller towns he left large garrisons, in all numbering 80,000 men, not one of whom returned to France before the fall of the empire. He was to miss these troops cruelly in the months that followed. It was a major strategic error.

On 9 November Napoleon arrived in Paris and immediately set to work to reconstitute the forces of the empire.[227] On hearing of the French defeat at

226. François Franconin, 'Lettres et souvenirs du commandant Franconin', in: *Carnet de la Sabretache*, 2e série, Paris, 1909, p. 799.
227. *Journal de l'Empire*, 10 novembre 1813, p. 1, 2e colonne.

Leipzig, Holland rose and drove out the French troops. On 3 November the kingdom of Württemberg abandoned the French alliance. On 9 November the allies announced that they agreed that France should confine itself to its natural limits, which were the Rhine, the Alps and the Pyrenees, and that a town on the right bank of the Rhine should be neutralised for negotiations, but without suspending military operations. The Grand Duchy of Frankfurt was occupied by Bavaria on 11 November. On leaving Saxony, Napoleon had left a strong garrison (36,000 men) in the capital, Dresden, under the command of Marshal Gouvion St-Cyr.

General Duc de Fézenzac was in the city. He recounted:

> Our last attempt to leave had taken place on 6 November, and the very next day negotiations for the capitulation began. I learned later that Marshal St-Cyr had had the idea of putting me in charge. The Count of Lobau told him that it was a sad commission to give to the youngest general in the garrison, and fortunately I was spared. Nothing would have been more painful than having to deal with a capitulation. It was soon concluded; both sides were in a hurry to get it over with. Thirty-three generals, including several wounded and sick, and 33,000 men were included in the capitulation of Dresden ... It was agreed that the garrison would lay down their arms and return to France via Switzerland, the officers would keep their weapons, their horses and their private property ... The capitulation was signed on the 11th, and the first column, made up of the first and second divisions, commanded by General du Monceau, set off on the 12th. ... We arrived in Altenburg on 17 November after a six-day march. The last column had left Dresden in the morning. The Russian general in command at Altenburg seemed very surprised by our arrival, of which he said he had received no notice. He suspended the march of the columns, awaiting orders. Soon a strange piece of news was circulating; nobody wanted to believe it. The Prince of Schwarzenberg refused to ratify the capitulation and declared us prisoners of war.[228]

Schwarzenberg offered Gouvion St-Cyr the option to return with his troops to Dresden. The French marshal refused and went into captivity with his men.

On 16 November Napoleon, aware of the difficult situation and the pressure of public opinion demanding peace, agreed to hold a congress with the coalition powers in the town of Mannheim. This congress never took place. On 30 November William of Orange, son of the former Stathouder, landed in

228. Raymond de Montesquiou-Fézenzac, *Souvenirs militaires de 1804 à 1814*, Paris, 1870, pp. 516–17.

Holland, supported by English troops. On 1 December, meeting in Frankfurt, the allied powers proclaimed that they were not waging war against France, but against the preponderance that the Emperor Napoleon exercised outside the limits of his empire; they gave assurances that they would leave France a larger area of territory than it had had under its kings, and declared that they would not lay down arms until the political state of Europe was once again consolidated, and general peace assured.

On 15 December the allies agreed on a plan to invade France. Prince Bernadotte would attack from Holland with 155,000 men. His objective would be Paris. Marshal Schwarzenberg would pass through Switzerland with 200,000 men, while a third army, under Marshal Blücher, would cross the Rhine between Koblenz and Mannheim.

It was not only in Germany that the situation was difficult for the French armies. In Spain, Wellington had defeated Joseph Bonaparte at Vitoria on 21 June. The troops commanded by Marshal Jourdan fled back across the Pyrenees, evacuating all of Spain except Catalonia. On 7 October Wellington's troops won the battle of Bidassoa, on 10 October the battle of Nivelle, and on 9–12 December the battle of La Nive. The south of France was gradually invaded and for the French the year 1813 ended under gloomy auspices.

Civilians and soldiers alike were largely demoralised. The brand new General Boulart of the artillery of the Imperial Guard recounted a discussion he had at the start of the campaign with one of his friends:

> I received my friend, battalion commander Renaud, whose artillery was parked near mine, and I made him share my room. We did not fall asleep without talking at length about the misfortune of our position and the vague and gloomy prospects for the future. I was certainly not reassured; I only had to open my eyes to judge the seriousness of the evil; but my poor friend's premonitions went further than mine: he lacked that confidence in the Emperor which I did not completely lose until the moment of his fall, although I did not really see how he could pull himself out of it; he was, finally, greatly demoralised.[229]

In Italy Viceroy Eugène was under heavy attack from Austrian troops. After leaving the French army in Saxony on 19 October 1813, the day after the battle of Leipzig, Joachim Murat, King of Naples and Napoleon's brother-in-law, in the hope of keeping his crown, entered into negotiations with the Austrians and abandoned the French camp. He signed an alliance with Austria on 8 January 1814.

229. Jean-François Boulart, *Mémoires militaires du général baron Boulart sur les guerres de la République et de l'Empire*, Paris, no date, p. 309.

Marbot wrote about the beginning of the 1814 campaign:

> On 1 January, the enemies, after hesitating for three months before invading France, crossed the Rhine at several points, the two most important of these being firstly at Kaub, a market town situated between Bingen and Coblentz, where a rocky gorge greatly reduces the width of the river, and then at Basle where the Swiss handed over the stone bridge, in violation of their neutrality, a neutrality which they maintain or abandon according to their interests. It is estimated that some five to six hundred thousand allied soldiers entered a France exhausted by twenty-five years of war, half of whose troops were prisoners in foreign lands, and many of whose provinces were ready to defect on the first suitable occasion.[230]

The campaign that began in January 1814 was atypical. General Boulart remarked at the beginning of his reminiscences of that year: 'The particular character of the campaign that was beginning against an enemy that was advancing on all points at once, and numerous enough to present considerable masses everywhere, was that it had no plan. The Emperor went, as it were, from day to day; he took advice only from the reports he received; that was where he drew his inspiration, and it was after receiving them that he improvised his decisions. There were frequent examples of this during this short campaign.'[231]

The first major encounter between the enemies took place on 24 January. Marshal Mortier, at the head of 5,885 infantrymen and 2,567 cavalrymen, came up against a corps of 12,500 Austrians. The advantage remained with the French, who lost 500 men killed or wounded, and 200 taken prisoner. The Austrians lost 1,400 men killed or wounded. On 27 January, in a less important encounter, General Milhaud's 2,000 cavalrymen defeated 1,500 Russian hussars at St-Dizier. After entrusting the regency to the Empress on 23 January and appointing his brother Joseph lieutenant general of the empire on 24 January, Napoleon left Paris on the night of 24/25 January to take command of the army. On 29 January, for the first time in this campaign, Napoleon saw action. At the head of 36,000 men, he encountered a corps of 28,000 Prussians and Russians, commanded by Marshal Blücher, at Brienne. Jean-Marie Félix Girod de l'Ain, a battalion commander, took part in this battle:

> From Châlons, we marched via Vitry and Montiérender to Brienne, where, for the first time since crossing the Rhine, we encountered the enemy in force; he had seized the castle of Brienne, situated on a hill. When we arrived in sight of this position, it was almost dark and, a

230. Marcellin Marbot, op. cit., t. II, p. 559.
231. Jean-François Boulart, op. cit., p. 309.

few moments earlier, the Emperor had almost been kidnapped by a party of Cossacks who had been led by chance across the fields to the very spot where he was stopped, with only the duty squadron of *chasseurs à cheval de la garde*, who usually followed him, as escort. The appearance of the enemy at this point on the main road which leads from Montiérender to Brienne, at a time when numerous troops of the Guard and other corps were already further forward, was so unexpected and so swift that it caused confusion around the Emperor for a moment; but the service squadron soon repulsed the enemy, who probably did not even suspect the important capture he was about to make.

General Decouz's Young Guard division was put in charge of this night attack and had to tackle the position head-on, while Colonel Château (Marshal Victor's son-in-law) was ordered to turn it around at the head of a brigade from the Duhesme division; This last attack was the only one that succeeded, and the château remained in our power; but General Decouz's column, having come up against superior forces, was repulsed and completely separated from Colonel Château's column, so that the latter's successes were ignored and he was even thought to have fallen, with all his people, into enemy hands. For his part, General Decouz fiercely renewed his attacks, and the whole night was spent in furious fighting, illuminated by the burning of part of the town.

The enemy, giving up the hope of retaking the castle, had finally decided to retreat; but, as the castle was still believed to be occupied by the Russians, even after they had evacuated the town, [Decouz's men] continued to direct the fiercest attacks at it. For his part, Colonel Château, who had so vigorously protected the castle against the Russians after taking it, continued to defend it against the French, whom he mistook for enemies, while the same French were making the same fatal mistake with regard to him.

Judge for yourself the surprise of both the besieged and the besiegers when, at daybreak, they recognised that they were wearing the same uniform![232]

At the end of the battle of Brienne, Napoleon was almost killed by a Cossack. The story was told by Baron Fain, Napoleon's secretary:

The French army established its bivouacs in the plain between Brienne and the woods of Maizières. Our artillery convoys sped along the main avenue to take up the positions assigned to them; and Napoleon,

232. Jean-Marie Girod de l'Ain, *Dix ans de mes souvenirs militaires de 1805 à 1815*, Paris, 1873, pp. 343–5.

> after giving these last orders, returned along this same avenue to his headquarters at Maizières ... The weather was very dark, and in the confusion of this night camp, we could hardly recognise each other except from a distance, by the light of a few fires. At that moment, a band of Cossacks, attracted by the lure of booty and the noise of our caissons, slipped through the shadows of the camp and reached the road. General Dejean felt a sudden rush, turned round and shouted 'To the Cossacks!' At the same time, he wanted to plunge his sabre into the throat of the enemy he thought he had; but the latter escaped, and rushed at the horseman in the grey frock coat who was marching in front. Corbineau threw himself across; Gourgaud made the same move, and with a pistol shot at point-blank range, he cut down the Cossack at Napoleon's feet. The escort rushed forward, some of the Cossacks were sabred, but the rest of the band, seeing that they had been recognised, jumped the moat and disappeared.[233]

On the morning of the 30th the French army was completely in control of Brienne and the enemy withdrew towards Bar-sur-Aube. Blücher's retreating corps joined up with Schwarzenberg's army, which, having learned of Napoleon's success at Brienne, rushed to the aid of its Russian and Prussian allies. Napoleon, faced with the numerical superiority of his opponents, decided to retreat. However, it was impossible for him to make this move immediately, as the bridge over the Aube had been cut to stop Blücher when he marched on Troyes. The two armies therefore clashed at the battle of Rothière on 1 February 1814. The French army numbered 45,000 men and faced 120,000 Russian, Prussian, Austrian, Württemberg and Bavarian soldiers. The encounter ended with the allied army defeating Napoleon. The French lost 4,600 men killed or wounded, as well as 1,000 soldiers taken prisoner by the enemy and 73 cannon. Taking advantage of the night, Napoleon retreated via the bridge over the Aube, which had been repaired and was then cut off again to prevent pursuit. The allied troops, although victorious, were unable to take full advantage of the victory because they were too cautious. Nor were they able to prevent the retreat of Marshal Marmont, who had remained on the right bank to protect the army's retreat.

Napoleon went to Troyes, where he learned of the opening of the Congress of Châtillon-sur-Seine on 3 February. France was represented by the Duc de Caulaincourt, who faced representatives of Austria, Russia and Prussia, as well as Lord Castlereagh, the British foreign secretary. Abandoning the proposals made in Frankfurt in December, the allies affirmed their determination that France should return to its 1792 borders and be excluded from the future

233. Agathon Fain, *Souvenirs de la campagne de France* (manuscrit de 1814), Paris, 1914, pp. 17–18.

reorganisation of Europe. Napoleon refused these demands. On 6 February the army set off for Paris. According to Baron Fain, the morale of the troops was not very high at this time: 'The abandonment of Troyes and the prolongation of our retreat dissipated our last hopes. The soldiers marched in a dreary sadness that cannot be described. Where will we stop? This question was on everyone's lips.'[234]

The situation seemed all the more difficult because the latest news was bad: 'the couriers who came to join us in Nogent continued to bring unfavourable news: from the North, the enemies have occupied Aix-la-Chapelle and Liège, immediately after the departure of the Duke of Taranto; the Anglo-Prussian army is blockading Antwerp ... General Bulow, after having attempted a futile attack on the town, has left the English and Saxons there for observation; with his Prussians and Russians, he is advancing on Flanders; his advance guard has entered Brussels; Belgium is lost.'[235] Another piece of news reached Napoleon: Marshal Blücher had separated from Schwarzenberg's corps and was marching on Paris: 'It was up to Blücher's soldiers and Schwarzenberg's soldiers who would be the first to reach Paris. The Prussians were trying to get ahead of everyone; General York could already see the steeples of Meaux. The Russian general Sacken, who supported him, was at La Ferté. Two more marches and they would be bivouacked at the foot of Montmartre!'[236]

The division of their forces was a strategic error on the part of Napoleon's adversaries. The Emperor decided to attack Blücher on his flanks unexpectedly. On 10 February a small Russian corps of 3,700 men was surprised and defeated at Champaubert. Two generals were captured. On 11 and 12 February Napoleon, at the head of 25,000 men, attacked General Yorck's 32,000 Prussians and Russians at Montmirail and Château-Thierry. These French victories seemed to signal a turning point. The fighting continued apace. On 14 February Napoleon attacked General von Kleist at Vauchamps and defeated him. Also on 14 February the Russian general Tchernychev took the town of Soissons, where 800 Frenchmen were killed and 3,500 taken prisoner. On 16 February the Cossacks seized the town of Nemours, where they took prisoner the 600 men guarding a depot of the Imperial Guard.

Napoleon changed direction. On 17 February, with around 20,000 men, he defeated 4,200 Austro-Russians commanded by Wittgenstein at Mormant. On 18 February, at the head of 25,000 infantry and 5,000 cavalrymen, he won the battle of Montereau over Austrian and Württemberg troops. The French lost 2,000 men, while the allies suffered 1,400 killed or wounded and 3,600 of their soldiers were taken prisoner. On the 18th Squadron Leader Mathieu wrote in

234. Agathon Fain, op. cit., p. 33.
235. Agathon Fain, op. cit., p. 34.
236. Agathon Fain, op. cit., p. 46.

his diary: 'On the 18th, we took Montmirail; I was shot twice in my clothes while charging at Russian skirmishers; I took three of them to my battery! The Marshal said to me, 'Don't you want us to finish the campaign together? You can see how close we came to being deprived of your good services.'[237]

On 26 and 27 February Marshal Oudinot led an army of 30,000 men against Marshal Schwarzenberg, who commanded Austrian, Russian and Württemberg troops, also 30,000 men, at Bar-sur-Aube. Schwarzenberg was victorious. The French suffered 2,600 casualties and 500 prisoners, while 250 Austrians, 400 Bavarians and 1,250 Russians were killed, wounded or missing. The battle of Bar-sur-Aube marked a turning point in the campaign of 1814. From then on, the initiative largely belonged to the allies. A series of small battles, often to the enemy's advantage, showed that the French were no longer in control of the situation: Macdonald was beaten by the Austrians on 28 February at La Ferté-sur-Aube, while on the same day Marshal Marmont, with 14,500 men, beat 12,000 Prussians at Gué-à-Tresmes; on 1 March General Marchand, with 11,000 men, was beaten by the Austrians at Saint-Julien; on 3 March the Prussian von Bulow and the Russian Wintzingerode took the town of Soissons, whose garrison was taken prisoner. This capture, attributed by Napoleon to the treachery of the general commanding the town, enabled Marshal Blücher's troops to escape pursuit by the imperial army. On 3 and 4 March Marshal Macdonald and his 20,000 men were defeated by Schwarzenberg, commanding 32,000 Russians and Bavarians.

On 7 March Emperor Napoleon gave battle to the Russians commanded by General Wintzingerode at Craonne. The French army of 31,000 to 33,000 men faced 19,000 infantrymen and 4,000 cavalrymen. This battle was the bloodiest of the 1814 campaign. Both sides considered themselves victorious. The French lost between 5,400 and 8,000 killed, wounded or missing, while the Russians lost around 5,000 men, including two generals. It was in fact a victory for the allied army. The heavy French losses in this battle were mainly due to the action of the Russian artillery. Mathieu Hubert, in his diary, gave this battle only a brief mention: 'On the seventh, the battle of Craonne, which had no result.'[238] On the other hand, the *Bulletin* of 7 March 1814, intended to calm the worries of the Parisians, declared: 'Craonne, 7 March 1814. There has been a very glorious battle today for the French armies. The Emperor defeated the corps of Wintzingerode, Woronzow and Langeron combined with the debris of Sacken. We already have 2,000 prisoners and several cannon. Our army is in pursuit of the enemy on the road to Laon.'[239] The *Bulletin* of

237. Hubert Mathieu, *Souvenirs militaires du chef d'escadron Mathieu de 1787 à 1815*, Paris, no date, p. 37.
238. Hubert Mathieu, op. cit., p. 38.
239. *Bulletin de la Grande Armée*, 7 March 1814.

9 March reviewed in detail the events of the past few days and concluded: 'The battle of Craonne was extremely glorious for our arms. The enemy lost six generals; they estimate their losses at between 5 and 6,000 men. We lost 800 men killed or wounded.'[240]

On 8 March the coalition powers meeting at Chaumont, in the presence of Lord Castlereagh, impressed by Napoleon's successes in this campaign and arguing over the reorganisation of Europe after the victory, signed a treaty. The allies undertook not to negotiate or make a separate peace with France; they promised to provide 150,000 men each and to conclude a defensive alliance for twenty years. Britain would provide £5 million to the coalition. Austria obtained the assurance that Holland would be independent, as well as Switzerland and Italy.

On 9 and 10 March Napoleon, at the head of 31,000 infantrymen and 8,000 cavalrymen, was defeated by Blücher at the head of 75,000 infantrymen and 25,000 Prussian and Russian cavalrymen at Laon. The French lost 4,000 men killed or wounded and 2,500 taken prisoner, while Blücher's army suffered only 166 dead, 566 wounded and 12 missing. On 11 March an Austrian corps of 8,000 men defeated 6,000 French troops commanded by Major General Musnier at Mâcon. French losses amounted to 800 soldiers killed or wounded, and 500 taken prisoner. On 12 March the Russians and Prussians captured the city of Reims, whose garrison was largely made up of men from the Imperial Guard. The next morning Napoleon retook the city. It was his last victory of the 1814 campaign.

On 12 March, following a revolt in Bordeaux in support of the royal cause, the Duke of Angoulême and the British army entered the city, which proclaimed Louis XVIII King of France. These events made a strong impression on both the French population and the allied sovereigns.

On 14 March General Merlin's 1,600 cavalrymen were beaten by 650 Prussian cavalrymen at Berry-au-Bac. General Janssens' young aide-de-camp Ferdinand de Cussy recounted a small encounter he had at the time:

> On the road we had a few engagements with the Russians, in particular at Sillery on 17 March, where we had to dislodge them. There were not many of them, but we found that they had drunk and broken nearly 3,500 bottles of champagne. After removing the necks with a sabre stroke, they broke the glasses, which was of no use to them, but in accordance with Moscow custom.[241]

240. *Bulletin de la Grande Armée*, 9 March 1814.
241. Ferdinand de Cussy, *Souvenirs du Chevalier de Cussy*, t. 1, Paris, 1909, p. 16.

On 20 and 21 March 1814 Napoleon's army met Marshal Schwarzenberg's army at Arcis-sur-Aube. Napoleon was defeated because of the disproportionate size of his army. He only had 23,000 infantrymen and 7,000 cavalrymen under his command, whereas Schwarzenberg had almost 100,000 soldiers. The French lost 3,400 killed or wounded in this battle, and had 800 soldiers taken prisoner; the allies had more than 3,000 killed, mainly Russians. This battle had major consequences for the French army:

> Up until then, Blücher had been beaten in detail, but Schwarzenberg had not been significantly affected: the failure at Montereau was nothing to an army as large as his, which was ultimately the main army, the army on which all events depended. The fact that we were forced to retreat in front of it, in the execution of a strategic movement during which the Emperor did not expect to meet it, manoeuvring on the same ground as himself, was significant and the direction we were taking was even more so. So there was a great deal of consternation and, from that day on, despondency set in. Where would we go? What would be the outcome of such a disproportionate struggle, in which the ratio between the combatants on both sides was like 10 to one? The field open to conjecture was vast, but none of it was reassuring.[242]

The soldiers were not the only ones to lose morale. Civilians began to despair of victory and sometimes even wanted Napoleon to be defeated. General Paul-Philippe de Ségur recounted an incident indicative of the mood of at least part of the French population:

> In the early hours of that night, we noticed that a Russian officer at the head of a strong detachment was trying to slip through our outposts; he was seized and an infamous letter was found on his person; it was signed by a wealthy inhabitant of the area. This Frenchman warned the nearest enemy general that 50 French soldiers were staying with him; he told him the way, the place and the most favourable time to surprise them! The wretch, seeing himself discovered, avoided the fate he deserved by hiding; to add a useless cowardice to his crime, he sent to beg one of our own, Colonel de Turenne, to intercede for him with the Emperor. He was told, with horror and contempt, to trust only the obscurity of his retreat.[243]

242. Jean-François Boulard, op. cit., p. 319.
243. Paul-Philippe de Ségur, *Histoire et mémoires, t. 7*, Paris, 1877, pp. 2–3.

On 23 March General Boulard heard of Napoleon's new plan:

> On the 23rd, we arrived very early at St-Dizier. The next day the army was at Doulevent when it received the order to go back to St-Dizier. This movement was carried out quickly; there was only one rather lively cavalry engagement, to our advantage, before arriving at St-Dizier; the enemy was driven out of the town and some troops were directed towards Bar-le-Duc. There was then only one rumour in the army, and that was that we were going to operate in Lorraine, rally the garrisons of the strongholds and intercept the enemy's main communications to Mainz and Strasbourg.[244]

On the same day, 23 March, Napoleon wrote a letter to his wife, Empress Marie-Louise, in which he revealed the direction he intended to take in the following days:

> On the 20th, I took Arcis-sur-Aube. The enemy attacked me there at six o'clock in the evening: the same day I beat them, killing 4,000 of them. I took two cannon from him, he took two from me, so that's even. On the 21st, the enemy army went into battle to protect the march of its convoys to Brienne and Bar-sur-Aube. I decided to attack the Marne and its communications in order to push it further away from Paris and get closer to my positions. I shall be in St-Dizier this evening. Farewell my friend. A kiss to my son.[245]

This letter was intercepted by the allies. Having learned of Napoleon's plans, they decided to march en masse towards Paris, instead of following him.

On 25 March Marshals Marmont and Mortier, with 17,000 infantrymen and cavalrymen, met the Crown Prince of Württemberg, who commanded a troop made up of Prussian, Russian and Austrians and soldiers from various small German states, totalling 28,000 men. The French marshals were defeated; the army under their command was the last protection for Paris. Sources vary widely on French losses in this battle. They range from 3,000 killed, wounded or missing and 3,000 prisoners, to 8,000 killed, wounded or missing and 8,000 prisoners. In addition, many French soldiers took the opportunity to desert. Allied losses totalled around 2,000 killed, wounded or missing.[246]

---

244. Jean-François Boulard, op. cit., p. 320.
245. Napoléon Bonaparte, *Correspondance générale*, t. 15, *Les chutes (1814–1821)*, Paris, 2018, p. 454.
246. Digby Smith, op. cit., pp. 513–14.

Meanwhile, Napoleon, convinced of the soundness of his plan to cut off the enemy's communications in Lorraine, continued to move away from the capital. A dispatch arrived from La Valette, director of the post office and one of the men in whom the Emperor had the most confidence: 'the Emperor's presence is necessary; if he wants to prevent the capital from being handed over to the enemy, there is not a moment to lose'. Likewise, a courier from Paris announced: 'All the crossings within 15 leagues of Paris are in enemy hands. In the capital, the royalists distribute proclamations. There is talk of forcing the legislative body to meet to ask for peace. Surely, people say, the Russians will burn Paris to avenge the burning of Moscow.'[247]

The Emperor turned around and marched his army back to Paris, but he was too late. At dawn on 30 March 100,000 allied soldiers attacked the capital, which had been evacuated the previous day by the main dignitaries of the empire and the imperial family. Violent fighting took place from eight in the morning until 3.30pm. Marshal Marmont felt that the battle was too unequal and sent parliamentarians to the enemy. On 31 March the allied army entered Paris through the Porte St-Martin. At its head were Czar Alexander, Frederick William III of Prussia, Marshal Schwarzenberg and Grand Duke Constantine, Alexander's brother.

The allies in Paris

In a letter to his father, Lieutenant Franconin of the Imperial Guard expressed his despair at the lack of resistance put up by Parisians against the enemy army, and even at the joy felt by some at the arrival of the allied troops:

> Paris had at least 140,000 men armed and equipped as soldiers, including 80,000 men of the National Guard, perfectly well organised and trained for a long time. This Parisian army could, by manoeuvring alone and beyond the range of a cannonball, prevent the enemy from approaching the barriers and entering Paris ... I do not want to hear any more about the National Guards defending a city or waging war; men accustomed to the pleasures of an idle life and solely occupied with their grooming and pleasing women, love life too much to contribute to the salvation of the fatherland. How the French have degenerated! You would think you were at the centre of a foreign nation, if you did not still find a few courageous individuals who were sensitive to the setbacks of this same homeland that was once so dear to them. There is no more enthusiasm, in other words no more heart, no more love for her. The entire nation is

247. Cited by Jean-Paul Bertaud, op. cit., p. 226.

> almost indifferent to the unfortunate events that have just overwhelmed it and that affect its glory.[248]

Franconin's bitterness is justified if we read the following account. The Russian troops who entered Paris in 1814 seem to have enjoyed a favourable opinion among many of the capital's inhabitants. One French royalist aristocrat, the Countess de Boigne, described these foreign officers and soldiers:

> There were no battles, occupations, riots or disturbances of any kind in the city to influence women's grooming. On Tuesday, they strolled along the boulevards in their raincoats, among the wounded, facing the shells. On Wednesday, they had come to see the allied army on parade. On Thursday, they wore their elegant costumes to the Cossack bivouacs on the Champs-Élysées. It was a strange sight for the eyes and for the minds to see these inhabitants of the Don peacefully following their habits and customs in the middle of Paris. There were no tents or shelters of any kind; three or four horses were tied to each tree and their riders, seated close to them on the ground, chatted together in very soft voices with harmonious accents. Most of them were sewing: they were mending their clothes, cutting and preparing new ones, repairing their shoes and their horses' harnesses, or shaping for their own use their share of the plunder of the previous days. They were, however, regular Cossacks of the guard and, as they rarely did scout duty, they were less happy at marauding than their brothers, the irregular Cossacks. Their uniform was very attractive: wide blue trousers, a dalmatic tunic, also blue, padded at the chest and drawn tightly around the waist by a wide black patent leather belt, with very shiny copper buckles and ornaments, which bore their arms. This semi-oriental costume and their strange attitude on horseback, where they are completely upright, the elevation of their saddle exempting them from bending the knee, made them an object of great curiosity for the onlookers of Paris. They were easily approached, especially by women and children who were positively on their shoulders. I have seen women take their work in their hands to better examine how they worked. From time to time, they would make a sort of grunting noise, which would frighten the curious women away. Then they would let out cries of joy and burst into laughter, with the women they had frightened taking part. They were less inclined to let the men approach them, but they would only ward them off with a calm, gentle gesture of the hand, accompanied by a word that was probably

248. François Franconin, 'Lettres et souvenirs du commandant Franconin', in: *Carnet de la Sabretache*, 2ᵉ série, Paris, 1910, pp. 18–19.

> a response to 'Off you go', from our sentries ... there was good reason for them to keep close to their horses, because they never, under any circumstances, took a step. As soon as they were not sitting on the ground, they were on horseback. To move around the bivouac from one end to the other, they rode their horses. And you could also see them holding their spear in one hand and a jug or bowl, or even a glass, in the other, going about their household business ... These nomadic habits seemed so strange to us that they aroused our curiosity, and we satisfied it all the more readily because we were convinced that our business was going well. The success of our business disguised the bitterness of a foreign bivouac on the Champs-Élysées.[249]

Not all Frenchmen, of course, shared the same view of the allied troops as did a large part of the capital's bourgeoisie. The Comte de Lavalette, former head of the post office during the empire and a friend of Napoleon, remembered the French victories and angrily condemned the attitude of the Parisians described by the Comtesse de Boigne:

> Twenty-two years earlier ... when the Prussians flooded the plains of Champagne, Paris and the whole of France had rushed against the enemy. French youth, inexperienced, uneducated, but shining with the love of country, exalted by a generous anger, trampled underfoot these phalanxes instructed by Frederick the Great: now the barbarians of Russia, our vanquished of all Europe, parading in all our squares, insolently seizing our homes, were no more than a spectacle for our Frenchmen who had become polite again, softened up, irritated by prosperity and all the luxury of the court. We deserved our fate![250]

Lieutenant de Cussy also witnessed the entry of the allied troops:

> The parade passed without any notable incident; at the end of the Faubourg St-Martin, however, we heard a few cries of: 'Long live our allied friends!' from a group of women in hair, waving their handkerchiefs. I have since heard this attitude attributed to Parisian women of the upper-class; it may be that the reproach is well-founded, but, for my part, the women I saw like this on 31 March 1814 belonged, without any possible error, to the ranks of the people. Apart from any patriotic considerations, I write as an honest man that at that time the

249. Éléonore d'Osmond, *Mémoires de la comtesse de Boigne, née d'Osmond, I, Du règne de Louis XVI à 1820*, Paris, 1986, pp. 225–7.
250. Antoine La Valette, *Mémoires et souvenirs du comte de La Valette*, Paris, 1994, p. 294.

> female elements in France were extremely hostile to Napoleon. For the success and insatiable glory of this modern Minotaur, thousands and thousands of French corpses of all ages had lined the roads of Europe; youth and adolescence noticed little. And yet, ever since I followed General Janssens, I, a young man of 17 and then 18, had been struck by the fact that everywhere in France the civilian population consisted only of women, children, the elderly and the infirm. At the end of the empire, by necessity, the hearts of women – whether mothers, daughters, sisters, wives or lovers – were yearning for the fall of the regime ...
>
> If on 31 March the attitude of Parisians had been generally correct, I have to say that on the following day it was not the same; I saw, with my own eyes, on 1 April, the rabble ready to disown and drag through the mud the man they had until then praised, reaching for a kind of cable that had been attached to the neck of the statue of the Emperor erected on the Place Vendôme, and seeking to topple him from his glorious pedestal ... It has also been claimed that, while all this was going on in the Place Vendôme, some upper-class Parisian women, travelling in elegant carriages along the Place de la Concorde and the Champs-Élysées, were handing out white ribbons and white roundels to the screaming crowd. One would have seen them, kissing the horses and boots of enemy cavalrymen, a Prussian, a Russian, a simple Cossack stretched out at that moment for her, a hero, a sort of demigod! ... I find it hard to believe, despite the exaltation of political passions, and even though, I repeat, all the women were, at home, Napoleon's greatest enemies.[251]

A German officer confirmed the welcome given to the allies, and in particular to the Czar, by the Parisian crowds:

> What influenced me most of all was the crowd of women who, as it seemed, all had the same feeling, who kept on shouting at each other: 'Long live the Allies, long live Alexander!' There could be no concealment. Here, as everywhere, the explosion of joy was too general and, willy-nilly, we finally had to get used to the thought that Paris, in the name of the whole of France, was today celebrating its deliverance and shaking off its chains, throwing itself gratefully into the arms of its saviour. I have never seen a more burlesque scene in my life than on this, the most remarkable day of my life. We were carried away in a veritable whirlwind of joy. In the midst of the ever-increasing cheers of an infinite people and through an unparalleled crowd, we were slowly making our way towards the Champs-Élysées. I still do not understand

251. Ferdinand de Cussy, op. cit., pp. 24–5.

> why the Czar was able to keep a shred of his red uniform of the Knights of the Guard, so much he was pressed, so much he was kissed; he accepted everything. Lots of women hung on his boots and spurs and even tied themselves to the tail of his horse ... When they finally reached the Champs-Élysées, the monarchs stopped.[252]

In the evening the King of Prussia and the Emperor of Russia went to the opera to attend a performance:

> At nine o'clock, Their Majesties Emperor Alexander and King William entered their box in the amphitheatre together. On their arrival, the hall resounded with the most touching acclamations, to which they responded with the most affectionate bows. These shouts were prolonged for a long time ... The ladies threw white roundels, which were eagerly collected and displayed. Several voices called for the eagle whose wings spread out above Buonaparte's box to be knocked down. As this would have been a rather lengthy operation, we confined ourselves for the moment to covering it with a white veil, and the eagle fell after the show. Not content with hearing the aria 'Vive Henri IV!', the audience wanted Lays to sing the words. This actor came forward, paper in hand, and intoned the following impromptu on the cherished tune, whose excellent intention can only be judged:
>
> Long live William / And his valiant warriors / Of this kingdom / He saves the children / By his victory / He gives us peace / And counts in glory / By his many benefits. /
>
> Long live Alexander! / Long live this king of kings / Without claiming anything, / Without dictating laws, / This august prince / Has the triple talent / Of being a hero, of being just, / Of giving us a Bourbon. /
>
> The French, in general, had no idea of Russia; in their ignorance, they considered it to be a savage and barbaric country; nothing surprised them more than to see a lot of Russian by the French; on the road, we frequently met an inhabitant and asked him in French: – How many leagues is it to such and such a town? He would then show us two or three fingers. If we said to him, 'But my friend, we are talking to you and you are answering with a sign,' he couldn't help but say, 'Look! He speaks French, that one.' There was no shortage of curious onlookers when we made our solemn entry into Paris, and you could hear them saying that we were all wearing breastplates under

252. Baron de Helldorf, 'La vie du prince Eugène de Wurtemberg', in: *Feuillets d'histoire*, Paris, 1911, p. 231.

> our uniforms, so astonished were they to see the fine bearing of our soldiers, who stretched out their chests in front. When we stopped to regain our distance, they felt the uniforms to check whether there was any breastplate underneath. And we often heard them say: 'There! He speaks French!'[253]

Until the capture of Paris, the allies had not agreed on what should happen to France after the victory. The sovereigns of the coalition had proclaimed that they wanted to return the country to its 1792 boundaries, but had not decided what form of government it should have. There were several possibilities open to the victors: the proclamation of Napoleon II under the regency of his mother Marie-Louise, the establishment of a new dynasty in the person of Bernadotte, Prince Royal of Sweden, an appeal to Louis-Philippe, Duke of Orléans, whose liberal views were well known, or the recall of Louis XVIII, living in exile in England. The latter solution had the support of the British cabinet and was being considered by Russia, while it was obvious that a regency for Marie-Louise would have to meet with the favour of Metternich and Emperor Franz I. Marie-Louise's regency was considered dangerous, however, as it was anticipated that it might bring Napoleon back to power. As General Dessoles, head of the National Guard, told Emperor Alexander: 'Sire, the regency is just a word; the tiger is behind it, and it will not be long before it reappears if it is proclaimed.'[254]

On his arrival in Paris, Czar Alexander agreed to stay in the house of Charles-Maurice de Talleyrand-Périgord, former minister of foreign affairs. That same evening Talleyrand-Périgord and a circle of friends set about convincing the Czar of the form the government of France should take. During the discussion, Talleyrand and his friends agreed with the Russian emperor that a provisional government was needed, that the Senate would be tasked with discussing a constitution and that Louis XVIII would be recalled to the throne. The following day, 1 April 1814, the senators present in Paris were summoned. Before entering the session, some of them were invited to dinner by the Emperor Alexander who, at the end of the meal, raised his glass and drank to the health of King Louis XVIII. In the morning a declaration signed by Alexander had been pasted on the walls of the capital, which read in part:

> The allied sovereigns proclaim that they will no longer deal with Napoleon Bonaparte, nor any member of his family; that they respect the integrity of ancient France, as it will exist under its legitimate kings; they cannot do even more, because they still profess the principle that,

253. Arthur Chuquet, *L'année 1814*, Paris, 1914, p. 158.
254. Duc de Rovigo, op. cit., t. VII, p. 114.

> for the happiness of Europe, it is necessary that France be great and strong; They therefore invite the Senate to designate a provisional government which can provide for the needs of the administration and prepare the constitution which will suit the French people. The intentions I have just expressed are shared by all my allies.[255]

A provisional government under Talleyrand was appointed. The form that the French state was to take was not yet decided. On 2 April sixty-six of the ninety senators present in Paris voted for Napoleon Bonaparte's impeachment. As soon as the declaration of forfeiture was known, the other institutions (City Council, Court of Cassation, etc.) rushed to support it. A commission set up with the consent of the allied powers set to work drafting a new constitution. On 5 April it was agreed by 63 votes – in other words, all the senators in session. Inspired by liberal ideas, it stipulated that Louis Stanislas Xavier de France, brother of the last king, was freely called to the throne of France by the French people. Louis would become King of France once he had signed the Constitution and sworn to accept and observe its terms.

Napoleon at Fontainebleau

As mentioned above, Napoleon had led his troops back towards Paris in the hope of getting there before the allies. This hope having been dashed by the surrender of the capital's defenders, he set up camp at the Château de Fontainebleau in order to regroup his remaining forces.

The allies, now masters of Paris, expected Napoleon to make one last effort to retake the capital of the empire:

> Napoleon was at Fontainebleau and a battle was still expected; it was possible to believe that Napoleon would still risk a battle; it is true that he had only 60,000 men left, many of whom were conscripts, but he had in his guard and in the rest of his troops from Spain former comrades-in-arms who would still have fought for him fiercely if they had fought one last battle, which his former military glory and his present position made equally necessary. Every precaution was taken for a general battle, which was to be expected by all those who judged Napoleon only by the role he had played until then, and who were far from believing him capable of ending a stormy and often so brilliant military life with an inexcusable weakness. General Bülow had the order to leave some troops in front of Soissons and to come to replace me at Montmartre; the corps of Sacken ... to advance on Charenton; the guards and grenadiers remained in Paris, and on 2 April, the corps

255. Duc de Rovigo, op. cit., t. VII, p. 87.

> of Yorck, Kleist and Vorontsov and mine went through the capital on the road of Orleans close to Palaiseau and Longjumeau where I took my district.[256]

Despite the French emperor's desire to go back on the offensive to retake Paris, this was impossible due to the opposition of Marshals Maret, Berthier, Lefebvre, Oudinot, Ney and Moncey. The army chiefs advocated a withdrawal to the Loire, where the Empress Marie-Louise, the young King of Rome and the imperial government were located. Napoleon nevertheless prepared a plan of attack on 1 and 2 April. On 4 April he explained his plan to the marshals but they again refused to fight. During the discussion, news came through of the senate's vote of disqualification. Napoleon wanted to bring the battle to the capital. The marshals unanimously refused and told him that abdication was the only solution. The Emperor finally agreed to a conditional abdication in favour of his son. Ney, Macdonald and Caulaincourt were instructed to take the document drawn up by Napoleon to Czar Alexander and to agree with him the next steps.

Marshal Marmont had been secretly approached by royalists and agents of the provisional government, who promised him that he would retain all his ranks and titles if he turned his coat. Marmont had concluded a secret agreement with Marshal Schwarzenberg which provided for the defection of his army, but he had asked that Napoleon's fate be guaranteed, which was granted. Marmont ordered one of his subordinates, General Souham, who was in favour of his leader defecting, to lead the troops towards the allied army:

> General Souham had the troops take up arms during the night, they set off towards Paris, they convinced themselves that it was a general movement, and the whole army followed them. The generals were at the head of their column; precautions had been taken to ensure that the encounter with enemy outposts would not cause difficulties before the whole column reached the territory occupied by the Russian army; The Russian army took up arms, and at the tail of General Souham's column passed a large cavalry which deployed itself, and took up position to oppose the retreat of these unfortunate troops, who were beginning to realise the perfidy of their generals.[257]

Chef d'escadron Mathieu wrote about this episode in his diary:

> On the 5th, at 5 a.m., we left Essonne and expected to come up against the enemy. Just as we left Essonne, on our left, I heard cavalry fanfares.

256. Alexandre de Langeron, op. cit., pp. 479–80.
257. Duc de Rovigo, op. cit., pp. 137–8.

> It was barely daylight. 'What does that mean?' I said to the good colonel Girardot of the 3rd cuirassiers. 'I do not know,' he said. I jumped the ditch, ran towards this cavalry and what did I see? Enemy cavalry. I got very close and was told nothing. I came back and said to Colonel Girardot: 'I think, my dear Colonel, that we are being made to desert the great man's eagles.' 'My God, if that is the case, what a crime!' I went to see the colonel chief of staff of the artillery of Marshal Marmont's army corps, Monsieur Marillac, to whom I said: 'but what does all this mean, my dear colonel, do you not know anything about what is going on?' 'I swear to you, my dear Matthieu, that I do not know any more than you do.' I then ran to General Bordessoulle who was marching at the head of the corps with Lieutenant General Souham, and I said to him: 'But, General, please be so kind as to tell me what role we are being asked to play here. We have enemy cavalry on our rear, are you aware of that? Are we deserting the great man's eagles, yes or no?' 'Yes, my dear Mathieu, yes, by a treaty we are leaving the insatiable man, the man who would have left us nothing but civil war. We are going to take up billets and you will be at peace and happy.' 'How, my general, we are being made to commit a crime that is fortunately unknown to us until now, and all for the sake of rest! There are only a few men who think like that, I do not follow you!' I ran to my men and told them: 'my children, we are being betrayed, he who loves me follows me!' When I wanted to go back through Essonne, the enemy cavalry was on horseback on the road and would not let us pass. I was forced to follow the movement towards Versailles, where we arrived after having crossed the enemy army and escorted by a very large enemy cavalry.[258]

When the movement had begun, Napoleon's envoys, unaware of what was happening, and in accordance with the orders they had received, were announced and informed their colleague of the events in progress. Marmont decided, on his own initiative, to accompany the delegation to the Czar. The Czar, informed of the conditions Napoleon had set for his departure, hesitated for a moment, fearing a resumption of fighting by a French army devoted to its leader. Just then, he was informed of the arrival of troops led by General Souham. At that moment, all hesitation disappeared: the number of soldiers at Napoleon's disposal made any attack impossible. All that remained was a pure and simple abdication.

On 10 April Marshal Soult, who commanded the last army still able to fight, was defeated at Toulouse by Lord Wellington. The next day Armand de Caulaincourt and Marshal Macdonald signed an agreement with the allied

258. Hubert Mathieu, op. cit., pp. 43–4.

leaders giving Napoleon sovereignty over the island of Elba, allowing him the title of emperor and guaranteeing the payment of an annual annuity. His wife, whom his father, Emperor Francis I, intended to keep separate from her husband, became Duchess of Parma, with the right to pass the duchy on to her son.

On 12 April Napoleon seems to have attempted suicide by absorbing a poison that he always carried with him. On the same day the Count of Artois, Louis XVIII's brother, made his solemn entry into Paris, acclaimed by the crowd, and the British fleet lifted the blockade on the French coast. On 13 April Napoleon resigned himself to signing the agreement negotiated by his envoys. He left Fontainebleau on 20 April after a final speech to the Old Guard. The prisoners of war held in France were released and returned to their respective powers. Those held in the British Isles were released under the agreement reached in London between Louis XVIII, en route to France, and the Prince Regent.

On 1 May Alexander went to meet Louis XVIII, who was at Compiègne. He was accompanied by a deputation of the legislative body, the Senate, the marshals and several generals, who recognised him as King of France. The following day Louis XVIII announced that he did not recognise the constitution decreed by the Senate, which would be replaced by a constitutional charter drawn up by himself. Two days later Louis XVIII arrived in Paris, where he was received by an enthusiastic crowd.

The war was over. General de Langeron recounted the end of the stay in France and the return to Russia:

> We stayed another seven days in the vicinity of Paris, then all the Prussian troops under the command of Marshal Blücher marched into Normandy, Picardy and Artois, where they were billeted. The Austrians, Bavarians and Württembergians were sent to Champagne, on the Seine, on the Aube and in Burgundy; all the Russian troops were placed under the orders of Count Barclay; General Wittgenstein's corps at Senlis, General Winzingerode's at Laon and mine at Châlons, Reims, Epernay and Commercy. It was only with the deepest sorrow that my corps separated from these brave companions in arms and glory, the Prussian soldiers, whose work and dangers we had shared. At the end of May, all the allied troops returned to their homeland. I marched through Mannheim, Nuremberg, Bayreuth, Dresden, Bautzen, Goldberg, Swidnica, Brieg, Krakow and Lublin to Dubno, in Volhynia, where the quarters of my corps were designated. Throughout Germany and especially in the states of the King of Bavaria and those of the King of Prussia, we received the most flattering welcome from the inhabitants and the worthiest reward for our work and our successes. Everywhere,

> people rushed to lavish us with the most touching care and the most distinguished reception; at the gates of every town and even every village, the inhabitants had erected triumphal arches, and came to meet us with flowers and laurel wreaths.[259]

On 30 May the peace treaty between France and the allied powers was signed in Paris. This treaty established France's return to its 1792 borders, with a few minor modifications, including the transfer of small territories from the Papal States to the Kingdom of France. On 2 June Emperor Alexander and King Frederick William III left Paris and began a visit to the United Kingdom, while Emperor Francis I returned to his states. The dissolution of Napoleon's empire, however, did not put an end to the territorial conflicts between the various European states. The four main victors (Austria, Prussia, the United Kingdom and Russia) were now fighting either to extend their domination or to recover the territories they had lost over the previous two decades. As a result, a European Congress opened in Vienna on 1 November 1814. Initially, only the four great victorious powers were to be allowed to decide on important matters. Talleyrand, representing the Kingdom of France, managed to get himself admitted to the discussions, and then found a way to include representatives from Spain, Sweden and Portugal on the small committee. Discussions were progressing with difficulty when, in March 1815, news arrived of Napoleon's landing in the south of France on 1 March, followed by the gradual rallying of the French army and the restoration of the empire. On 13 March the sovereigns meeting in Vienna proclaimed Napoleon to be a disrupter of the world's peace and declared that he should be excluded from civil and social relations and handed over to public vengeance. In March Napoleon arrived in Paris, which Louis XVIII had just left.

On 20 March Napoleon announced to the ambassadors of the foreign powers that he would faithfully observe the Treaty of Paris signed on 30 May, and that he hoped the said powers would do likewise. This announcement had no influence on the congress taking place in Vienna, where the various nations continued their preparations for war. The major European powers decided to increase the number of men destined to fight the new French empire to 930,000. The Russian troops immediately set off on the march and on 1 April reached the Oder. On 2 April, from Frankfurt, the allied powers declared that they would guarantee each other's thrones, and that they regarded the legitimacy of the princes as the safeguard of the tranquillity of the peoples; they gave Napoleon ten days to return to Elba, and the French army ten days to submit to the authority of Louis XVIII. In the event of disobedience, Napoleon and his army would be declared enemies of France and Europe.

---

259. Alexandre de Langeron, op. cit., pp. 484–5.

On 10 April the first Russian columns arrived in Prague. On the same day Czar Alexander transformed the Duchy of Warsaw into a kingdom and took the title King of Poland. On 11 April, 18,000 men of the Russian imperial guard arrived in Lübeck. On 15 April, 245,000 Russian soldiers arrived in Silesia. On 23 April the sovereigns represented at the Congress of Vienna officially refused Napoleon's offers of peace. On 27 April General Barclay de Tolly arrived in Breslau with 50,000 Cossacks, crossing Silesia towards the borders of France. On 3 May the Russian army in Poland marched towards the Rhine under the command of Generals Sacken, Jermanoff and Langeron. The first Russian columns crossed the Rhine at Cologne. On 3 June the Russians arrived on the Mein. Ten days later a Russian column under the command of General Vorontsov prepared to enter Switzerland. On 25 June a Russian corps under the Bavarian general Wrede crossed the Saar, occupied Sarreguemines and threatened Lorraine.

On 18 June Napoleon's empire collapsed on the plain of Waterloo, defeated by British, Belgian-Dutch and Prussian troops. Napoleon quickly returned to Paris, where he intended to reorganise the defence of the empire, but he came up against the hostility of the political world, which forced him to abdicate for the second time, in favour of his son. He decided to leave France and seek hospitality in the United Kingdom. On 15 July Napoleon boarded HMS *Bellerophon*, which sailed for the United Kingdom the following day. Meanwhile, the allied armies had arrived in French territory, and Wellington and Blücher entered Paris. The Emperors of Russia and Austria and the King of Prussia entered the city on 10 July. Napoleon's abdication had not suspended military operations. The allied armies had invaded fifty-eight départements, which were treated without mercy.

Further negotiations led to the signing of a new treaty between the allies and France on 20 November 1815. The conditions imposed on the defeated were harsher than those contained in the previous treaty. France was reduced to its 1790 borders rather than those of 1792. It lost territories to Bavaria, the Kingdom of Belgium and the Netherlands, and Prussia. It was required to pay compensation of 700 million francs. In addition, it would have to maintain for five years 150,000 men in an army of occupation intended to prevent the return of unrest.

During the campaign of 1814 Emperor Alexander had emerged as the true leader of the coalition against Napoleon, but the speed of the operations and the region where the French emperor had chosen to stage the war did not allow the Russian army to play a role of primary importance. This time, the leading role had passed to Wellington and Blücher, victorious on the battlefield.

Conclusion

On entering the European political stage under Czar Peter the Great (1672–1725), Russia was viewed as a peripheral and enigmatic nation by its peers. The victory over the Swedish king Charles XII at Poltava (1709) was acknowledged, yet failed to elevate the authority of the Muscovite empire as a significant military force. Empress Elisabeth (1709–1762) joined forces with Austria to combat Frederick II's Prussia. Elisabeth's untimely passing and Czar Peter III's sudden allegiance shift reversed the Prussians' fate, despite Catherine II's near-fatal contribution. Subsequently, Catherine II (1729–1796) joined the Kingdom of Prussia and the House of Austria in three partitions of Poland. Nonetheless, Catherine's regime primarily centred on aggressive action against the deteriorating Ottoman empire. On his ascension to the throne, Czar Paul (1754–1801) redirected Russian policy towards Europe, while maintaining the policy of expansion through conflict with the Ottoman Turks. The following seventeen years were a pivotal period in Russian politics and shaped European perceptions of their eastern neighbour.

The initial engagements between the French and Russian armies favoured the former but unveiled among the latter steadfast troops resolved to triumph or perish. Following the assassination of his father on 23 March 1801, Czar Alexander kept up the interest in European affairs. As a political neophyte, he was content to monitor the situation on the continent until 1805. Although initially neutral upon his accession to the throne, Alexander's allegiance shifted to the anti-Napoleon camp after the execution of the Duc d'Enghien in 1804. He subsequently joined the Third Coalition and on 2 December 1805 participated in the decisive battle of Austerlitz, where Napoleon emerged victorious but mercifully allowed the struggling Russian army to escape. In 1807 Alexander joined the Fourth Coalition and provided military assistance to Prussia, which was in dire straits following the battle of Jena. The Russian army confronted Napoleon at Eylau, a brutal battle with an ambiguous result, and at Friedland, which ended in the victory of the French forces. Following this, Alexander suggested a ceasefire to Napoleon, and the two leaders, alongside Alexander's Prussian counterpart, later convened at Tilsit. Here, Napoleon secured Alexander's endorsement of the continental blockade against Britain, in exchange for no territorial concessions.

In 1808 Napoleon suggested a partition of the Ottoman empire to benefit the Czar. The two monarchs convened again in September in Erfurt to reconcile their disagreements regarding Poland, which was of concern to the Czar since he had influence over part of the country while Napoleon appeared inclined towards its reconstitution. Throughout the negotiations with Napoleon, Talleyrand covertly urged the Czar to defy the French requests. The two men parted amicably, but reasons for dissatisfaction were brewing for both. It is likely with this period in mind that Napoleon painted the following word-portrait of the Russian ruler eight years later on St Helena: 'For the Emperor of Russia, he is a man infinitely superior to all that. He has wit, grace, education and is easily seduced, but one must be wary of him. He is a Greek of the Lower Empire.'[260]

Just as the two emperors were meeting in Erfurt, news spread across the continent of General Dupont's defeat by the Spanish at the battle of Baylen and Marshal Junot's defeat by the British at Cintra. Europe thus learned that the French army *could* be defeated. This revelation was to make its way into the mind of Czar Alexander, whose real friendship for his French interlocutor was, like Napoleon's later, open to doubt. For the time being, Napoleon had succeeded in diverting the interest of the Russian monarchy in other directions. Further friction arose when Napoleon decided to divorce his wife and approached the court in St Petersburg with a view to marrying a Russian archduchess. The Czar, who was not in favour of a possible union between one of his sisters and Napoleon, did not respond to the French advances.

In 1812 a crisis erupted as a result of the extension of French territory into northern Germany. This encroachment included the Duchy of Oldenburg, which was a possession of Alexander's father-in-law. Other contributing factors were Napoleon's attitude towards the Grand Duchy of Warsaw and the abandonment of the policy to blockade Britain. Despite numerous warnings and misgivings from those close to the French emperor, the Russian campaign began in June. The crossing of the Niemen by the largest army in European history marked a significant moment, and it would lead to one of history's most catastrophic military failures. However, Napoleon was able to assert his interpretation of the campaign and attribute his loss to the premature winter. It could be argued that the Russian army, while not always eager to fight, acted more than honourably and inflicted heavy losses on the invaders. Additionally, the actions of the light cavalry hindered communication between the withdrawing troops and their base. It is worth mentioning that during the retreat the Russian troops endured equally harsh temperatures as their foes and with limited resources traversed regions already made desolate by Napoleon's forces. Furthermore, the Russian army was severely impacted by the challenging conditions in which it fought, making any continuation of its offensive difficult.

260. Emmanuel de Las Case, *Le mémorial de de Sainte-Hélène*, Paris, 2019, p. 350.

The campaign in 1813 did not truly commence until the spring. This was due to Napoleon taking the time to rebuild his forces before going on the offensive against Russia. By now Russia was no longer on its own, as it had received support from Prussia and Austria, and eventually from all the German states and Sweden. In October the French were finally driven out of the areas on the other side of the Rhine after the defeat at Leipzig. In January 1814 the allied forces crossed the Rhine, marking the start of the invasion of France. Napoleon was in a challenging position as his army was outnumbered by his opponents. Although his campaign had been brilliant and possibly marked the peak of his military genius, on 31 March the coalition troops took over Paris. The Emperor wished to carry on the fight, but his marshals, themselves exhausted and mindful of the dire circumstances that Napoleon was facing, declined to take a chance with another battle.

Alexander, nicknamed 'the Agamemnon of this crusade' by several authors of the time, was the master of the situation. He agreed that Napoleon should be given possession of the island of Elba and be allowed retain his title of emperor. The armies of the coalition then evacuated French territory, which had returned to its boundaries on 1 January 1792.

In March 1815 Napoleon eluded British surveillance and capitalised on the errors of Louis XVIII's administration to disembark in southern France. The military had maintained strong Bonapartist sentiments and soon rallied behind the Emperor. The Congress of Vienna proclaimed Napoleon an outlaw, precluding all negotiations, and the anti-French coalition was promptly resurrected. Napoleon's assault faltered and failed in June on the battlefield of Waterloo. On this occasion, the wreath of victory no longer graced the head of the Russian emperor but instead adorned the heads of Generals Wellington and Blücher. The coalition forces had been caught off guard by the swift French offensive. Nevertheless, it is worth mentioning that the significance of the battle of Waterloo may have been somewhat overstated over time, as, in the event of a victory, Napoleon would still have had to contend with close to a million adversaries. France, fatigued after two decades of relentless warfare and the depletion of its resources, would likely have succumbed sooner rather than later.

Despite the loss of lives, the advent of peace transformed Russia from a remote power, almost alien to Europe, into a crucial player in the continent's politics. Czar Alexander had bolstered his domain with the acquisition of the Grand Duchy of Finland and the re-established Kingdom of Poland, both of which served his interests.

As shown in this book, the French soldier viewed his Russian counterpart as a valiant, orderly and proficient soldier, especially compared to troops from the German states, for instance. As the Russian army comprised diverse ethnic groups, this generated a considerable amount of interest. This diversity was also highlighted by French contemporary witnesses in their writings. In Europe's memory of the conflict between France and Russia, the catastrophic campaign of 1812, which resulted in the start of Napoleon's downfall, is the most remembered. In 1854 Napoleon III's involvement alongside the British in the Crimean War may have been prompted by the memories of this era.

Nevertheless, the Napoleonic Wars definitely marked Russia's arrival on the European political scene.

Bibliography

Primary sources

Archives

Archives de l'État à Liège (AEL), Fonds Français Préfecture, 1043, 1044

Newspapers

Bulletins de la Grande Armée, 1805–1813
Journal de l'Empire, 1805–1813
Journal de Toulouse, l'Observateur républicain, ou l'Anti-Royaliste, 19 vendémiaire an VII, 9 vendémiaire an VIII
Journal des débats politiques et littéraires, 3 April 1814
Pièces officielles et Bulletins de la Grande Armée, Paris, 1812

Books

Anonymous, *Campagne de la grande armée et de l'armée d'Italie, Supplément, Relation officielle de la bataille d'Austerlitz, présenté à l'empereur Alexandre par le général Kutusow, et observations d'un officier français,* Paris, 1806
Anonymous, *Lettres interceptées pendant la campagne de 1812*, Paris, 1905
Béniton, Étienne, *A la conquête de l'Europe, souvenirs d'un soldat de la révolution et de l'empire*, Paris
de Berthezène, Pierre, *Souvenirs militaires de la République et de l'Empire*, t. II, Paris, 1855
Bonaparte, Jérôme, *Mémoires et correspondance du roi Jérôme et de la reine Catherine*, Paris, 1861, 7 vols
Bonaparte, Napoléon, *Correspondance* générale, t. 3, t. 6, t. 7, t. 10, t. 12, t. 13, t. 15, Paris
Boulart, Jean-François, *Mémoires militaires du général baron Boulart sur les guerres de la République et de l'Empire*, Paris, no date
Bourgogne, Adrien, *Mémoires du sergent Bourgogne (1812–1813)*, Paris, 1910
de Bourgoing, Pierre, *Souvenirs militaires du Baron de Bourgoing, 1791–1815*, Paris, 1897
de Brandt, Henrich, *Souvenirs d'un officier polonais, Scènes de la vie militaire en Espagne et en Russie, 1808–1812*, Paris, 1877
Bréaut des Marlots, Jean, *Lettre d'un capitaine de cuirassiers sur la Campagne de Russie*, Paris-Poitiers, 1885
de Cambacérès, Jean-Jacques-Régis, *Mémoires inédits*, t. 2, Paris, 1999
de Castellane, Boniface, *Journal du maréchal de Castellane*, t. 1, p. 175
de Caulaincourt, Armand, *Mémoires du général de Caulaincourt, duc de Vicence, grand écuyer de l'empereur*, t. 1, t. 2, Paris, 1933
——, *Recollections*, t. 1, London, 1838
Chlapowski, Désiré, *Mémoires sur les guerres de Napoléon, 1806–1813*, Paris, 1908
Chuquet, Arthur, *Lettres de 1812*, Paris, 1911
Combe, Julien, *Mémoires du colonel Combe*, Paris, 1896
Compans, Jean, *Général Compans (1769–1845), d'après ses notes de campagne et sa correspondance (1812–1845)*, Paris, 1912
Constant, *Mémoires intimes de Napoléon Ier*, t. 2, Paris, 1967

Curély, Jean-Nicolas, *Itinéraire d'un cavalier léger de la Grande Armée (1795–1815), publié d'après un manuscrit authentique par le général Thoumas*, Paris, 1887
Delmarche, Joachim, *Les Soirées du grenadier ou Mémoires de Joachim Delmarche, de Philippeville, Cerfontaine*, 1980
Denniée, Pierre-Paul, *Itinéraire de l'Empereur Napoléon pendant la campagne de 1812*, Paris, 1842
Dupuy, Victor, *Souvenirs militaires de Victor Dupuy, chef d'escadron, 1794–1816*, Paris, 1892
Fain, Agathon, *Souvenirs de la campagne de France (manuscrit de 1814)*, Paris, 1914
François, Charles-François, *Journal du capitaine François*, Tours, 1913
Franconin, François, 'Lettres et souvenirs du commandant Franconin', in: *Carnet de la Sabretache*, 2e série, Paris, 1909
Girod de l'Ain, Jean-Marie, *Dix ans de mes souvenirs militaires de 1805 à 1815*, Paris, 1873
d'Hauterive, Alexandre, *Lettres d'un chef de brigade 1793–1805*, Paris, 1891
Labaume, Eugène, *Relation circonstanciée de la campagne de Russie*, Paris, 1814
de Langeron, Alexandre-Louis, *Mémoires de Langeron, général d'infanterie dans l'armée russe, Campagnes de 1812, 1813, 1814*, Paris, 1902
Lévi, Camille, *Mémoires du capitaine Duthilt*, Paris, 1909
de Marbot, Marcelin, *The Memoirs of Baron de Marbot*, London, 1913
Martha-Beker, Félix-Victor, *Le général Beker, comte de Mons*, Paris, 1876
Mathieu, Hubert, *Souvenirs militaires du chef d'escadron Mathieu de 1787 à 1815*, Paris, no date
von Metternich, Clemens, *Mémoires du Prince de Metternich, Chancelier de Cour et d'État*, t. 2, Paris, 1880
de Montesquiou-Fézenzac, Raymond, *Souvenirs militaires de 1804 à 1814*, Paris, 1870
Noël, Jean-Nicolas, *Souvenirs militaires d'un officier du Premier Empire*, Genève, 1971
d'Osmond, Éléonore, *Mémoires de la comtesse de Boigne, née d'Osmond, I, Du règne de Louis XVI à 1820*, Paris, 1986
Pagan, Thoran, *Mémoires d'un prisonnier en Russie, par M. Pagan, ancien chef d'escadron*, Lyon, 1843
Picard, Alexandre, *Le journal de route d'un soldat de la Grande armée*, Gilly, 1946
Puybusque, Louis-Guillaume, *Lettre sur la guerre de Russie en 1812, sur la ville de Saint-Pétersbourg, sur les mœurs et les usages des habitants de Russie et de Pologne*, Paris, 1816
Robinaux, Pierre, *Journal de route du capitaine Robinaux, 1803–1832*, Paris, 1908
Roos, Heinrich, *Avec Napoléon en Russie, Souvenirs de la campagne de 1812*, Paris, 1913
Roy, Just-Étienne, *La Tour d'Auvergne dit le premier grenadier de France*, Tous, 1870
Schlumberger, Gustave, *Lettres du Commandant Coudreux*, Paris, 1908
de Ségur, Paul-Philippe, *Histoire et mémoires*, t. 7, Paris, 1877
Surrugues, Abbé, *Lettres sur l'incendie de Moscou écrites de cette ville, au R.P. Bouvet de la Compagnie de Jésus, par l'abbé Surrugues, témoin oculaire et curé de l'église de Saint Louis à Moscou*, Paris, 1823
Ternaux-Compans, Maurice, *Le général Compans (1769–1845), d'après ses notes de campagne et sa correspondance de 1812 à 1813 par son petit-fils M. Ternaux-Compans*, Paris, 1912
la Valette, Antoine, *Mémoires et souvenirs du compte de la Valette*, Paris, 1994
Wilkin, Bernard, Wilkin, René and Remy, Christian, *Mémoires des campagnes de Jean Gheerbrant*, Brussels, 2021

Secondary sources

Articles and book chapters

Les carnets de la Sabretache, 1895
Kerautret, Michel, 'Napoléon et le mirage récurrent de l'alliance russe', in: M.-P. Rey and T. Lentz, *1812, La campagne de Russie*, Paris, 2012, p. 34
Lentz, Thierry, 'La formation de la troisième coalition. Un grand succès de la diplomatie anglaise', in: *Revue du Souvenir Napoléon*, n° 459, July–August 2005, pp. 7–12

Books

Anonymous, *Victoires, conquêtes désastres, revers et guerres civiles des Français de 1792 à 1815*, t. 15, Paris, 1819

Boudon, Jacques Olivier, *Lettres de la campagne de Russie*, Paris, 2012

von Clausewitz, Karl, *La campagne de 1812 en Russie*, Paris, 1987

Fairon, Emile and Heuse, Henri, *Lettres de Grognards*, Paris, 1936

de Jomini, Antoine, *Précis politique et militaire des années 1812–1814*, Lausanne, 1868

de Longchamps, Buret, *Les fastes universels, ou tableau historique chronologique et géographique contenant siècle par siècle depuis les temps les plus reculés jusqu'à nos jours*, t. 10, Brussels, 1827

Martinien, Aristide, *Tableaux par corps et par batailles des officiers tués et blessés pendant les guerres de l'Empire (1805–1815)*, t. 1, t. 2, Paris, 1899

Madelin, Louis, *Histoire du Consulat et de l'Empire*, t. 2, Paris, 2003

Perrot, Aristide-Michel, *Itinéraire général de Napoléon, chronologie du Consulat et de l'Empire, indiquant jour par jour pendant toute sa vie, le lieu où était Napoléon, ce qu'il y a fait et les événements qui se rattachent à son histoire*, Paris, 1845

Pinkerton, John, *Modern Geography, a Description of the Empires, Kingdoms, States, and Colonies; with the Oceans, Seas, and Isles; in All Parts of the World*, vol. 1

Quintin, Danielle and Bernard, *Dictionnaire des colonels de Napoléon*, Paris, 1996

Roy, Just, *Les Français en Russie*, Paris, 1886

Smith, Digby, *Napoleonic Wars Data Book*, London, 1998

Vandal, Albert, *Napoléon et Alexandre Ier*, Paris, 1896

Index